SAGE was founded in 1965 by Sara Miller McCune to support the dissemination of usable knowledge by publishing innovative and high-quality research and teaching content. Today, we publish over 900 journals, including those of more than 400 learned societies, more than 800 new books per year, and a growing range of library products including archives, data, case studies, reports, and video. SAGE remains majority-owned by our founder, and after Sara's lifetime will become owned by a charitable trust that secures our continued independence.

Los Angeles | London | New Delhi | Singapore | Washington DC | Melbourne

WOMEN IN
SOCIAL CHANGE

Thank you for choosing a SAGE product!
If you have any comment, observation or feedback,
I would like to personally hear from you.

Please write to me at **contactceo@sagepub.in**

Vivek Mehra, Managing Director and CEO, SAGE India.

WOMEN IN SOCIAL CHANGE

Visions, Struggles and Persisting Concerns

Social Change in Contemporary India

Series Editor: Manoranjan Mohanty

Volume IV

Edited by

GHAZALA JAMIL

Los Angeles | London | New Delhi
Singapore | Washington DC | Melbourne

First published in 2021 by

SAGE Publications India Pvt Ltd
B1/I-1 Mohan Cooperative Industrial Area
Mathura Road, New Delhi 110 044, India
www.sagepub.in

SAGE Publications Inc
2455 Teller Road
Thousand Oaks, California 91320, USA

SAGE Publications Ltd
1 Oliver's Yard, 55 City Road
London EC1Y 1SP, United Kingdom

SAGE Publications Asia-Pacific Pte Ltd
18 Cross Street #10-10/11/12
China Square Central
Singapore 048423

Published by Vivek Mehra for SAGE Publications India Pvt. Ltd. Typeset in 10.5/13pt Bembo by Fidus Design Pvt. Ltd, Chandigarh.

Library of Congress Control Number: 2021932187

ISBN: 978-93-5388-771-1 (HB)

SAGE Team: Amrita Dutta, Syed Husain Naqvi and Kanika Mathur

Contents

Section I: Women's Rights Movement

Sectional Introduction

Section II: Women as Workers

Sectional Introduction

Section III: Political Participation
Sectional Introduction

Section IV: Culture and Identity
Sectional Introduction

Section V: Law and Violence
Sectional Introduction

List of Abbreviations

AFSPA	Armed Forces (Special Powers) Act
AIDWA	All India Democratic Women's Association
AIWC	All India Women's Conference
BAMCEF	Backward and Minority Communities Employees Federation
BDO	Block development officer
BKU	Bhartiya Kisan Union
BSP	Bahujan Samaj Party
Cr.PC	Criminal Procedure Code
CRPF	Central Reserve Police Force
CSD	Council for Social Development
CSDS	Centre for the Study of Developing Societies
CSWI	Committee on the Status of Women in India
CWDS	Centre for Women's Development Studies
HUF	Hindu Undivided Family
IPC	Indian Penal Code
J&K	Jammu and Kashmir
JRY	Jawahar Rozgar Yojana
MKSS	Mazdoor Kisan Shakti Sangathan
MPs	Members of Parliament
MS	Mahila Samakhya programme
MTP	Medical termination of pregnancy
NCRB	National Crime Records Bureau
NES	National Election Study
NFHS	National Family and Health Survey
PRI	Panchayati Raj Institutes
PWDVA	Protection of Women from Domestic Violence Act
RCR	Restitution of Conjugal Rights
SCs	Scheduled Castes
SEWA	Self-Employed Women's Association

STs	Scheduled Tribes
UCC	Uniform Civil Code
UN	United Nations
UP	Uttar Pradesh

About the Series

Social Change in Contemporary India is a series of thematic volumes carrying selected articles from the journal *Social Change,* which is celebrating its golden jubilee. The articles are offered as important contributions capturing the momentous experience of people of India and their institutions since Independence.

Social change in independent India has gone through three distinct phases. The first two decades saw the impact of the freedom struggle in most arenas where policymakers and common people shared some perspectives to initiate concrete steps to reduce poverty, hunger and scarcities with the objective of making progress towards the goals enshrined in the Constitution of India. Planned development with a focus on industrialization, the Green Revolution in agriculture, building educational institutions of high quality and, above all, promoting democratic institutions and procedures to meet the aspirations of all sections of society characterized most of this era. The pluralistic character of Indian society, culture and polity was acknowledged, and some important policy initiatives emerged.

But by the late 1960s, the crisis of this model already surfaced. The food riots in 1966, the Naxalbari uprising in 1967 and the beginning of non-Congress governments in many states were symptoms of the emerging environment. This heralded the second phase—1970 to 1990—which witnessed the unfolding of most major contradictions in the Indian Republic. Assertion of rights by ethnic groups in different parts of the country was responded to by a certain centralization of power by the union government which, in turn, was challenged by the emergence of strong regional parties and movements. Poverty eradication was prominent on the agenda, but progress was tardy. Education and health facilities expanded but not to the extent needed. An Indian middle class did emerge but was increasingly alienated from the masses. Challenges accumulated leading to mass movements and the republic saw the declaration of emergency followed by rule of alternative forces and return of the Congress to power. In the process, civil society organizations pursuing citizens' rights emerged and the struggle for democratic rights continued to expand. Internal disturbances, communal riots and atrocities on Dalits, minorities and women occurred from time to time. But the democratic structure continued to get consolidated and people's consciousness to defend constitutional values continued to grow.

In 1991, the neoliberal economic reforms were launched in the wake of a serious economic crisis. At that time, India was also experiencing a social upsurge over the rights of Dalits, backward classes, religious minorities and women. By this time, environmental issues had also acquired much attention. Thus began the third phase. The Indian elite cutting across the dominant political parties accepted the agenda of globalization, liberalization and privatization. Mobilization on caste and religious issues took a new turn with Hindu nationalist forces becoming stronger by the day. Initially, the Congress, through its alliance of parties, was able to stem this trend. They handled contradictions for a decade by a strategy that promoted rapid economic growth, tried to provide rural employment and food security to the poor and addressed the grievances of minorities. But corruption and inefficiency made them unpopular and a BJP-led government came to power. This third phase of neoliberal growth, steered by Hindu nationalism, is in full swing though alternative forces continue to occupy a significant space.

This story of independent India is captured by scholars and commentators as it unfolded during the past 50 years as contributions to the Council for Social Development's social science quarterly, *Social Change*. They narrate the multidimensional dynamics of social change experienced by various sections of people at local, regional and national levels and also in the global context. We decided to share these contributions on specific themes in several volumes with a wider readership for good reasons.

First, *Social Change* is a unique, interdisciplinary journal that covers not only research papers in social sciences but also policy analysis and reports from the field in areas of social development. Right from the start, Durgabai Deshmukh, the founder of the Council of Social Development, wanted theory, policy and ground-level experience to be integrated, each benefitting from the other. So, each volume in this series has papers by authors defining concepts, explaining theoretical frameworks, analysing policies and presenting survey results and other evidences from rural, urban and tribal areas.

Second, the journal carried contributions from not only senior scholars such as Nirmal Kumar Bose, B. N. Ganguly, T. N. Madan and B. K. Roy Burman, policymakers like C. D. Deshmukh and social activists like Devaki Jain but also from a large number of young academics from all over the country who used the forum to present their findings from their most important research projects. Some of them later became eminent academics and important policymakers. The contributions by these writers over a 50-year period can help us identify key points in the history of policymaking as well as discourses during the three major phases of contemporary India. Some contributions clearly impacted public discourses and the policy process. Thus, we are able to capture shifts in policy in the early 1970s, when the state took many active initiatives, and also the big change in 1991, when a new role of the state was visible in the economy giving a substantial role to the private sector. That trend continued in the first two decades of the 21st century. We may note the changing perspectives and the linkage with the global processes not only on theoretical issues of social development but also on policy debates concerning questions such as the privatization of health, education, rural development, forest and environment. Their implications for people's welfare and human rights were also dealt with by many authors in the recent years.

Third, an equally important consideration underlying these volumes is the fact that the Council for Social Development (CSD) has a mission to serve the interests of marginalized groups—its research, publications, advocacy and, indeed, this journal reflects that commitment. Therefore, the volumes carry articles on selected themes such as health, education, poverty and agriculture with special focus on the marginalized groups including the Adivasis, Dalits, minorities, women, and urban and rural poor. Each of these volumes reflects what has been done in respect of the specific marginalized groups and analyses the nature of the development experience from the vantage point of the marginalized.

Each volume is edited by an expert who has done considerable work on the subject. A major and substantive introduction by the editor of the volume not only puts the papers in perspective but also identifies the strengths as well as the gaps in the treatment of the subject. The editor's introduction also addresses current concerns in theory and policy, discourse and practice and presents suggestions for further thinking and action. These volumes are designed as studies on a theme for ready reference and use by students, researchers and general readers.

Manoranjan Mohanty
Series Editor

Foreword

The year 2020 marks the 25th anniversary of the momentous World Congress of Women which adopted the Beijing Platform for Action and the 45th year since the historic report on the status of women in India, *Towards Equality*. Both had put on their agenda a 'transformative vision' of advancing towards gender equality in all spheres of society and both recorded enduring concerns about the inadequate results, failures and even setbacks on many fronts during the succeeding decades, even though considerable progress had been made on gender justice all over the world. The vision and the concerns as mentioned in the title of this volume, *Women in Social Change: Visions, Struggles and Persisting Concerns,* run through the selection of articles that profile the evolving discourse on the gender question in India during the past five decades as reflected in the contributions carried in the journal *Social Change.*

Thanks to the vision of the founder of the CSD, Durgabai Deshmukh, the issue of gender has been a central concern of the Council and *Social Change* since its inception in 1970. The perspective that India's development had to be mainly about uplifting disadvantaged sections of society, especially women, children, Dalits, Adivasis and the rural poor, has guided the academic programme of CSD throughout its history. Within that, the focus on women's issues was unmistakable. As the editor of this volume points out, this engagement was graphically communicated in the cover of the very first issue of *Social Change* where women's work in agriculture, in a science laboratory, as a mother and as a right-bearing citizen are boldly illustrated conveying the multidimensional perspective on the women's question that the founders of this initiative had. This thinking was reflected in the kind of articles that the journal carried on its pages. That education was a principal mode of women's development was evident in many articles. Special issues on women's literacy and field reports on the experience in schools in different places illustrated this. Health, including reproductive functions, was another area of focus where state policy was assessed, and alternative policy proposals were put forth. Women's employment opportunities and performance records in various sectors were scrutinized on the basis of evidence from the ground. Political participation was yet another area. In all these spheres, gender disparity and patriarchal hold remained conspicuous, even though there was a rising consciousness in society about the need for gender justice which was gradually seen in public policy.

From the late 1980s onwards, two shifts in women studies gradually crystallized. One was the adoption of the perspective of women's rights as the key element of women's liberation from multiple oppressions. Thus far, the attention was on women's welfare through various measures such as education, healthcare and employment. Hereafter, the discourse on women's empowerment captured the entitlement to women to not only social and economic rights as was guaranteed in the Constitution and UN documents but also the demand for an equal share in political decision-making. The rising consciousness about women's rights led to several state initiatives in India. The establishment of the National Commission on Women in 1992 as a statutory body, the Indian Constitution's 73rd and 74th Amendment giving at least one-third representation to women in panchayats and municipalities in 1993 and having a special section on Women's Development in the Five-Year Plan documents and also having gender components in annual budgets and many other legislative and executive decisions by the union and state governments reflected this trend.

The other major shift was to enlarge women studies into gender studies which not only covered varieties of sexuality and corresponding gender identities but also pointed out a gender dimension in every aspect of life and society. That patriarchy pervaded society, economy and the state in multiple forms in the immediate surrounding, as well as nationally and globally, latent as well as manifest, was the new reference point. Subtle modes of domination through cultural practice—old and new, as also in everyday social behaviour became a subject of enquiry as well as intervention. That caste, class, ethnicity and gender relations merged in a variety of ways in multiple degrees was realized in the course of studying social experiences on the ground. Dalit women studies in India, Black feminism research in the US and Muslim women studies in many parts of the world had a pathbreaking impact. Gender was now seen in an intersectional perspective. These developments revolutionized social science, the policy process and social behaviour and brought to the fore dimensions of domination and oppression and, therefore, freedom and emancipation not discovered before, leading to fresh approaches in understanding and action possibilities. From then on, gender studies pioneered elements of freedom discourse, influencing all disciplines of knowledge and practice.

This trajectory of gender discourse in India is captured effectively in the editor's introduction. A distinguished feminist in her own right, whose studies on multiple forms of exclusion have drawn much attention in the recent years, Ghazala Jamil's essay is a contribution by itself to understanding the history of women's development and the dilemmas and crisis points that India has reckoned with on the gender question. She highlights major strides in women's studies and women's movement captured on the pages of the journal and, at the same time, does not hesitate to boldly record the dimensions and areas missing or under-represented. The volume carries contributions of many legendary figures of women's movement in India who have shaped policy and critical understanding of the nature and course of Indian women's journey and stalwarts—all including Vina Mazumdar, Devaki Jain, Mina Swaminathan besides Durgabai Deshmukh, herself. Incidentally, the very first official initiative to usher in equal rights for women by the Indian government was the setting up of the National Council of Women in 1958 with Durgabai Deshmukh as Chairperson.

One theoretical question had to be handled carefully in planning this volume. It is now widely accepted that the gender issue, like other such issues as caste and ethnicity, had to be treated both autonomously as well as a part of all other general initiatives. Hence, our other five volumes in the *Social Change Golden Jubilee Series on Social Change in Contemporary India*—volumes on Tribes of India, Agriculture, Education, Health and Poverty—also have gender-related essays. In addition, we thought it absolutely necessary to have a special volume on women. For good reason, we decided not to repeat the gender essays from other volumes in this book; readers need to visit the other volumes for that. We reiterate that moving towards gender equality is a multidimensional programme and any narrow preoccupation with any one sector to the exclusion of others will leave voids that can create new hurdles. In this volume, the dimensions of rights, work, political participation and culture have been given the main focus and they do capture the reality of contemporary India that is battling to contend with the rising cases of sexual violence on the one hand and commodification, insecurity and loss of work in a growing market economy on the other. The discourse has been drawn to cope with a sociopolitical environment characterized by the Nirbhaya case of December 2012, the plight of women workers during the COVID-19 lockdowns and the gang rape incident in Hathras of October 2020 in Uttar Pradesh, where the role of state agencies and communal forces have created new contingencies. While the Nirbhaya case shook up the conscience of the nation leading to adoption of new legal safeguards against sexual violence and added initiatives on the economic and educational fronts, the Hathras incident, which happened in the height of a raging pandemic of COVID-19, invited mixed messages from the state itself; thus, showing how much more distance India has yet to travel on the road to equality.

In the face of serious challenges from the state withdrawing its principal welfare role while strengthening its coercive and surveillance apparatus, society, experiencing shocking reversals to sectarianism, and the global market bulldozing on a profiteering track, the struggle for equality continues through heavy odds. *Social Change's* golden jubilee offerings are part of the process to reduce the odds. The year 2020 has particularly been very significant in reaffirming CSD's gender agenda. While the predicament concerning women's world of work, paid and unpaid was the theme of the special issue of *Social Change* in March 2020 edited by Vibhuti Patel, the golden jubilee lecture by feminist historian Uma Chakravarti on persistence of sexual violence from home to the border, focusing on the phenomenon of impunity by state forces, even in the face of increasing resistance, captured the major threats to gender equality in contemporary times. And this volume of essays takes forward the mission initiated by Durgabai Deshmukh 50 years ago.

Manoranjan Mohanty
Council for Social Development
New Delhi
November 2020

Shifting Frames in the Women's Rights Discourse in India
A Critical Reading

Ghazala Jamil

The first issue of *Social Change* appeared in 1971 with an evocative imagery of social change on its cover. The banner had the title in simple block letters. The journal announced itself with a tagline that simply said, 'Journal of the Council for Social Development'. Under the banner title, four circular figures reveal the place of gender in social change in the view of the journal. On the bottom left was an image of a grand building with an impressive road leading up to it—possibly a symbol of institution building or infrastructure development. Moving counter-clockwise, the next image was that of agricultural workers toiling in a field, a woman's form in the foreground. Next was a scene from a science laboratory with two scientists (gender neutral figures) in lab coats and, finally, was an image of a woman with a baby tied on her back casting her vote in a polling booth while several other women wait outside in a queue for their turn. Women are highlighted as workers and as political agents, but, simultaneously, their reproductive and care roles are also underlined. The vision is clearly transformative—it communicates that the goal of social change is to usher in a society which is free from dehumanization and has opportunities for each of its member—especially women, to contribute to well-being of the society, but seen closely, the vision also conveys certain continuity. The images appear not to be too anxious about the systemic disadvantage women face in the society and do not pose them as victims.

This vision probably came from the shared view of CD Deshmukh and Durgabai Deshmukh—founders of CSD, and the founder-editor of the journal, Kamla Mankekar, journalist by profession and a leading women's rights activist of the time. From the very beginning, the contents of the journal clearly reflected this same confidence in the role and place of women in bringing about development in Indian society which reflected in the iconography of its first cover. Even the colour of the cover page, a brilliant sea-green, exuded an optimist, confident outlook. Mankekar was to later describe her years at the helm of *Social Change* as 'rewarding work' (Rai, 2019). The proof that this imagery was not merely incidental also lies in the fact that an article or two on gender and women's rights was included in almost every other journal issue thereafter.

It is also reflected in the fact that apart from these articles, since April 1971, when the first issue of Volume 1 of *Social Change* was published, over 20 issues were dominated by articles around gendered concerns or were special issues of the journal. While the initial approach seems to go for diversity, later, most special issues with a gender focus were tied up to one theme noticeably. During the tenure of Amar Kumar Singh, who was the editor of the journal for over 20 years from 1979 until his death in 1999 (Dubey, 1999), the journal developed the practice of inviting a guest co-editor sometimes. The co-editor would write a contribution which was more like an introductory article on the theme of the special issue rather than an editorial piece tying up all the other contributions. September–December 1980 issue seems to be themed around a social-psychological perspective in which the lead article by Amar Singh, the editor, explores empirically the prejudices faced by women as a group (Singh, 1980). The September–December issue in 1981 was focused around abortion/medical termination of pregnancy (MTP) and fertility. The special issue in June 1990 was themed *Status of Women and Employment*, another was focused on tribal women (December 1993), and one was on concerns related to girl children (June–September 1995). There was a special issue in June 1996 titled *Family in Historical and Contemporary Time* and one in September 1998 focused on population policy.

Still, occasionally, some special issues were very broadly defined and contained a collection of articles that had little connecting them. For example, the special issue in September 1988 was titled *Indian Women: Tensions and Conflicts*. Similarly, an issue in June 1992 was titled *Indian Women: Perceptions and Problems* and another one in March 1993 was titled *Studies on Women in India*.

Later, when Manoranjan Mohanty took over as editor in 2006, invited guest editors began writing editorial introductions tying the pieces together in one analytical framework, while some of them would also contribute a research article to the issue. This is seen in the December 2007 special issue on women's marginalization put together by geographer Saraswati Raju as guest editor and another in December 2011 on gender and education edited by Janaki Rajan. During the tenure of Mohanty's editorship, *Social Change* has also had, in Rakhshanda Jalil, Purnima Joshi and Mannika Chopra, an impressive line of managing editors who are notable women journalists and popular writers, in the tradition of Mankekar.

The articles—whether in the special issues or otherwise—raise important questions and discuss challenges confronting women at the time and, therefore, are also a testament to the development of discourse around the gender question in India. An important part of the history of feminist movement in India is the evolution of the field of gender/women's studies. A small subset of concerns in this regard is related to changes in the conventions and forms of academic research writing in the backdrop of changes in the society.

From the initial confidence of the early 1970s in state-led legislative interventions to promote equal rights of women, one can discern a growing disquiet of a persistent nature of most of the problems that plagued Indian society. Still, in the 1990s not only was the largest number of special issues of *Social Change* on gender and women's rights were brought out but the themes in which published articles utilized a gendered lens diversified drastically too. When the broad semantic field for discussing women's issues shifts, it is not because the erstwhile problems have been solved but that the nature of problems themselves have changed and a different set of actors or actions have been introduced in this field.

This introduction uses the research insights, theoretical frames and opinions published on an array of themes around women in *Social Change* as a window to comment upon the broader discursive evolution of the women's rights movement in India and scholarship on gender. It is not my intention for this narrative to be a chronological catalogue of events in the movements, although, as you will see, the manner and timing of appearance of issues and debates is tied to these events.

THE INITIAL FRAMES OF THE DISCOURSE

The journal began publication in 1971, which coincidentally was also the year when the Committee on the Status of Women in India (CSWI) was constituted. This was a follow-up of the United Nations General Assembly having adopted the Convention on the Elimination of All Forms of Discrimination in 1969, asking member-states to submit country reports on the status of women by 1975—designated as International Women's Year. The convention was the result of efforts made by women's rights movements all across the world expressing dissatisfaction with the developmental paradigm in the post-second World War scenario—as men workers returned from the war and re-joined the workforce, women not only had to struggle to retain some of the freedoms gained during the war but they also had to struggle for equal wages and entry into professions considered inappropriate for them. In the 1950s and 1960s, women in large numbers joined the trade union movement the world over, including in India. In India, since the results of planned development and the long-awaited fruits of a trickle-down effect had failed to materialize, the committee particularly signalled a moment of reckoning for women's struggles in India.

The report, which has been hailed as 'the founding text' for the Indian women's movement in independent India (Tharu & Lalitha, 1991), was tabled in the Indian Parliament in February 1975. Titled *Towards Equality* (CSWI, 1994), it contained findings that were characterized variously as 'shocking', 'revelatory' and 'eye-opening' to the true realities of women in India. In an event held over two decades after the publication of the report, the members of the CSWI met to reminiscence how the document was prepared and assess the progress made on the problems discussed therein since then (CWDS, 1988). Several members, using the benefit of hindsight, discussed how their approach was bound by their assumptions and they had to develop or almost invent frameworks within which to place their scrutiny. Reading their assessment, one can also discern generational differences between the positions of the members. The second article included in this volume is a sharp review of this landmark report by Mina Swaminathan (1975), who was a member of the committee but had resigned early on following differences. From a close reading of her critique, it is easy to see that the features and the flaws of the report became the very features of the approach in understanding women's questions in India and, consequently, the scholarship on gender.

A roundup of all the articles published in *Social Change* in the first decade (1970s) shows that the gendered enquiries expressed can be broadly categorized by their manner of framing. Not surprisingly, the most prominent one among these was the very idea of 'status of women'. Numerous articles published in the first decade sought to conceptualize different aspects of women's status. It was correlated with other important concerns of the time, for example, women's education (Wasi, 1971) or within the family by marriage (Mukherjee, 1974). Women's status as agricultural or rural labour was also a subject of several studies (Chakravorty, 1975). Theoretical conceptualization of 'status' was also attempted (Mukherjee, 1975). This framing of assessing the status and efforts to ameliorate the same continued thereafter too and has lingered on (Bhagat, 1990; Firoz, 1990). The problem of the framing appears to have a methodological consequence, too. It directed efforts towards bargaining for a better or higher place in the social hierarchy and is bereft of any critique of the structure of this hierarchy itself.

The other dominant ideas were national development and nation-building, which echoed in all other explorations including gender. The shortcomings of planned development in bringing about a more 'prosperous nation' were heaped upon India's large and 'unwieldy' population. In the gender discourse, this manifested itself in the still often-repeated articulation of worry and nervousness around fertility. It has to be remembered that this discussion is taking place in *Social Change* during and after the Emergency (1975–1977). The discourse about population control and controlling fertility can be seen in attempts to correlate various factors such as family welfare (Ganguli, 1971), social security (Bose, 1972), cultural milieu (Dandekar, 1974), educational status (Vig, 1976), family structure (Reddy, 1978) and the like to women's fertility behaviour.

The articles published in the journal also show a sustained interest among scholars to girl's education in the first two-and-a-half decades.

Several micro-studies were published on school education but only a few on higher education and gender. This is an intriguing trend because it is also reflective of the fact that there appears, clearly, to be a prioritization of needs and scholars were focusing on more acute or more basic problems. While women in higher education seem to have made some gains in absolute numbers and visibility, the improvement in the retention rates of girl children in primary, middle and secondary school levels has not been anything to feel complacent about even today (Datta & Kingdon, 2019).

Not just the girl child but the advocacy for child rights or protection has been a gendered responsibility and child right activists have functioned within the domain of women's rights activism. To begin with, child rights were articulated by activist writers like Tara Ali Baig (1972, 1979) more in terms of children's protection from exploitation. Beyond just the issues of discriminatory treatment meted out to the girl child, childcare and women's welfare were underscored as being intricately linked (Chaudhuri, 1984). Surprisingly, it took several decades before child rights could be framed around the more basic rights of children to access good education and nutrition.

Put together, this makes for a reading that, on the one hand, invests in women the responsibility to bring about social change by taking care of children and other familial responsibilities, contributing as workers, and by getting themselves educated—without which true and sustainable national development was said to be impossible. On the other hand, their bodies were identified as the site of control where ideally a spanner could be put to stop the 'uncontrolled population explosion' which was blamed for jeopardizing the project of national development.

If we pay attention to several articles published in the journal about women's rights in foreign countries, we notice that these were to do with complicating the western notions of women's liberation (Hursh, 1973; Paul, 1989; Rosenmayr, 1974). Several articles also focused on the situation of women's rights in South Asian and South East Asian countries (Nakane, 1975; Nayar, 1977; Papanek, 1977). The authors—sometimes of the same nationality as the society they were describing—placed the question of women's rights vis-à-vis prevailing levels of development of that society. The critical scrutiny of the outcomes of the women's liberation movements in the western world, especially in terms of their labour rights, is revelatory. Reading these articles, which point out the limits of western women's liberation movement, in conjunction with several other articles that discuss the achievements or goals of the Indian women's rights movement, we come to note a set of dissonances.

FRAME DISSONANCE

Foremost among these dissonances is the expression of complete faith in the Constitution of India as a framework which adequately responded to Indian women's aspirations. In her review of *Report of the Committee on the Status of Women in India*, Mina Swaminathan (1975) reports that the committee called the Constitution a 'radical' document 'embodying the objectives of a social revolution'. Reading her comments, one realizes that the committee read the Constitution as a cryptic document for clues to yet unattained objectives of social change. But because of this, the committee, and indeed the movement, found itself in the middle of a quandary. For example, Swaminathan commends the report thus: 'Far from being a Women's Lib inspired *trumpetting for personal freedoms*, it is commendable for the thoroughness of its survey and the *sobriety of its tone*' [emphasis added].' According to her, the Fabian approach of the Constitution brought the committee 'into conflict with both the traditional Indian approach and with the emerging modern group and family oriented way of thinking.' (Swaminathan, 1975, pp. 21)

We can see that the Indian women's rights activists of the time were aware of being torn between appearing distinct from the western liberal women's movement and pledging unwavering allegiance to a liberal Constitution. They are keenly aware that the domain of women's rights lies squarely within the improvement of the lot of a, largely, poor-toiling society. Meanwhile, they fail to notice that it is the constitutional framework itself that places the amelioration of women's status within the domain of (Hindu joint) families and (religious/ethnic) communities but props up the individual (woman) citizen as the locus of rights.

The dissonance within the constitutional frame was not the only dissonance that was pointed out by the votaries of equal gender rights.

There was also the contradiction of India 'living in its villages' and the rural societies being beset with social problems and economic woes. In the previously mentioned studies of the 1970s, the women being discussed are mostly rural women and agricultural labour, who were also assumed to be more backward than the rest. The enquiries published in *Social Change* were keenly interested in changes in roles that rural women performed (Dhillon, 1981; Singh, 1990). Later, the articles included a look at aspects such as the health of rural women, their child-rearing practices and migration patterns. Social-psychological perspectives were used in the analysis of most village and microstudies to examine regressive attitudes and prejudiced outlooks prevalent against women.

The third dissonance was to do with the continued portrayal in scholarship of the institution of family as being one of the most-privileged marker around which womanhood continued to be defined, but on the other hand, the crushing poverty and demands of nation-building mandated women to participate in wage work or paid labour.

WOMEN AS WORKERS: FROM NATIONAL DEVELOPMENT TO ECONOMIC AUTONOMY

Perhaps, it can be said with a certain degree of confidence that the research pertaining to gendered study of labour and employment is one of the most sustained and robust part of the scholarship on gender published in *Social Change*. But empirical research on women workers began slowly and picked up only in the 1980s. Prior to the CSWI report, we see that the little writing on women workers is only in the manner of assertion of women's right to wage/paid employment, the impediments to the same and demands for what ought to be. In 1975, economist Leela Gulati published an article in the *Economic & Political Weekly* on the issue of women's work participation (Gulati, 1975), inspired, in part, by the International Decade of Women and, partially, by a book on women's work participation in Africa by Ester Boserup (cf. Gulati, 2003). In an interesting narration, Gulati recounts that economists were doing interesting work at the time that stirred the questions of poverty, unemployment and development; secondary data was easily available but there was practically no interest in these same issues from a gendered lens.

This trend is reflected in *Social Change,* too. What triggered the robust body of research on women and employment was the awareness about the collection and availability of vast amounts of data for and by state's project of planned development. It was this data which also made it difficult (if one went scrutinising it) for scholars to jump to conclusions that were closest to their personal (class) realities. For example, while the public perception about the increased number of working women was well established due to the visibility of urban, elite women in higher-paid jobs, the committee found in its analysis of existing data that women's work participation rate had been declining since the beginning of the century and the trend had not been arrested by independence nor by centralized planned development. This was a shocking revelation and the reasons were not attributable merely to attitudes or even factors like educational attainments because it was easily observable that the quality of employment was in overall decline, jobs in organized sectors had shrunk and work in traditional crafts and small-scale industries was vanishing fast. The causes were structural and impinged upon the women more because they were the first to be edged out of the shrunken job market.

As mentioned earlier, women appeared as workers framed within the scholarship as equal sharers of the burden of national development (Kara, 1972). Their claim to wage work or paid work outside homes was not yet framed in the discourse of economic autonomy (Shariff, 1990). Although because of the census and labour commission surveys the work participation of women was known to be in mostly lowest-skilled and lowest-paid job sectors, there existed discourse which today—over four decades later—appears pandering to sexist notions of work and women's gender roles. What makes it interesting for the younger generation of feminist scholars is that this discourse was not inadvertent. A reading of the guiding principles adopted by the CSWI (cf. Bagchi, 2013, pp. 11–12) shows that this was a conscious construction.

The knowledge about women inhabiting particular sections of labour markets resulted in a propensity of gendered labour research to focus on those sectors. Reading the articles published in *Social Change* over the years and in the special issues that appeared in 1985 and 1990, one can see the diversity of sectors in which women went on to engage in paid work—namely in the agricultural sector, home-based work, for example, bidi-making, handicrafts and entrepreneurship, in the urban, informal construction sector and even in the urban service sector. These studies often bring great nuance to the specific issues of women belonging to different communities, regions, or cultures, for example, the role of caste and tribal identity in work participation (Bose, 1985).

From late 1990s, one can discern the attention scholars paid to the newer sectors of work which engaged Indian women, for example, export-oriented manufacturing (like garments), domestic work or IT-enabled industries. With the advent of neoliberalism, the idea of nation-building and national development seem to recede from these studies and themes of exploitation, drudgery emerge. Apart from such notable and well-recorded examples such as the Self-Employed Women's Association (SEWA), there are not many studies in *Social Change* that record the attempts of women to unionize and gain bargaining capacity for economic autonomy.

DISCERNING STRUCTURE: POLITICAL PARTICIPATION

To look for the trajectory of how Indian women found themselves in such a situation where their scholars and advocates were surprised by their 'status' being more deplorable than expected, we will need to step back to examine the stand taken by the Indian women in the national public sphere at the founding moments of the republic. Indeed, to the feminists who came of age many generations later—and admittedly built upon the freedoms gained by these foremothers in hard battles—it is astonishing that leading Indian women of the time found the idea of reservations repugnant to their 'intelligence'. It is profound that to entertain the thought they would be accepting that they are of lower intelligence or of a lower status. In the Constituent Assembly where there was only one Dalit woman member and one Muslim woman member, they put their undoubting faith in the promise that all shall be equal in the newly-independent India. To them, the biggest proof of this promise was the extension of adult franchise universally.

The rejection of special provisions was not only to have a debilitating consequence on the political future of women and their stake in decision-making in independent India, but it was to have repercussions for other sections who were demanding these protections.

Muslims were wholly unsuccessful in getting even the job reservations that the Scheduled Caste/Scheduled Tribes (SC/ST) were successful in getting, and the demand for a separate electorate was scuttled entirely. Appreciating the women's stance on the matter, Dr Pattabhi Sitaramayya said in the Constituent Assembly debates,

> It is a gentleman's agreement that we have entered into, a terrible responsibility that we have taken upon our shoulders, when we asked them to give up their reservations and their separate electorates. We have to find as many representatives from the Muslim community through the medium of the joint electorate as would have been their legitimate share, if they had their separate electorates. Even so with the Indian Christians and others. And the way to all this was pointed by our women. I admire the women who in the Provincial Model Constitution Committee and in the Central Constitution Committee came forward and said, 'No separate electorate for women, no reservation for women'. Of course, they stand to gain now. But it required courage and imagination to say so then. They showed the way to the Muslims. (Constituent Assembly debates on 25 November 1949)

Instead of a structural provision that ensured representation, women opted for a gentleman's agreement and approval of the upper-caste men. Later too, this tendency was frequently on display. Even if the law gave women a right, for example, in property, Indian women were to routinely exercise their agency to waive off these same rights. This conformed to the national image of Indian women crafted during the nationalist movement of being 'dignified' in sacrifice and garnered them approval for being superior citizens for having put lofty national interests ahead of the 'narrow' group interest, unlike SC/ST and Muslims.

A view of the structural nature of patriarchy was still not common when *Social Change* began publishing. As we have seen in the iconography of the inaugural cover page, it was considered enough that women performed their duty of voting in their representative diligently. But this would soon change. Representation of women became an issue as a means to ensure that women's voices and opinions mattered in arenas of policymaking having direct implications for women. The demands to increase the participation of women in the legislation and policymaking began to be raised also because it was argued that women's experience can enrich the policies and laws. The overwhelming absence of women and a hegemonic usurping of political space by men was undeniable.

A good example of this realization or shift in understanding of 'the absence'—not just as an issue of status but that of structural exclusion—can be discerned in an article published in *Social Change* in 1978 included in this volume titled 'Indian Women and their Participation in Politics'. Usha Mehta, the author, discussing women's participation in electoral politics reports,

> In a survey conducted amongst the women candidates contesting for 1971 parliamentary and 1972 assembly elections an attempt was made to find out if this low participation was due to women being afraid to violating the traditional Indian norms or because of their lacking motivation to enter the fray. A majority of them blamed the discriminatory policy of the political parties. Political parties, they complained, not only failed in encouraging them to participate in politics but sometimes adopted positively discriminatory and discouraging attitudes. (Mehta, 1978, pp. 33)

At the end of the article, Mehta proposes a set of remedies that include a few focusing on creating awareness and transforming attitudes, but most are more structural in nature and pertain to fundamental changes in the way political parties function.

The CSWI report had, among other things, brought to light the 'worsening political position of women, and the inadequate positive impact of government-sponsored programmes and policies on their status' (Hasan, 2018, pp. 129). Hasan argues that, 'it was the first unequivocal indictment of the government's promise of gender equality' (ibid). While the majority of the members of the committee, including its chairperson, still did not wish to take the path of reservation, two members of the committee, Vina Mazumdar and Lotika Sarkar, in fact, envisioned reservation at the highest level, such as in the Parliament. The report eventually carried their recorded dissents on this matter (Sarkar & Mazumdar, 1999). A quarter of century after the promulgation of the constitution, leading women's rights activists and scholars again voiced a resounding no to staking a claim in political decision-making at the highest level of India's polity.

The CSWI did register the concern and its response was to 'widen' the discussion to talk of ensuring not only the representation of women but a substantive representation which could potentially make a difference at the grassroots level (Bagchi, 2013). But the aspirations expressed by Mazumdar and Sarkar were to only grow. The question of women's representation remained an issue of mobilization outside the state, in the arena of civil society. Besides, the participation of women in electoral politics as voters was swelling gradually by every general and state election.

In the 1980s and 1990s, the demand for greater presence of women in different political activities in civil society began to gather momentum (Menon, 2000) and the institutional spaces within the state could not remain oblivious to it. By the mid-1990s, various women's organizations appealed to all political parties to ensure women's representation in state assemblies and parliament. The demand took the shape of ensuring a minimum number of women through reservation in parliament so that the issue is not left to the internal dynamics of political parties. However, as might be expected, these assertions would not easily convert into reality. The Parliament of India saw democratization after the 1990s with the advent of leaders from various marginal sections of society in parliament (Rai & Sharma, 2000). Women parliamentarians like Pramila Dandavate and Geeta Mukherjee played a pivotal role in shaping the 108th Constitution Amendment Bill, popularly known as the Women's Reservation Bill which was introduced in parliament in 1996 and has been pending since. But the bill is marred by controversies within the movement about the recognition of difference and diversity among the women, as much as it is hampered by patriarchal impediments (Menon, 2000). The demand for a sub-quota for women from backward sections within this 33 per cent quota for women in parliament is found unreasonable by a sizable section of the women's movement.

The late 1990s and the first decade of the millennium witnessed repeated attempts by successive governments to introduce the Women's Reservation Bill to reserve 33 per cent seats in the Parliament of India but all in vain. Meanwhile, women were ensured reserved seats in the Panchayati Raj elections. It ranged from 33 per cent going up to 50 per cent seats reserved for the women in panchayats and municipalities in different states. How substantive has been this representation has been a matter of great deal of research in political science. Farah Naqvi's qualitative study on the first-generation elected women representatives, included in this volume, is an excellent example of this body of work. Several other village studies published in *Social Change* have attempted to evaluate the potential of the PRI (Panchayati Raj Institutes) reservations for women for transforming gender dynamics.

Unfortunately, there is little sign that women's participation in electoral politics at the panchayat levels acts as a launching pad for them to reach bigger platforms or national-level politics. Drawing on the experience of quotas and sub-quotas for women from the SC/ST/OBC communities at the panchayat level, it could be argued that, possibly, the women's rights movement has been committing the same blunder that it did at the founding moments of the republic.

In the decade of 2010, the demand for the Women's Reservation Bill seemed to have lost traction. Both the political class and the civil society seem to have moved on to more pressing matters. In the current (17th) Lok Sabha, 14 per cent seats are occupied by women candidates (as compared to 12 per cent in the 16th Lok Sabha), which is greater than any previous Lok Sabha. So, one could draw slight consolation from this marginal rise in the proportion of women parliamentarians, if one wanted to feel content. But when it comes to state assemblies, the average percentage of women legislators in all states is less than 10 per cent. The percentage of women who turn out to vote is still continuing its rising trend in each subsequent polls.

RECOVERY, REPRESENTATION AND PRESENCE

Concomitant with the issues of political representation, the voices of women from marginalized sections also gain capacity to articulate their lived experiences, thereby challenging their stock representation in mainstream discourses. In some of these fresh articulations within gender studies, scholars use feminist methods of recovery of lost history and suppressed voices. Like in the other aspects, here too the motivations began in form of writing a national narrative of the country's past that can provide the resources for the anti-colonial struggle, but this method came to be used also for the struggle for equality in Independent India and the struggle of women to appear in the Indian public sphere as equal citizen invested equally in its future.

> The past was thus an important item in public debates to do with women's modernity. The central question around which this discourse evolved was whether the past produced the disadvantages that women had to overcome in order to be fully participating citizens, or whether it was a resource that made Indian women especially suited to participation in national life, either as virtuous mothers and wives at home or as dutiful members of the public sphere. (Mazumdar, 2003, pp. 2131)

Feminist historians used religious, mythical and literary historical texts to glean a view of a past which was more emancipated, so that Indian women could walk towards a modern future without breaking ties with their past. These efforts involved putting together narratives that established women as revered and autonomous beings who wielded power in ancient India. This feminist 'invention' of a past which allowed for modernity yet was sanctified by the nationalist discourse is an intriguing phenomenon. Trouble is that it mostly resurrected and projected a Hindu past, conspicuously forgetting other diversities. But soon enough feminist scholars of later generations began to use this method as a tool of critique. Textual analysis of media texts helped women first discern and then resist unedifying representation. Feminist media persons and feminist critics also complicated the field further and it was more and more common to observe what scholars have called 'mediatization' of the women's movement (Gopal, 2019) to denote actual media representation while the movement was still negotiating the issues involved in women's representation.

Since the discussion is on the matter of textuality, a comment on the form, length and complexity of argument contained in the selected articles is warranted. The persistent nature of most gendered concerns meant that scholarship has grown in complexity. From the small sample of selected articles published in *Social Change* included in this volume, it can be discerned that discussions on persistent problems and enduring concerns have grown more and more intricate. The questions posed demand sophisticated data collection and analysis, and scholars continually innovate on the sources of information or data. The research techniques and discussion of findings show more interdisciplinarity and fine-grain reading of realities. For example, literary sources and media texts in feminist studies are not just read to see and recover a simplistic narrative of what women are doing or being treated as in the story, but they are seen as important records of dominant forces of their time and the contemporary forms of resistance.

But the representation of women from marginalized communities, SC or Dalit women, tribal women and Muslim women remained ensconced in the same framing of backwardness, status, health status, educational status, attitudinal impediments to development and problems of attitude. Some niches within these did make some progress. For example, there are a notable number of articles on the employment, income and landlessness among tribal women farm workers. The issue of cultural specificity of tribal women and their rights was something not explored even in the special issue titled *Status of Tribal Women in India,* published as late as 1993.

Dalit women's personal or autobiographical narratives were recorded using oral narrative methods or recovered from material from personal archives or oral testimonies in ground-breaking work, for example, by Sharmila Rege (2006). But the issues of positionality and self-reflexivity of Hindu, upper-caste women scholars who were doing this work was raised first by Dalit men scholars and then, later, by Dalit women themselves. Gopal Guru (1995) and Rege debated the Dalit feminist standpoint in the *Economic & Political Weekly*. In 2009, Vivek Kumar wrote in *Social Change* to discuss the issue of representation of Dalit women within the women's movement. The debates were often adversarial and the leading feminist scholars in India, surprisingly, continue to indicate aversion to demands of reflexivity about their dominant positioning, while in western academia, Indian origin women scholars, such as Chandra Mohanty (1988), raised the discourse of difference of women of colour.

The studies on women from marginalized identities were not only very few in numbers but also, methodologically, they were also cast in static frames. Quite recently, ethnographic works are appearing which have begun challenging the stereotypical representations of the experiences of the women of difference.

A BREAK FROM STATE-LED CHANGE: RECOGNIZING IMPUNITY

For the movement to come out of the shadows of post-colonial nationalism, it took innumerable instances where women got into the hair of the exploitative development state when it was asserting its eminent domain over Adivasi land, or the military state crushing secessionist forces in Kashmir and in the north-eastern states, or the cunning state that looked the other way while providing criminal impunity to state and non-state actors in instances of mass violence against minorities, or the hegemonic state exercising its soft cultural might to exploit, violate and regulate women's lives though limiting representation and manipulating narratives. It took Indian women's rights movement a long time to walk out of a sometime paternalistic relationship with the Indian state that had now turned violent. It was not long before the honeymoon period was over and the toxic patriarchy inherent in the modern nation-state, through its monopoly over violence, began to manifest itself.

To being with, the view on the matter of law and women was that legislating social gender relations in the framework of the Indian Constitution was largely progressive by design, and the problem was the non-implementation of these laws. Often, the articles published in *Social Change* also argued—following the CSWI report—that some laws pertaining to gender inequity, for example, the Dowry Prohibition Act or Child Marriage Act had unintended 'loopholes' or were not as strongly punitive as required. The only big problem in this domain, they kept repeating, was the existence of Muslim personal law. The committee has unequivocally recommended the adoption of a Uniform Civil Code (UCC). But another important recommendation that the committee made was 'the establishment of family courts to deal with the *settlement of all family problems* as opposed to the present system' (emphasis added). The contradiction of the two recommendations needs to be brought out in sharp relief. The committee in its wisdom thought that Muslim women needed to be brought into the same civil justice system which the other women had been disappointed in. While there are unending laments about Muslim women still caught within patriarchal Islamic law, a comparable amount of ink has not been spent on evaluating and recording the 'seminal' role that family courts have played in protecting the 'sanctity and integrity of family' at the price of individual women's rights.

The valorisation of women's 'status' in the Indian family was necessary because it was the family which was the unit of the national community in the post-colonial nationalist discourse and not the individual citizen. The nation was also said to live in its villages. For these two reasons, it could hardly be a modern, liberal democracy. The articulation of women's rights was caught up in the paradox of this post-colonial moment. The palimpsest of a national narrative which the movement was also seeking to selectively delete and rewrite was a hypertext. It not only had the text of nationalist narrative of the colonial era written on it with a persistent pigment, but there were several other authors simultaneously working on it and contesting the changes. Problems were bound to arise when the feminist narratives did not quite fit with the new image in which the post-colonial state was trying to build the nation.

This is reminiscent of Partha Chatterjee's (1989) characterization of anti-colonial struggle as having simultaneously opened up the possibility of women's participation in the nationalist movement and also edged out the women's question from a political sphere to a cultural, domestic sphere. The reformists in the early colonial period and the nationalists of the late colonial period both shared the reluctance to demand any radical restructuring of family relations. As the previous discussion shows, postcolonial feminists seemed also to have inherited this reluctance. Eulogizing family remained the norm in the few decades after independence. But there are exceptions to this norm, and we will see later how this norm itself had to give way in the face of burgeoning evidence of violence. But meanwhile, the discourse had to go through a dangerous liaison with the state and the paradox of nation-building framework strengthening the patriarchal structures.

The issue of ineffective prevention of child marriage despite the law was further extended into the debate on discouraging early marriage not only as a measure conducive to increased educational attainments but also as a cure for the problem for fertility and population. Regrettably, abortion or MTP were also discussed in the light of the same anxieties. But soon, the discourse took the form of discussing MTP as reproductive autonomy for women. Reminiscent of the debate around the questions of political participation, Indian women received the gift of legalized abortion just like they got voting rights from the Indian state. Just as voting rights did not mean political agency, legalized abortion was not meant to translate into reproductive autonomy for women. With the benefit of hindsight, scholars have debated if the state expressly meant abortion as a measure for population control (Phadke, 1998). Later, easy availability of the amniocentesis technology was facilitated by the government to allow Indian families to indulge in their male-child preference without giving birth to too many 'unwanted' girl children (Das Gupta & Mari Bhat, 1997). Accessible sex determination and legalized abortion combined together to create a nightmare (Kumar, 1983) for the women's movement in India. This aspect raises an important consideration that the women's movement has often been instrumentalized by the modern nation state to further it projects (Menon, 1993). This, of course, is not a phenomenon that is unique to India. World over, women's right or women's liberation movements often find themselves co-opted by the agenda of capital or state but having open discussions about the same is found difficult (Fraser, 2013, 2017).

Continuing well into the 1980s, the debate on MTP intensified around the time the bill was tabled and passed into a law. As such, *Social Change* contains a mini archive that records the opinions of the proponents of development as population control and public opinion around MTP and the critics of the statist approach.

Unfortunately, female foeticide remains an enduring concern until today and articles continued to bring to light the various empirical realities created by the legal, technological and cultural semantic field around this issue on the pages of *Social Change* over the years. Related to this is the gender imbalance and sex ratio. One odd article raising interesting issues on the role of technology diffusion and the question of women's empowerment (Singh, 2011) has appeared in *Social Change* but, more generally, the connection of technology and biopower of the state over women's bodies and life worlds has not seemed to catch on much within gender studies in India until the recent work on surrogacy.

Later, in the decade of the 2000s several articles were published based on micro-studies that show the impact of the lopsided sex ratio on family structure, property and social fabric of society. In states such as Haryana, where the deficit had been acute, the phenomenon of the missing girl child had become the matter of missing women and survey studies conducted in villages showed invention of practices that further dehumanized women (Ahlawat, 2009; Mukherjee, 2013). Inevitably, interest in marriage (or the lack of it) continued and articles kept appearing on such things as conversions in inter-religious marriages, unmarried (single) working women and plight of widows.

Another problem that has proven to be tenacious has been of dowry and related violence. While the issue seems to have been passionately raised throughout the late 1970s and even in the 1980s, it seems to have lost currency later among the gender scholars working on violence against women, although there is no evidence that the role of dowry in domestic violence has abated. The exhaustion of the women's movement and debate on the issue of dowry-related killings and violence is a perfect illustration of fatigue that sets into the movement after it succeeds in getting laws with harshest penalties enacted (Menon, 2004). In addition, there is a bare savagery about dowry-related violence, especially 'bride burning', which is difficult to couch in any kind of discursive jugglery. The matter does not lend itself easily to continually evolving discourses and philosophical explorations, unlike other enduring concerns such as the thorny issue of political representation or, even, ethics of sex-selective abortion. The phenomenon being very specific to the dominant cultures of the Indian subcontinent may have added to the fatigue in discussing it.

Because of their faith in the constitutional framework treating women as equal, women's rights advocates in India neglected the study of law beyond enumerating the constitutional provisions and the fate of post-independence legal reforms. Even the CSWI limited itself to a scrutiny of the legal texts. In their consultations, whenever they heard problems related to criminal law, their response was how to think of ways in which the text of the law could be improved. So, on rape, the committee recommended only two changes. One, the rationalization of age of consent between the IPC offence of rape and the Medical Termination of Pregnancy Act, and the second was that consent obtained by coercion was not to be read as consent. Lotika Sarkar was to later confess that the committee members did this because, 'It had not occurred to (them) that rape was such a major problem in our society.' (CWDS, 1998, pp. 97). A few years later, this misconception in the movement was to be challenged in 1980 by the rude reality of prevalence of rape as a tool of routine violence against women, especially Dalit, Adivasi and Muslim women, by men from dominant groups and police forces with impunity. It has taken scholars over two decades of study to evolve a complex understanding of rape not only as an offense against body of an individual woman by a criminal but as a systemic oppression enabled by impunity created through a whole cluster of laws and sociopolitical/geopolitical realities for raping women who bore certain identities (Baxi, 2000).

Regrettably, this long and arduous learning experience of the movement is yet to fully become part of its quick recall memory. Acid burning by stalkers and honour killings (of men as well) by families of women who exercise their choice in selection of partners, especially breaking the taboo for inter-caste and inter-religious marriages, are reported frequently in the media but have not received the deserved attention of researchers and scholars or even the movement. The response on acid burning has been to demand regulation of acid sales, and the violent hostility to interreligious marriages has triggered debates on religious conversions, religious freedom and even calling into question what a constitutional practice of secularism might entail in India!

The history of debates on Personal Law in India, especially the communal nature of the discourse around Muslim Personal Law in particular, is long and tortured. I have flagged some of the problems on this account in the preceding discussion. Muslim women make an appearance only in the discussion on UCC which is used and understood in most of the literature on women's questions, or the movement in India as a code for abolition of only Muslim Personal

Law. There is hardly any discussion that divulges as to what would be the exact contents of the UCC. Moreover, the gendered exploration of legal pluralism has been absent in women's studies and has gone unremarked for a very long time. The customary laws of tribal communities and many other regional differences in customary laws do not get space in the discussion on UCC. But in every discussion on Muslim women—when it happens—the same hackneyed discussions on Shahbano, triple talaq and so on is regurgitated, or a story of economic and/or educational backwardness that hinges only on their religion, as if they inhabit a watertight world in which no other social force has a sway but Islam.

The question that interests me here is this—after the usual trajectory of movement mobilization for demanding a (stricter) penal provision on the matter has been traversed and succeeds in getting a legislation, what form should/does a feminist response take to the continuance of that violent social or cultural practice?

For a long time, the story seemed to reach some kind of dead end after the enactment or amendment of the desired law. Recently, the answer that many scholars have given to this conundrum is that feminist praxis must follow the law and see what happens to it and to the lives of its subjects/actors. In other words, instead of leaving vaguely vexed comments about loopholes and lax implementation, study law in action—conduct feminist practice and research in judicial spaces. This can take form of court ethnographies (Baxi, 2014) or even critical reflective accounts of feminist lawyering (Grover, 2002). An article by Flavia Agnes included in this volume 'Has the Codified Hindu Law Changed Gender Relationships?' is one such example of enquiry that utilizes feminist lawyering to create knowledge. As such, this is not only a legal studies' push to gender studies to explore hitherto unexplored sites of research but also a feminist contribution to the sociology of law (Baxi, 2008).

Feminist scholarship and praxis have moved from articulating aspirations for equal rights for women in India to appear as a perspective to evaluate and critique any and all spheres of life. This is, obviously, not to claim that it faces no challenge but that many frontiers remain yet to be explored.

A NOTE ON THE SELECTION OF ARTICLES FOR THE VOLUME

The selection has been mindful in, at least, affording a glimpse of the work of some of the illustrious scholars, lawyers and trade-unionists such as Durgabai Deshmukh, Maniben Kara, Mina Swaminathan, Vina Mazumdar, Devaki Jain, Uma Chakravarty, Mathreyi Krishnaraj, Kumkum Roy, Farah Naqvi and Flavia Agnes, among others. In addition, care has been taken to create space for lesser-known scholars whose articles are excellent contributions to illustrate the development of the discourse on the theme in the journal and elsewhere.

While many men have also written and contributed their works on gender in the journal, wherever possible, my attempt was to prioritize inclusion of articles written by women scholars. Three articles written by men included in the volume are important contributions in that theme that signpost a major turn in the development of the discourse. Their inclusion is also an example of the fact that gender concerns have also been of interest to men researchers, not only because of their feminist convictions or passion for equality and social justice but also because of disciplinary or methodological, or just historical, importance of that issue.

The selection of articles in this volume is aimed at giving the readers and researchers a bird's eye view of the expansive academic research and writing on women's rights in India. The selected articles are organized in five, theme-based sections, namely Indian Women's Rights Movement, Women as Workers, Political Participation, Culture and Identity and, finally, Law and Violence. Each section has three or four articles which are chronologically organized. Each section has a brief introduction in which my attempt is to highlight the importance of the arguments contained in the individual pieces and to present a brief assessment of their place in the shifts or continuities of the discourse on that issue in India.

It appears to me that one will not be entirely amiss if the articles published in *Social Change* are taken to lie in a sphere where academic writing crosses over to influence civil society and vice versa. Some articles do that on their own, but all these articles put together constitute a record of a feminist praxis in India. The micro and survey studies, and the observations and critiques of experts in their field record the empirical signs or indication of the existence of a certain social reality or of social change occurring in different sections of Indian society. And, sometimes, one sees an expansive exploration that challenges an existing framework in which an issue is examined and proposes a new one in its place. Often, it is difficult to categorize the contributors of *Social Change* selected in this volume as being either activist or scholar, or even whether they are activists first or scholars first. Even in terms of their professional locations, they keep traversing boundaries—from lawyers to trade unionists, journalists, economists, historians, development workers and even to areas further afield.

Apart from the selected articles, I am mindful of articles on themes that were published in *Social Change* but they are not included in the volume. In the discussion in this introductory essay, I have commented on some of these issues. Broadly, I have not included any articles on the issue of tribal women, education, health and the land question for women because this volume is part of a series which contains volumes on these issues. Although where necessary in this introduction, I have mentioned these issues to forward my arguments, I have refrained from making any extensive remarks on these themes. I also decided to exclude from consideration any reviews of literature that seemed not to propose any fresh argument or formulation on the issue at hand. I have also not been able to include articles that were too specific and limited to a case study or a microstudy, even though some of them were extremely well done and interesting, purely because of space constraints and the broader objective of mapping the discourse. Throughout this introduction and the section introductions, I have commented on methodological issues wherever there was something striking but I found it tough to discern any patterns in methodological innovations and developments. Perhaps, I could have expended more effort on scrutinizing this further but, be that as it may, I could only observe a happy polyphony and eclectic approach of the scholars to methodology.

Gender concerns have reflected in the pages of *Social Change* within articles on myriad other issues such as displacement, urbanization, land, poverty and crime. This is in no way an exhaustive list but only an enumeration of prominent themes appearing in the journal. There are also other issues which are of great importance in women's or gender studies that were not reflected in articles published in *Social Change*. Articles on sexuality, in general, and non-binary gender identities, in particular, make a late appearance. This is, perhaps, because the scholars working on these issues considered *Social Change* an academic space which was for more developmental view of social change while the issues of sexuality and the lesbian, gay, bisexual, transgender and queer community may have been considered more in the domain of the studies of politics of lifestyle (Giddens, 1991). Possibly for the same reason, the studies of masculinity do not appear in the pages of the journal as gendered concerns, although some articles do note the changes on notions of masculinity as one of the peripheral concerns. Of grave concern is that there were too few articles on Dalit and Muslim women to choose from. In my assessment, this paucity of articles on the issue is, for the most part, indicative of stunting and staleness of the discourse on the issues of Muslim and Dalit women for a long time.

Finally, a personal note: I have served on the *Social Change* editorial team from 2014–2019 as its book review editor. Most academic journals can be expected to publish quality research catering to specialized scholarly interest and niche audience. *Social Change,* however, goes several steps further to mentor young scholars, and to prod and invite senior scholars to contribute to the understanding and practice of social change in India. It is not just an institution for having published regularly for 50 years now but for conceptualizing social research as a method of intervention. As a Muslim woman scholar, it was an absolute privilege for me to be asked by the CSD to comment on the scholarship around gender and women's rights movement in India. I hope that my standpoint has brought an edge to the analysis of the debates on gender, particularly in *Social Change*. To read and comment on the margins of the pages of 50 years of *Social Change* was a task that was its own reward.

REFERENCES

Ahlawat, N. (2009). Missing brides in rural Haryana: A study of adverse sex ratio, poverty and addiction. *Social Change, 39*(1), 46–63.

Bagchi, J. (2013). Towards equality. *Social Scientist, 41*(11/12), 11–23.

Baxi, P. (2000). Rape, retribution, state: On whose bodies? *Economic & Political Weekly, 35*(14), 1196–1200.

———. (2008). Feminist contributions to sociology of law: A review. *Economic and Political Weekly,* 79–85.

———. (2014). *Public secrets of law: Rape trials in India*. Oxford University Press.

Baig, T. A. (1972). Protection for the child. *Social Change, 2*(3), 31–38.

———. (1979). SOS children's villages—Care for the abandoned child. *Social Change, 9*(4), 29–34.

Bhagat, R. B. (1990). Status of women and age at marriage. *Social Change, 20*(2), 20–25.

Bose, A. (1972). Family planning and social security. *Social Change, 2*(3), 21–26

Bose, S. (1985). Caste, tribe and female labour participation. *Social Change, 15*(2), 15–20.

Centre for Women's Development Studies (CWDS). (1998). Making of the 'founding text' report. *Indian Journal of Gender Studies, 5*(1), 87–113.

Chakravorty, S. (1975). Farm women labour: Waste and exploitation. *Social Change, 5*(1–2), 9–16.

Chatterjee, P. (1989). Colonialism, nationalism, and colonialized women: The contest in India. *American Ethnologist, 16*(4), 622–633.

Chaudhuri, M. (1984). Sex bias in child nutrition. *Social Change, 14*(3), 50–52.

Committee on the Status of Women in India (CSWI). (1994). *Towards equality: Report of the CSWI*. Ministry of Social Welfare, GoI.

Dandekar, K. (1974). Trends of fertility behaviour reflecting the status of women. *Social Change, 4*(3–4), 30–41.

Das Gupta, M., & Mari Bhat, P. N. (1997). Fertility decline and increased manifestation of sex bias in India. *Population Studies, 51*(3), 307–15.

Datta, S., & Kingdon, G. G. (2019). Gender bias in intra-household allocation of education in India: Has it fallen over time? *IZA Discussion Papers*, No. 12671, Institute of Labor Economics (IZA), Bonn.

Dhillon, G. (1981). The changing role of rural women. *Social Change, 11*(2), 21–30.

Dubey, M. (1999). Professor Amar Kumar Singh: A tribute. *Social Change, 29*(3–4), 6–11.

Firoz, N. (1990). Status of women in Islam. *Social Change, 20*(2), 13–19.

Fraser, N. (2013). *Fortunes of feminism: From state-managed capitalism to neoliberal crisis*. Verso Books.

Fraser, N. (2017). Crisis of care? On the social–reproductive contradictions of contemporary capitalism. *Social Reproduction Theory, 23*.

Ganguli, B. N. (1971). Family welfare and the variables of population dynamics. *Social Change, 1*(3), 15–22.

Giddens, A. (1991). *Modernity and self-identity: Self and society in the late modern age*. Stanford University Press.

Gopal, P. (2019). Media meddlers: Feminism, television and gendered media work in India. *Feminist Media Histories, 5*(1), 39–62.

Grover, V. (2002). The elusive quest for justice: Delhi 1984 to Gujarat 2002. In S. Varadarajan (Ed.) *Gujarat: The making of a tragedy* (pp. 355–388). Penguin Books.

Gulati, L. (1975). Female work participation: A study of inter-state differences. *Economic & Political Weekly, 10*(1–2), 35–42.

Gulati, L. (2003). Full circle: Women's studies sans institutions. In D Jain, & P. Rajput (Eds.), *Narratives from the women's studies family: Recreating knowledge.* SAGE Publications.

Guru, G. (1995). Dalit women talk differently. *Economic & Political Weekly, 30*(41–42), 2548–2550.

Hasan, Z. (2018). *Agitation to legislation: Negotiating equity and justice in India.* Oxford University Press.

Hursh, G. D. (1973). Women's liberation in the United States. *Social Change, 3*(1–2), 20–27.

Kara, M. (1972). National development and women workers. *Social Change, 2*(1), 51–58.

Kumar, D. (1983). Male utopias or nightmares? *Economic & Political Weekly, 18*(3), 61–64.

Menon, N. (1993). Abortion and the law: Questions for feminism. *Canadian Journal of Women & Law, 6*(1), 103–108.

Menon, N. (2000). Elusive 'woman': Feminism and women's reservation bill. *Economic & Political Weekly, 35*(43/44), 3835–3844.

Menon, N. (2004). *Recovering subversion: Feminist politics beyond the law.* University of Illinois Press.

Mohanty, C. M. (1988). Under western eyes: Feminist scholarship and colonial discourses. *Feminist Review, 30*(1), 61–88.

Mukherjee, B. N. (1974). Status of married women in Haryana, Tamil Nadu and Meghalaya. *Social Change, 4*(1), 4–17.

Mukherjee, B. N. (1975). A multidimensional conception of status of women. *Social Change, 5*(1–2), 27–44.

Mukherjee, S. (2013). Skewed sex ratio and migrant brides in Haryana: Reflections from the field. *Social Change, 43*(1), 37–52.

Nakane, C. (1975). Women in cross-cultural perspective. *Social Change, 5*(1), 3–8.

Nayar, U. (1977). Women of Sri Lanka. *Social Change, 7*(3-4), 31–46.

Papanek, H. (1977). Women in South and South-East Asia: Issues and research. *Social Change, 7*(1), 24–35.

Paul, M.C. (1989). Colonialism and women's education in India. *Social Change, 19*(2), 3–17.

Phadke, S. (1998). *Pro-choice or population control: A study of the Medical Termination of Pregnancy Act, Government of India, 1971.* https://www.academia.edu/270056/Pro_Choice_or_Population_Control_A_Study_of_the_Medical_Termination_of_Pregnancy_Act_Government_of_India_1971

Rai, S., & Sharma, K. (2000). Democratising the Indian Parliament: The 'reservation for women debate'. In S Rai (Ed.), *International perspectives on gender and democratisation* (pp. 149–165). Macmillan.

Rai, U. (2019). Kamla Mankekar (1928–2018): Founder-editor, Social Change. *Social Change, 49*(1), 186–188.

Reddy, P. H. (1978). Family structure and fertility. *Social Change, 8*(1), 26–33.

Rege, S. (2006). *Writing caste/writing gender: Narrating Dalit women's testimonies.* Kali for Women.

Rosenmayr, L. (1974). The underdeveloped position of the woman in industrial society. *Social Change, 4*(2), 4–14.

Sarkar, L., & Mazumdar, V. (1999). Note of dissent by Lotika Sarkar and Vina Mazumdar. *Indian Journal of Gender Studies, 6*(1), 134–137.

Shariff, A. (1990). Women workers: Gender equality and female autonomy. *Social Change, 20*(2), 46–51.

Singh, A. K. (1980). Women: The most disliked group—Ranking of prejudices. *Social Change, 10*(3–4), 3–9.

Singh, M. (2010). Empowerment of women: gaps in technology diffusion. *Social Change, 40*(4), 563–576.

Singh, U. (1990). Changing socio-economic conditions and rural women. *Social Change, 20*(2), 52–57.

Swaminathan, M. (1975). Miles to go. *Social Change, 5*(1–2), 21–26.

Tharu, S. J., & Lalita, K. (Eds.). (1991). *Women Writing in India: 600 BC to the early twentieth century* (Vol. 1). Feminist Press at CUNY.

Vig, O. P (1976). Neglect of female education: A risk for family planning programme in controlling fertility in India. *Social Change, 6*(3–4), 22–28.

Wasi, M. (1971). Educating India's women for social change. *Social Change, 1*, pp. 24–30.

Section I

Women's Rights Movement

Sectional Introduction

Ghazala Jamil

After more than seven decades of independence, it is to be expected that several accounts of the women's rights movement in India have been written. Most began by tracing the antecedents of the movement in the reform efforts during the colonial period, although there is near unanimity that the opinions of reformist men shaped these efforts. The participation of women in the anti-colonial movement is highlighted. Almost all chroniclers of the movement mark activities around the setting up of the Committee on the Status of Women in India (CSWI) in 1971 and its subsequent report in 1975 as the beginning of a concerted women's rights movement in independent India.

Thereafter, scholars such as Neera Desai and Vibhuti Patel (1985), Vina Mazumdar and Indu Agnihotri (1995), Shilpa Phadke (2003), Anupama Rao (2010) and Radha Kumar (2014) have written the story of the movement giving us almost a decadal assessment. These authors have used a combination of several approaches to develop a movement perspective. The most-frequently employed approach in these narratives is to discuss the movement issue by issue—tracing the discussions on each. The second approach is to recount the movement as a series of collective efforts, namely women's organizations and protest events. Another approach is to tell the story of the movement through the lives, work and opinions of individuals considered main actors of the movement. The fourth approach is to chronicle the expansion of women's rights through legislative action or policymaking and women's advocacy for the same.

In this volume, my attempt has been not to present a comprehensive and historical account of the movement but to critically comment on some important debates. With the advantage of hindsight, I have also been able to interpolate the implications of the framing of these debates by mainstream gender-rights activists. The directions in which discourses developed, the privileging of certain viewpoints and the silencing/forgetting of different voices has had a material impact on the lives of not just women but also communities because of the gendered nature of realities.

The four articles included in this section are examples of writing by women's rights scholars which assumes a movement perspective. Each of the articles exemplify different challenges that confronted the movement and its response.

The first article in this section 'Indian Women: Some Reflections on a Two-sector Analysis' is authored by economist Devaki Jain. The article is important for several reasons. First and foremost, it illustrates attempts of scholars of the time to search for and invent frameworks. As Jain's discussion shows, the primary concern is to examine manifest realities in a manner that suggests ways to intervene effectively. It should be clear that Jain is writing in the absence of reliable data that could point to the cause of prevailing problems. Her categorization of the variety of views prevalent about the status of women at the time is the second reason why this article is important. She identifies 'death, disease and exhaustion' due to childbearing and strenuous wage/unpaid labour as the burden of poor women which needed immediate finance outlays and planned infrastructure development, whereas it was assumed that women in the 'rich sector' had overcome these burdens and the interventions they required were understood to be more intangible and difficult to plan for short-term impact. Thirdly and notably, even though the article acknowledges the different experiences of women belonging to different classes and advocates a differential response, the framing is not that of a Marxist-class analysis. The persistence of subservience in different ways is explained by the presence of adverse economic conditions and interventions are judged through cost-benefit exercises.

Mina Swaminathan's article 'Miles to Go' is emblematic of the self-awareness of the women's rights movement which comes to fore as women scholar-activists engage with the empirical realities of the Indian women beyond the legal provisions made for them in independent India. The article demonstrates that disagreements and constructive criticism have always existed in the movement. This seemingly axiomatic point needs to be highlighted because the disagreements are not fully acknowledged and quickly papered over in the service of upholding a unifying or universal narrative of a sisterhood. It is not uncommon in women's rights writing to exaggerate differences of opinion as having (potentially) divided the movement and describe the moment as 'cleavages'.

Though critical comments on the CSWI report come later from its original authors, they represent the failings of the report as personal naivete or the less-developed stage of the discourse prevailing at the time. Indeed, in most references of the report in movement literature, it is difficult to find a mention of its critics. Mina Swaminathan's review of the report published in *Social Change* in March–June issue in 1975—soon after it was discussed in the parliament and made public—shows the contemporary existence of a critical discourse. Swaminathan delivers a sharp yet constructive criticism of the report, especially pointing out aspects that, in her judgement, had not received due attention.

Vina Mazumdar's article contains a complex argument on the impact of international relations, and the position of India as a Third World developing economy caught in an increasingly globalized world while addressing the women's question in India. The article is an incisive reading of the political economy of UN diplomacy from the perspective of the international women's movement. Mazumdar flays the UN marking the occasion of its 50th anniversary as the International Year of Family rather than of Human Rights. Towards the end of the article, Mazumdar focuses on how the UN upholding 'family' and linking development with population control affects a regressive limiting conceptualization of women merely as reproductive beings. This, she shows, also reflects in the Indian policy framework that links population and poverty.

The article is part of a critical body of work that Third World feminists produced in response to the 1990s neoliberal globalization while assuming the representation of a global movement. It illustrates the coming of age of the movement which earlier held that the lower status of women in the given structure was a cause of worry but now was forwarding a structural critique of conditions that perpetually undermined women's concerns to allow for an unrestricted flow of capital in global markets.

Finally, Maithreyi Krishnaraj presents a sweeping, century-long account of the movement in her article 'The Women's Movement in India: A Hundred-Year History'. This shows the evolution of self-reflexivity of the movement to look back at events about which newer questions have been raised. The article is a useful summary of the movement employing the techniques and approaches mentioned at the beginning of this introduction. Krishnaraj seems acutely aware of the charges on the movement being largely limited by concerns and viewpoints of Hindu society. She seems to stop short of actually addressing various counterfactuals, explaining them as eventually having a universal undercurrent, exemplifying that the movement still had miles to go indeed.

REFERENCES

Phadke, S. (2003). Thirty years on: Women's studies reflects on the women's movement. *Economic & Political Weekly, 38*(43), 4567–4576.

Rao, A. (2010). Women's movement. In Jayal, N. Gopal, & P. B. Mehta (Eds.), *The Oxford companion to politics in India* (pp. 409–422). Oxford University Press.

Agnihotri, I., & Mazumdar, V. (1995). Changing terms of political discourse: Women's movement in India, 1970s–1990s. *Economic & Political Weekly 30*(29), 1869–1878.

Desai, N., & Patel, V. (1985). *Indian women change & challenge in the international decade 1975–1985.* Popular Prakashan.

Kumar, R. (2014). *The history of doing: An illustrated account of movements for women's rights and feminism in India, 1800–1990.* Zubaan.

Chapter 1

Indian Women*
Some Reflections on a Two-Sector Analysis

Devaki Jain

What is the position of women in the Indian society? No one dares answer that question. There are so many societies in India, each with its own beliefs and habits that only micro-level surveys and analysis can hint at the answer. Yet the debate is on and positions are being taken by those involved in it.

There are a number of views on the status of Indian women. Three of these models are given as follows:

1. Women are born for a certain role. They are like mother earth—all-embracing, endless and protective. In the role of mother, there is the element of sacrifice and this self-denial uplifts her into godliness, sublimation. Since mother is one who can be trusted, who is forever loyal, who never asks but always gives, there is total confidence in her. In playing this role according to its ruled, she receives the regard, in fact, the worship of the men of the family.

2. A more sophisticated version of this model brings in institutional and sociological factors. In this version, the belief system which prevails upon women to be devoted wives and mothers is supported by the functioning of joint family, rules of marriage, practices in child-bearing and rights and obligations allocated to different members of mainly larger social organizations. Indian women are self-confident, powerful persons because they have always been

---

* *Social Change* (March–June 1975), 5.

given respect in their society. The hierarchy in society is not through sex but age. The fact that the girl is always made responsible for the boy and is relied upon to look after others whether as a sister, wife or mother has given her a superior, rather than equal, status. Men are, in fact, dependent on women both physically and emotionally. The joint family offers not only social security but also collective mothering, removing the pressures of motherhood on the young women. Arranged marriages remove the problem of soliciting, at a personal level, for man's favours; the fact that every girl can almost be sure of marriage prevents the kind of humiliation forced on the unmarried mother in the West. Further, women have their own social occasions and festivals, dancing, singing, preparing of food or what have you. Purdah or segregation is not repressive; in fact, there is more peace and harmony in socialization within the sex than between the sexes.

3. The even more modern model brings in the effects of the nationalist movement. In this model, the position of women in India today is, de jure, one of the most advanced. The Indian heritage, the freedom struggle, the constitutional guarantees and legal provisions have combined to give Indian woman an almost perfect status. However, social attitudes and practices have prevented full enjoyment of the rights and privileges guaranteed under the law. Once this is taken care of, an ideal status can be ensured for Indian women.

Parallel to each of these three models are arguments denying every one of the inferences drawn, if not the premises on which each model rests. Ancient texts including the sayings of the Buddha are quoted to show the derision and humiliation hurled at women in India from time immemorial. Manu is not alone in ordaining that the woman is no more than a slave of man. Fidelity and motherhood may be deified but at what cost? Any deviation from the Sita image or from marriage and motherhood is considered intolerable. In other words, outside this context and the rules relevant to it, woman is not acceptable—she is inauspicious, polluted, barren and wicked. Girls have no options.

The so-called ideal constitutional and legal provisions are for the birds of upper classes, though, even for these classes, the laws and the opportunities and immunities are still far from satisfactory. Religious and communal obscurantism, male-dominated councils and institutions, the argument runs, inhibit the formulation of laws and other institutional arrangements from really emancipating the woman from her handicapped position.

As for the poorer sections, they need relief, sheer physical relief from physical strain. Poverty may be common to men and women, but at the poorest levels, women work both at home and in the fields and roads. Girls do not go to school or play as freely as boys. Discrimination and neglect haunt the Indian woman from birth to death.

THE TWO SECTORS

With this kind of variety of views—and it must be admitted that nothing which is said is totally incorrect—choosing a course of action cannot only become difficult but clouded. There are those who would concentrate on attitudinal change, those who would like to make women into a subject like steel or mines with ministers and lobbies, those who feel that women's needs can be taken care of if maternity and child welfare services are made efficient and available, and, finally, those who think that no women have had it so good as the Indian women.

It seems to me, however, that much of the suspense as well as the differences can be resolved if women in India are divided into two classes—the rich and the poor. The division becomes even more useful if the income-based classification is superimposed on the classification between the scheduled castes and tribes together and the others. By 'poor' it means the lowest five deciles, by 'rich' all others. The Scheduled Castes and Tribes account for 21.5 per cent of the population (1971 census). Most of them (almost 95 per cent) would belong to the lowest five deciles, therefore, it could be said that 20 per cent of the population are poor and belong to the category of Scheduled Castes and Tribes; 30 per cent are poor, but outside this category.

The lowest five deciles are chosen on the basis of Pranab Bardhan's poverty studies. Though 50 per cent of the population are below the poverty line of ₹15 per month at 1960–1961 prices, most observers would suggest that at least 70 per cent are still in need of a minimum level of living, that is, in need of literacy, health, nutrition and other amenities. So, this 50:50 division can be modified to a 70:30 if the poverty line is shifted upwards on the basis of social indicators, or to 20:80, if only the scheduled castes and tribes are considered poor.

Whichever percentage breakdown is taken, the needs of women from the 'poor' sector are for physical amenities. The statistics, though very inadequate, indicate that women die at a higher rate than men, girls more than boys. In the case of the former, the major hazard is that of childbirth and, in the latter case, the effort required to treat sickness is lacking. A boy's sickness would call forth the physical and financial effort required which the girl's illness may not.

Many years ago, long before studies on women were even thought of, Alva Myrdal reflected on women's two roles: frequent childbearing and performance of strenuous manual work. The havoc caused amongst the poor by the performance of these two roles is a grim reminder of her perception. Work in poor countries is, basically, hard, manual work and the options are limited. Women have to work more for less wages than men because, in theory, they are supposed to be less capable of hard, manual work. Surveys of women in the 'poor' sector show that they do undertake extraordinarily strenuous work. Whether they work on the roads, in the fields or in the homes, they work very hard. Fetching water or firewood, sometimes, can take five hours walking and carrying a heavy load. Frequent childbirths and a low amount of nutrition undermine their health.

Good medical facilities for women within easy reach of every home can make a dramatic difference to female morbidity and mortality. Drinking water sources and fuel supplies close to village homes can be another great boon. Hence, for the 'poor' women the immediate need would be of provision of material benefits and services which will lessen the strain of hard and exhausting work at home and on the farm.

Women in the 'rich' sector, we will assume, have overcome the elementary hazards of death, disease and exhaustion. They would be, presumably, ready for education and employment, and as they move up the ladder of sophistication, legislative help for preventing humiliation and exploitation, in various forms, such as a ban on dowry, facilities for divorce, acquisition of property rights, etc., would have great significance. The re-ordering of society's attitude to women's behaviour, especially in the higher castes, would be an important step in the direction of women's 'emancipation'. Manu's ghost has to be laid, and that would require fairly long-term persistent effort.

OLD MYTHS AND NEW REALITIES

At the level where policy is made, the decision-makers themselves have to be re-educated. The report by the Committee on Status of Women in India identifies several myths and sets out to explore them. For example, there are the following myths:

1. The notion that it is the special provisions made for the benefit of women workers in factories that inhibit their employment. The authors of this report are able to show that the downward trend in the employment of women began before the enactment of welfare laws, rather than succeeded them.
2. The productivity of the women is lower than that of men and hence the wages have to be lower. The authors of this report argue that such an inference is drawn after denying women access to new skills through education and training and condemning them to less-productive jobs, thus creating a stereotype.

Coming back to the needs of women in the 'rich' sector, we notice the emerging role of a vigorous women's movement. Organizations of women, religious and social reform agencies, the media—not to mention the educational channels—can be mobilized to expose the cruel attitudes to women, for example, as revealed in the treatment of widows.

The advantage of the 'two-class analysis' outlined in this paper is that it tends itself to the planning methodology. For example, it is possible to suggest that the tangible and basic physical needs of 'poor' women can be met in the short term, that in the short period of, say, five years the goal can be to bring the most elementary social services and amenities to the poorest women.

This target can be worked out in terms of financial and physical planning. After an identification of the beneficiaries and the types of benefits (varying with region and historical situation) it is possible to estimate the requirements of finance and personnel over a five-year period.

The needs of the 'rich' women, on the other hand, are, by and large, intangibles and require long-term efforts. The long-term goals in their context would be to bring about attitudinal and institutional changes to ensure the equality of women with men in society. This effort does not lend itself to physical and financial planning. The distinction suggested here is no par with the old Bhoodan distinction between 'constructive work' and 'propaganda' or '*vichar-prachar* work' The 'poor' sector needs the former, mainly, and the 'rich' sector the latter.

REORDERING SOCIAL ATTITUDES

Obviously, this type of compartmentalizing the needs and methods creates a hiatus. Interconnections can be introduced in the presentation made above. For example, the 'poor' women also need changing social attitudes. Neglect of girl infants, insistence on childbearing and on performance of menial tasks, wife beating and the abandonment of women are evils which have to be countered along with better provision of 'social services'. Similarly, in the cities or in the 'rich' sector itself, there is a positive need for such 'social services'. However, I would like to argue that in the 'poor' sector attitudes can best be changed only through 'back door' effort, namely through the expansion of 'social services' themselves. For example, if health services are more readily purchased for boys than for girls, provision of medical aid at low cost would make it possible for girls not to be discriminated against. It is obviously ridiculous to believe that Indians would deliberately kill girl babies. One has to believe that adverse conditions—mainly poverty—followed by stress puts them into the cruel position of being discriminated against. This is also true of the lag in girls' school education. Girls are not sent to school because of inhibition about letting them go alone far and mix with boys as well as because of the exigencies of domestic work and childcare. If schools exclusively for girls are within easy reach and the time and trouble of preparing the family meals can be reduced, the girls would be sent to schools.

To reduce the inequities in the 'rich' sector, propaganda will have to be prevalent attitudes. If dowry is to be abandoned, what has to be done by way of changing the inheritance law in favour of girl? Who is to pay for the education of the boy, which is usually paid for by means of the dowry he receives? If the girl and boy are to be educated on an equal footing, what benefits, social and financial, accrue to the parents? Would the girl get an opportunity to become an income earner? What institutional changes would be required for that opportunity to become real? The society or those who observe double standards will have to be persuaded by showing the tangible gains that non-discrimination will generate. In order for the gains to be tangible, many interrelated arrangements will have to be examined and re-ordered. Hence, the needs of this sector have to be identified by means of research and analysis, apart from *vichar prachar*.

The two-sector analysis does not suffer even if these complex considerations are introduced. When, however, the 'poor' sector has overcome its elemental physical distress and deprivation through national effort, such a piece of analysis would become superfluous.

Chapter 2

And Miles to Go*

Mina Swaminathan

In tune with the times, the Committee on the Status of Women in India has brought out its solid and well-documented study to coincide with the celebrations of the International Women's Year. The report assumes great significance, because it is the first comprehensive study of this kind undertaken in India since independence, or for that matter, ever, and should, therefore, be welcomed as a baseline and a much-needed reference point for all future discussion on women's problems. Far from being a Women's Lib' inspired trumpeting for personal freedoms, it is commendable for the thoroughness of its survey and the sobriety of its tone.

Ironically enough, the first question that strikes one is whether the report is not out of date even before the printer's ink has dried on its pages. The basic assumption underlying it, that the problems of women can be considered in isolation from those of the family or of society in general, is itself, being increasingly questioned. The committee itself is fully conscious of this dilemma, which it discusses in the opening chapter on its approach to the study, but bound as it is by the terms of reference, it proceeds to grapple bravely with the assignment. However, the basic weakness of this assumption dogs the efforts of the committee, and is largely responsible for the various ambivalences and contradictions that run throughout the report.

---

* *Social Change* (March–June 1975), 5.

A review article on report of the Committee on the Status of Women in India, Government of India, Ministry of Education and Social Welfare 1975.

The major conclusion of the report, which can be summed up in the phrase 'And Miles to Go', is that the process of development itself in the course of the last quarter century has positively worked to the detriment of women's status. The evidence for this conclusion lies largely in the decline in the labour participation rates in respect of women and the implications of this trend thereof. However, this trend is not peculiar to women but applies to the underprivileged as a whole. Has not development, as it as a whole. Has not development, as it has been so far, made the rich richer and the poor poorer? In the last few years, the view has gained increasing popularity that the very nature of the development process has adversely affected the landless labourer, the unskilled urban worker and other groups which, under the blanket definition 'the poor', form the overwhelming majority of the population in underdeveloped countries such as India. Would not women, being one-half of this overwhelming majority, suffer from lack of employment opportunities and could they not be considered merely as one-half of the population lacking these opportunities. The evidence marshalled by the committee strongly suggests that, while sharing the disabilities of their groups, women have, by virtue of these low social status, and lack of education and skills, suffered relatively more in this process. However, the status of poor women is not likely to improve, except in the context of a general improvement in the social and economic condition of the poor.

RIGHTS AND FREEDOMS—A FABIAN APPROACH?

The committee takes as its starting point the rights and freedoms guaranteed to women, as to other under the Indian Constitution, which it describes as a 'radical' document 'embodying the objectives of a social revolution'. The committee then rightly proceeds to explore the dimensions of the unfinished social revolution hinted at in the Constitution and the gap between the ideal and actual achievement becomes the focus of its attention. At the end of the first chapter, the committee summarizes its guiding principles in a short paragraph entitled 'We believe'. While it is, in this context, overtly acknowledged that the constitution-makers were themselves the inheritors of a 'liberal' tradition of thought based on the British 19th-century Fabian socialism, it is also apparent in the unremitting commitment both to the rights of the individual and to the nuclear family as a model. This brings the committee into conflict both with the traditional Indian approach and with the emerging modern group and family-oriented way of thinking.

The second chapter is a masterly presentation of the demographic perspectives with particular reference to Indian women. The committee highlights the most alarming aspect of Indian population, namely the low ratio of females to males (contrary to the trend in the developed world). Even more disturbing is the persistent decline in the sex ratio over the last 50 years. The committee surveys and discusses this trend and the reasons for it in some detail both in this chapter and in a later one devoted to female health and points out that the very paucity of statistics relating to female health, malnutrition and mortality and the consequent difficulty of drawing firm conclusions is a reflection of the relative neglect of, and indifference to, the status of women—a point very well taken. At the end of this chapter, there is a useful little summary on male–female ratios in regard to selected demographic characteristics.

THE LAW—IS THE MEDICINE STRONG ENOUGH?

After a somewhat messy chapter entitled the 'Socio-Cultural Setting of Women's Status', which is obviously a hotchpotch hastily assembled from a number of sources of uneven quality and adding little to anyone's understanding of the diverse and complex problems involved, the committee proceeds to deal with women and law. As it is mentioned earlier, the Indian Constitution emphasizes the principle of equality, and subsequent social legislation is, by and large, progressive, thoroughgoing and calculated to remove all the legal obstacles to complete equality. The gap is between the ideal as laid down in law and what has been achieved in practice.

Nevertheless, there are still some lacuna in the law itself and the committee has done a thorough job in pointing these out and suggesting needed reforms, the most important of which relate to Muslim personal law and some of the laws regarding polygamy, divorce, inheritance, adoptions, child marriage and dowry. The most significant recommendation is the setting up of family courts to deal with the settlement of all family problems, as opposed to the present system. Other important recommendations are the adoption of a uniform civil code, compulsory registration of marriage and making the infringements of the Dowry Prohibition Act and Child Marriage Act cognizable offences.

With regard to the practice of dowry, which the committee has studied in depth, it points out the growing magnitude of this evil and its increasing strangle hold on all classes of society. It is significant that this practice, far from declining, has been on the increase in the last 25 years, so much so that communities that did not practise it and those which followed the opposite custom of bride-price have taken to it. The amount of dowry involved has shown a steady increase, and the spread of education, far from controlling the menace has only strengthened it, ironically, in ways wholly unexpected by the early social reformers. One could theoretically argue that the custom of dowry, insasmuch as it affects the relationship of men and women, is as much a question of the 'status of men' as of the 'status of women' (In this reviewer's opinion, the fact that husbands have to be 'bought' by the parents of brides indicates an extremely low status for men!). However, no one could disagree with the conclusion that the practice needs to be fought at all levels and by all conceivable measures. The committee recognizes that the argument of the conservatives that social pressures, education and social reform alone, rather than legislation, can put an end to this evil, has been given a long enough innings and has been proved a failure. The time for stronger measures has come. Yet the committee neither recommends revised legislation nor stronger measures of law enforcement but contents itself with the modest proposal that the offence be made cognizable under the present Prevention of Dowry Act. Surely this is not going anything like far enough. Drastic legislative action under something similar to Maintenance of Internal Security Act may be called for to turn the tide and support social action. The disease is well diagnosed, but medicine is not strong enough.

WOMEN AT WORK—DECLINE AND FALL

It is in the chapter on women at work that the committee really come into its own. The expression 'working woman' in common parlance conjures up the vision so dear to the urban middle-class of office-going girls in the cities, whose numbers have undoubtedly shown a phenomenal increase in the last two decades and has contributed to the illusion that the participation of women in the work of the economy has increased. The committee has done well to destroy this illusion for ever in no uncertain terms. Of the 31 million women constituting the female labour force, no less than 28 million are in the rural areas and 80 per cent of all women workers are engaged in agriculture. Taking the total population of women as 284 million, the labour participation rate for women is 11.6 per cent, while they constitute 17 per cent of the total working force. However, this may be a distortion of the true picture. The figure of 31 million is based on the census definition of full-time workers and does not take into account women who are returned as housewives or non-workers work. If this group and a still vaguely defined category of 'unpaid family workers', were given their full weight, the figure would be considerably higher. There is, therefore, no longer any justification for the view that Indian women are playing or have played a marginal role in the economy.[1]

The most disturbing conclusion of the committee is the inescapable one of the decline in the labour participation rate for women over the last few decades. There has been an overall decline in the percentage of female workers to the total of female workers to the total labour force since 1921. In the case of the organized sector of industry, it has even implied a decline in absolute numbers in certain industries. What is the nature and pattern of this decline, what are the reasons for it and, above all, what are the implications for the future? It could well be argued in certain contexts that the withdrawal of women from the labour force is an indicator of rising economic prosperity and social aspirations. It is well known that the leisure of its womenfolk is a feature of the bourgeoisie's ostentatious consumption. However, a study of the facts indicates that this is far from being the case in India. The glaring contrasts in employment patterns clearly show the nature and causes of the decline. In agriculture, there has been a steady drop in the number of cultivators and increase in the numbers of agricultural labourers. In the unorganized industrial sector, the decline of handicrafts and the small-case industries has itself contributed to the decline of female labour participation. In the organized industrial sector, there has been an absolute decline in certain industries, combined with deliberate measures against the employment of women in certain areas. Thus, along with the decline in labour participation rates, women are being pushed more and more towards the most precarious sector— that of unskilled, casual labour. This massive trend is by no means compensated for by the sharp increase in the employment of women in the tertiary sector, in which most of the increase is accounted for by public sector employment and which mostly concerns the upper and middle levels of employment. The phenomenon, in sum, is one of increased pauperization and downgrading of the quality of employment, and there is undoubted evidence for the conclusion that women as a group have been more affected than men by the limited growth of employment opportunities in relations to population, though the solution cannot be found within the perspective of women's problems.

TECHNOLOGY—A CLOSED SHOP?

In relation to agriculture, the findings of the committee are disappointing for though they start by reminding us that agriculture accounts for 80 per cent of all women's employment, they have little more to say on the subject. The paucity of statistical information contributes to the blankness of the canvas. Important issues are referred to, in passing, and are not given the attention they deserve. At one point, for instance, the committee mentions that, since most farm extension workers are men, they have tended to neglect women in the training programmes and connected with extension of new methods. This finding is neither substantiated nor followed up. At another point, the committee makes reference to the fact that the new technology associated with the Green Revolution has, in certain parts of the country, affected adversely the employment of women in certain traditional occupations and, thus, contributed to their economic displacement. What are the available alternatives? This is a point which deserves serious study, and surely should have been stressed more as an aspect of the impact of new technology which is rarely taken into consideration.

With regard to the unorganized sector, there is again very little available information, but that on the organized sector is well marshalled. The committee deplores the lack of vocational training and employment schemes for women. It is an astonishing fact that no such special schemes for women have been implemented by the concerned departments of government in any part of the country. The committee rightly stresses the need for vocational training, including training in production and marketing—so necessary for self-employment, the setting up of training-cum-production centres for women, extension of training programmes to illiterate and semi-literate women, etc., other important recommendations are the extension of the facilities under the Maternity Benefits Act to all classes of workers and the provision of crèches and part-time employment opportunities.

On crèches, the committee is somewhat lukewarm. It appears to concede the need for crèches without recognizing fully how they are an important bearing on women's employment and welfare, especially in a society composed of nuclear families that the committee would like to see. Here, the committee appears to have been grounded between the upper and lower milestones of the traditional Indian family-oriented approach with its reliance on the joint family and the Western horror of institutionalized childcare. There is no such horror in countries with a communist ideology—the countries like China, Cuba and the USSR; there is an appreciation of the link between childcare and women's welfare and participation in national development. It seems that the committee has missed a unique opportunity to develop the fact that the committee did not have any member with an especial commitment to child welfare.

EDUCATION—WRONG KEY TO THE LOCK

Well-reasoned and solidly documented, the chapter on women's education paints a gloomy picture of the dismal state of girls' education which covers barely 10 per cent of the female population, and there is an alarming increase in the absolute numbers of female illiterates. The territory is familiar, the conclusions well known and remedies suggested are not new either. The remedies do not go much farther than those of the Kothari Commission and, in a sense, they do not need to, since the malaise of Indian education—reflected in the growth of illiteracy, wastage and stagnation at the primary level, the weaknesses of the lowest levels of education, the unbalanced growth of higher education, etc.—is one which affects both boys and girls. There is more doubt whatsoever that women are more seriously affected. Besides the general remedies, which are needed for the transformation of the entire educational system to make it more relevant and meaningful to social needs, there is a crying need for special measures for women. As in the case of employment, the unprecedented growth of opportunities for higher education for women in no way makes up for the grim situation with regard to primary education and adult education.

Ambivalence dogs the footsteps of the committee here, too, and once more they have missed the opportunity to argue for unique situations. The committee is well aware that one of the main reasons for the non-attendance of girls in school and female dropouts is that they are required at home partly for household chores and mainly for the care of the younger ones. This is a phenomenon too widespread to be ignored. Yet the committee has evidently not thought of any special measures to deal with this situation. The combined crèche-*balwadi*-primary school is likely to be the only viable agency that can at once meet the needs of working mothers, provide childcare and pre-school education and also enable girls of school-going age to attend school. A few such experiments have been conducted successfully in the country, but the committee appears to be unaware of their existence. Instead of this, energy has been wasted on batting with dead dodos like the differentiation (or otherwise) of curricula for boys and girls. Due emphasis has, however, been given to the needs of adult education, including both functional literacy (based on vocational training and skills) and education bearing on the rights and opportunities of women. The mechanism for doing all this has been, somewhat, vaguely suggested in section on non-professional, community-based systems of non-formal education. One wonders how far such a system is likely to develop without more specific and detailed guidelines for linking it with the existing system.

Once, it used to be assumed that education was the key to social transformation. Educate the women, it was said, and you, at one stroke, raise the labour participation rate for women, eradicate social evils like the dowry system and open the door to political participation. That this does not hold good is being increasingly realized and nothing makes this clearer than the chapters on employment, education and the political process. In this last section, the committee has analysed the political attitudes, the status and extent of participation of women in the political process. On this issue too, the remedies suggested are hardly commensurate with the dimension of the problem, which might be even larger than the committee imagined. How does one involve women more in the political process? On this question, opinion seems to have been sharply divided, as it is only on reservation of seats for women in the legislative bodies that notes of dissent appear in the report. It is significant that the chairman and the secretary represent polar opposites, one calling for no reservation at all and the other for the maximum possible reservation. The official view is expressed by the harassed neutrals who take the middle position and timidly ask for reservation of seats only on municipal and local bodies but not at national or state level. The committee stresses vaguely the need to educate women on their roles, rights and opportunities in a modern State- but how? Strangely enough, though the committee included a leading trade unionist and several political workers, they do not suggest that trade unions or political parties should devote themselves to this cause. In fact, the trade unions have been let off very lightly and have not even been called upon to work for the uplift through unionization of the most-neglected categories of labour such as agricultural labour, construction workers, etc. Neither is it foreseen that women's organizations or political parties will do much in this regard. The total burden has been placed on government initiative through the various departments devoted to women's welfare and development. Government has been, as is usual in such cases, soundly berated for its lack of coordination, while the voluntary agencies and women's organizations go scot free.

NOT WOMEN ALONE

By the end of the report, then the weakness of the committee's approach appears in its true form. Who is to take responsibility for bringing about the needed changes? Must not better organization of women, greater opportunities for employment and training and education in the broadest sense go together? How can they be linked up? Must not all agencies work together to achieve this, and must this not be within a nationally accepted framework of goals? Ultimately, the committee is betrayed by its own terms of reference—the complete social transformation that it seeks, based on the principles of equality and justice— which is surely not a world of women or for women alone, but a new social order which can provide a better life for all, and the achievement which needs a social revolution in which both men and women must play a part. Economic transformation by itself cannot achieve much without a corresponding change in the social norms and expectations in respect of the roles and status of both men and women even further behind than they are—a concomitant effect of modernization, noted by the committee in relation to tribal women. A society in which women can play a full and equal part is not necessarily one in which roles are interchangeable. In most societies in the post-period war, defence and, perhaps, politics have been exclusively male occupations, while women have been responsible for child-rearing and homemaking. Some of this differentiation will continue, but the society of the future must be more flexible, offering a wider range of multiple roles for both men and women. To attain this, not merely goals but effort, too, must be shared and a mutually acceptable pathway found. In this context, the uncompromisingly 19th-century 'liberal' approach, with its emphasis on individual rights, may be not found to go far enough. The nuclear family is no longer seen as the desired objective in other parts of the world. The need for accepting multiple roles for both men and women is being increasingly perceived. The value of the group as well as of the individual is being increasingly recognized. Women alone cannot transform society any more than men alone, or education alone, or any one thing alone. The report provides an excellent vantage point from which to survey the present scene; but it fails to step on boldly forward even a few paces in the new direction. And we have miles to go.

NOTE

1. The reader may refer to the results of a survey presented in this number by Shanti Chakravorty.

Chapter 3

Globalization of the Family*
The Politics of Population Control

Vina Mazumdar

In one of his recent lectures, Upendra Baxi observed 'Globalisation seems to have achieved the death of Globalism.' On the one hand is the ideology of the sovereignty of the market—fast acquiring the external apparatus of a religion, which one is expected to profess, perhaps practice ritually, but not necessarily believe in.[1] On the other is the growing evidence of 'humanity's retreat' from the pursuit of some universal values, symbolizing a shared advance of human civilization as a whole.

As a student of history and politics, one is compelled to ask the question—why the 50th anniversary of the United Nations is becoming an occasion for projection of a global image of the 'family' as an abstract entity detached from its contemporary socio-economic, cultural and political contexts, rather than the Universal Declaration of Human Rights, which gave birth to the United Nations? Why, in particular, should the International Year of the Family coincide with the 4th World Conference on Population and Development which, to a considerable extent, sought to pre-empt the UN's first ever Summit on Social Development and the 4th World Conference on Women, both scheduled for 1995? Are we expected to believe that the UN is unaware that the two major battle arenas for the international women's movement through the International Women's Decade and beyond were:

* *Social Change*, Vol 24, Sep-Dec 1994.

1. Ignorance and misuse of such abstract notions regarding the family (reflecting the dominant social construction of gender roles in most societies) in all macro-policies for development, that is, mostly for economic growth with occasional lip service to social or 'infrastructural' services and

2. The nature of the politics surrounding women's reproductive roles—at national, regional and global levels?

Amongst the many deeply buried parts of social history uncovered by feminist scholarship is the fact that women all over the world had struggled desperately to control their fertility with whatever knowledge was available to them, including abortion—despite the ban prescribed by every organized religion. This was, and is, particularly true of women who bore the major burden of labour for production—of food and other goods and services—for their own survival and that of the collective of which they were a part. It is generally assumed that this collective is synonymous with the family. But even an undergraduate student of anthropology today knows that is not the case. Even today, there are communities with no sense of separate family units, the corporate/joint/extended/unclear family, the household, all represent different formations in a chain of collectives—whose functions and size are closely related to their regional (which includes ecology), occupational, cultural and historical contexts. Nor are these collectives unchanging or frozen in isolation. Linkages, migration and varied historical (including global) changes affect them.[2]

Even in the industrial countries of Europe and North America, where the nuclear family—of one pair of parents and their offspring is taken as the dominant, and assumed as the only model of the family—changing lifestyles and social mores are fast creating new models of the single parent, other types of units, along with the emergence of some experiments in larger collectives.[3]

Demographers and policy makers tend to forget that the words 'family planning' was invented by women, just as 'being in a family way' referred to women's state of pregnancy. The essence of the family, thus, is tied up with the woman and her children, which historically created lineage and the foundation for the collective. But along with mother-right and matriliny, what has disappeared from the major faces of human society is women's control over their own bodies, the products of their labour (both in the biological and economic sense) and their sexuality. The institutionalized forms (formal and informal) of these controls exercised by society, the rulers at various levels and technology are, what feminist scholars refer to as, 'the structures of patriarchy.[4]

A lesson from history is that nothing promotes stronger alliances than the desire to retain control that seems to be in danger of slipping. At the fag end of the 20th century, when national sovereignty itself has become part of the 'dissolving certainties', one may be allowed to reword the Palmerstonian statement as, 'In maintenance of controls enemies, only eternal interests.' The controllers exist in all societies. Today, one cannot use north/south as geographic entitles—since there are souths in the north and norths in the south.

For a few decades of the post-second World War in the postcolonial world—when a semblance of balance (or confrontation) between the super powers kept hegemonism and dominance in some check, the UN had begun to assume the appearance of an assembly of nations. Spaces and fora were created to debate issues and concerns of those who did not normally figure among the club of rulers and controllers. Human rights, workers' rights, women's rights, the rights of the child of exploited, marginalized indigenous people facing extinction, along with rights of self-determination, participation, education, health, development, etc., were incorporated into international covenants, as milestones in the advance of human civilization. They represented universal values of human equality, justice, dignity and freedom for which innumerable struggles had been waged by the oppressed and the deprived, as well as the wise and humane from the ranks of the non-oppressed.

Women's movements were among several such struggles. What gave them greater strength during this period was their internationalization. Women witnessed tremendous expansion of the base of these movements, within and across national boundaries, giving them strength to challenge the structures of patriarchy—new and old. Dominant models of economic growth; production technologies that increasingly displaced large masses of people from their livelihood and dignity; weapons of mass destruction that threatened the future of humanity; educational and knowledge systems that destroyed or marginalized people's laboriously acquired knowledge through generations of observation, analysis and transmission—depriving large sections of their pride and self-esteem; or the pursuit of science and wealth without ethical and humane values, that threatened the survival of the Earth itself—all came in for challenge. Gender equality required acceptance of human equality at all levels. And in a world of growing inequalities—of wealth, control over resources and power, and increasing violence and crime, of traffic in arms, drugs and human beings, 'which respect no national borders'[5]—gender equality or gender justice would soon become a mirage, as on many occasions in the past.

As in nature, everything in history also come 'in pairs'.[6] The global discourse on the 'Population Crisis' began roughly about at the same time as the beginnings of the Women's Liberation or Feminist Movement in the West. The latter was itself a product of the Civil Rights and anti-war movements in the USA, though many of its later participants often overlook this fact, or Feminism's older connections with the anti-slavery, anti-alcoholism (or the temperance movement, as it was known in 19th-century USA), anti-war or contraception and abortion the internal threat of the non–while population outnumbering the White on provided a rationale for pushing the discourse to al global arena. The historical coincidence of the Women's Liberation Movement and the Population Crisis discourse has not, however, drawn so much attention, at least not in the Indian subcontinent or other parts of the developing world.

The third world's persistent claim that 'development is the best contraceptive' found few supporters in the North, until the second World Conference on Population (Bucharest, 1974). Was this another historical accident, that should have taken place just one year before the first World Conference on Women, for equality development and peace (1975)? Very few persons in our part of the world are aware of the role that some feminists played in bringing about that change of heart in some leading spokesmen of the population crisis lobby.[7] They were certainly instrumental in introducing the roles and status of women as major factors to be studies and considered in population dynamics and population policy.[8] A trend analysis or population studies literature would reveal that studies on women's roles (economic, social, political), as distinct from their access to the trappings of modern status (education, paid employment, public offices), began mainly after Bucharest. Coinciding as it did with the International Women's Decade, such studies and dialogues often overlapped or got linked with the genre that came to be known as Women in Development (or WID/Women and Development/Gender and Development) studies.

If Bucharest opened the door to women's roles, Cairo, with its slogan of women's empowerment may well go down in history as the end of the chapter. The effort was made at the Rio Conference on Environment and Development (1992), also to pose the 'population bomb' as the main threat to the global environment. But the women's movement and sections of the environment movement joined hands in fighting back and the damage was contained. The strategy for Cairo was subtler slogans of the women's movement (empowerment, choice, unmet needs, reproductive health, abortion by rights/on demand, etc.) were appropriated, bringing in support from some sections of women. But the voices of dissent, of women from the third world and elsewhere, who asked what 'choice' meant in their context of growing economic squeeze, or could one feed one's children with contraceptives, or how would they continue their struggle for survival if they lost their health through dangerous hormonal implants which they could not remove themselves or whose implications for their health would never be explained to them—were not allowed inside the conference hall. Even the press faced problems in obtaining access to credible information on what went on inside.[9]

From the reports that have surfaced so far, three conclusions can be drawn:

1. Despite the compromise/consensus which took up more than 90 per cent of the conference's time and energy, religious fundamentalism, of Islamic, Catholic or other hues—has gained greater strength to deny many other rights to women to uphold the 'sanctity of the family,' and 'the conjugal bond'.[10]

2. Despite the statements by the United Nations Environment Programme Executive Director, Elizabeth Dowdeswell and United Nations Development Programme Administrator, Gus Speth—that

lifestyles and consumption patents in the North constitute a far graver threat to 'the planet's sustainability' than population growth in the developing world, Cairo deliberately avoided any reference to consumption from the developing countries (who represented by and large the 'control lobby'—or the north in the south) and accepted the responsibility, virtually a mandate—to control women's bodies and their reproduction, whatever the consequence to their roles, rights and responsibilities and their children's future— all in the name of their empowerment.

3. Science establishments (academies) from different parts of the world which men at the Science Summit, in Delhi in 1993, spelt out 'in terms of almost religious intensity—the great orthodoxies of the population control movement',—to a point of suppressing/ excluding all heretical views amongst scientists themselves. It was a demonstration 'that scientists, no less than economists, theologians or historians, are capable of allowing their attitude to objective evidence to be modified by predetermined ideas of truth'.[11] According to the Summit's joint statement, food production had declined in relation to population growth during the 1980s. According to the World Bank, however, 'world food production has more than kept pace with population growth, and rates of growth of food production show few signs of slowing.'

The net outcome of this exercise in 'women empowerment', in my opinion, is to shift the focus to women primarily as reproductive beings, away from the emphasis on their productive and developmental roles achieved during the last two decades.

The report of the Swaminathan Committee on Draft National Population Policy demonstrates the same kind of schizophrenia. The policy framework states that the 'unsustainable lifestyle' of the wealthy—nations and persons in our country—are responsible for using far more than a fair share of natural resources and causing grave threats to the environment.

> The current global development path-ways are leading to a continuous increase in the gap between the incomes of the poor and the rich and to jobless systems of land, water, flora, fauna, and the atmosphere. Development which is not equitable will not be sustainable in the long run.[12]

Having identified these causes, it then proceeds to put the blame for the environmental degradation on 'population and poverty' and states that 'access to food, education, health and work for all will remain illusory' without limiting population growth. Its recommendations do not contain anything to curtail consumption by the elites. The stress is entirely on containing the numbers of the poor. In a country like India, where a minuscule section of the population is responsible for consumption of about nearly three-fourths of the resources, how will squeezing the poor and starved majority further resolve any problems or achieve 'social justice' or 'equity', let alone 'gender equity'?

There is no critique of macro-economic policies that make the poor pay the price for the growing affluence of the wealthy. The basic focus of the recommendations is on limiting family size arbitrarily. The new set of proposed disincentives would silence the majority of Indians:

1. The committee holds up the anti-democratic and unconstitutional Panchayati Raj Acts of Haryana and Rajasthan which impose restrictions on the number of contesting elections to the Panchayati Raj institutions as models for the whole nation. Given the fact that the total fertility rate in India is estimated to be around 3.6, the committee's recommendations will disable the majority of women and men from holding any public office.
2. Having more than two children is also to be a disqualifier for getting employment in the organized sector.
3. Victims of child marriage, that is, all women married before the age of 18 or men before the age of 21 are to be debarred from employment in the organized sector. This is an extraordinary recommendation, because the perpetrators of these crimes, that is, the families, the community and the government—which does nothing to enforce the law against such marriages—are to be 'empowered'.[13] The committee has made no recommendation to improve enforcement of the law.

However, the committee would like population control programmes to acquire a 'positive image', hence the recommendation that they should provide choice to people and do everything to raise the status of women to make it equal to men. It is claimed that 'social empowerment mechanisms' and vigorous steps to abolish vicious forms of discrimination such as dowry, female foeticide and infanticide are necessary to enable women to increase the age at their marriage and have free access to contraception. The committee is silent on the social approval that practices like female foeticide and infanticide have obtained from a substantial section of the elites and government as they help reduce population growth or the role played by three decades of population propaganda and education in the construction of this mindset, among the educated, especially among the medical profession.[14] Are the promises of 'gender equality' designed to silence the women's organizations who have been consistent in opposing many aspects existing of policies?

The committee wants panchayat to draw up population goals based on resource availability but makes no reference to the redistribution of land and irrigation facilities or changing cropping patterns to conform to the needs of local residents. Can a rich farmer be asked by the local panchayat to use farm labour in preference to farm machinery? Are nationally fixed prices of farm inputs and outputs to be abandoned in favour of the panchayats? How, then, are the panchayats to achieve harmony between resources, consumption and population? Since the Population and Social Development Commission, recommended as a Super-Commission, equal (if not higher) in rank to the Planning Commission, is to formulate policies and control all resources—especially those coming from external agencies–this proposes a divorce between power and responsibility or centralization in the name of decentralization.[15] The proposal to use the army and paramilitary forces to promote the small family norm and population stabilization on the analogy of the Ecological Battalions currently involved in overcoming environmental degradation has already provoked a senior planner to describe the report as fascist.[16]

The section on Contraception and Biomedical Services reads most like the preparation leading up to Cairo. There is the same talk on 'informed choice'. The truth about the state of India's health services, about which the women's movement has cried itself hoarse, should now be realized by many others—since the plague scare. The fact that with so many economists and planners on the committee, no cost benefit analysis of the appropriateness of different technologies for a poor country like India was undertaken, which is more evidence of the schizophrenia. A Norplant costs ₹2,000, which is the medicine budget for an entire population under a sub-health centre. The cost of an imported injection of Depo Provera is close to $30 or ₹4,000 per year per woman, which the majority cannot afford. If such contraceptives are provided by the health department, these expensive items will compete with essential life-saving drugs. Neither can India afford research on all methods of contraception, just as its citizens cannot be provided with a menu card for every meal. Why not follow recent research and action research conducted by Indian Council of Medical Research, which found high utilization of existing methods following improvement of quality of services? Recent Kerala studies also indicate that availability of alternative methods of healthcare affect fertility more than levels of education or contraception.[17]

To conclude, the rationale for the title of this chapter, and the statement that Cairo's aim was to pre-empt the Social Summit and the Beijing Women's Conference, can now be substantiated by the papers coming from the Summit Secretariat. The Economic and Social Commission for Asia and the Pacific's strategy paper prepared in 1992 had frankly idolized the family and contradicted its own earlier evidence of its growing dysfunctionality under pressures of rapid socio-economic change. Having started off with load protestations of the need to change, 'stereotyped' gender poles to end discrimination against women, it ended up lamenting that increased social and spatial mobility and individualism was bringing family-member role expectations. However, since the state cannot perform the role of 'social provisioning', the family will have to be strengthened 'to carry out its traditional functions in the face of the corrosive influence of development'.[18]

The summit's first draft programme of action has a section titled 'Ending Discrimination in All Its Forms'. After two decades of information explosion on 'discriminations' based on gender, the summit's draft is unable to go beyond Article 16 of the Indian Constitution, now nearly half-a-century old.

'Given the long-standing discrimination against women, based on their traditionally subordinate roles to men, special efforts are needed to develop policies to end discriminatory practices in employment, education and access to public services, as well as in other domains.'[19]

Since this follows a paragraph regarding ending discrimination in the 'public sphere', only the meaning is clear, even if the Summit Secretariat is avoiding the word 'family' after the furious arguments around this word in the preparations for Cairo.

NOTES

1. John Kenneth Galbratith. The sting of Truth in Scientific America, May 1991.
2. K. S. Singh (1992). People of India—An Introduction, Anthropological Survey of India (National Series vol. 1) Calcutta.
3. This is based on a conversation with Judith Bruce of the Population Council, New York. She has been making a special study of the new types of family units.
4. Vina Mazumdar and Kumud Sharma in Tinker—Persistent Inequalities: Women and World Development, New York, OUP, 1990; Bina Agarwal, 'Structures of Patriarchy: State, Community and Household' in Modernising Asia, Kali for Women, Delhi 1988; Leela Dube and Rajni Palriwala, Structure and Strategy: Women Work and Family, SAGE Publications, New Delhi, 1990; Mainthreyi Krishnaraj and Karuna Chanana, Gender and the Household Domain: Social and Cultural Dimensions, SAGE Publishers, New Delhi, 1989. Andrea Menefee Shingh and Anita Kellis Vinan, S SAGE Publishers, New Delhi, 1987, Vina Mazumdar, Development Dialogue, 1983; While there is a steady increase in analysis of this phenomenon in the modern and contemporary period, historical research in scanty. See A. S. Altekar, The Position of Women in Ancient India. Motilal Banarasidas, 1959 (ed.); J. G. Phule, Collected Works. Government of Maharashtra, Education Department.
5. HDR'94 P. 1–2.
6. It is interesting to note that Jane-Addams, one of the founders of the Women's International League for Peace, which campaigned against the First World War (1914–1918) as an 'imperialist war', invited Rabindranath Tagore to the USA, acted as his host and organized his lectures. Mahatma Gandhi acknowledged the lessons he had learnt from British suffragists. Connections/ support from Western feminists to Indian radicals/revolutionaries is still missing from histories of India's freedom struggle.
7. Particular reference here is to late John D. Rockfeller III—Founder and Chairman of the Population Council, New York, and a leading member of the US delegation to the conference.
8. I had the privilege of listening to some of the women personally involved in this lobbying. They gave me JDR's speech at the conference—which

state these clearly. They were also instrumental in getting me appointed as a trustee of the Population Council in 1976. JDR was the Chairman until his tragic death in a car accident, a few years later. During this short association, he constantly supported my battles with the demographers—for a change in their perspectives. At the very last meeting, shortly before his death, he lost his temper with some of the senior professional staff, who used the phrase 'women's welfare' in their presentations before the board. 'We are not talking of welfare—but of women's roles. Vina, please explain the difference.'

9. Anne Shephered. 'Transparency in Short Supply as Cairo Conference Squabbles over Word'. Pioneer, Sept, 18, 1994.
10. This point became very clear form an official statement by one of the senior bishops in Manila, some weeks after Cairo—at the South East Asian Consultation on Population and Quality of Life.
11. William Oddie. 'The lie Explosion at the Cairo Population Meet'. Sunday Telegraph, London, reproduced in Pioneer, 14-9-1994.
12. Swaminathan Report, p. 1—6.
13. Ibid.
14. Vina Mazumdar, Amniocentesis and Sex Selection, paper presented at WIDER, Helsinki's Conference on Women, Equality and Reproductive Technology, August 1992, CWDS Occasional Paper No. 17, 1994.
15. Arun Ghosh, National Population Policy: Progression Towards a Fascist State, EPW, Vol. XXIV, No. 34, August 20, 1994, p. 2189.
16. Ibid.
17. K. C. Zachariah, CDS, Trivandrum.
18. SDS 2000—ESCAP ST/ESCAP/1124. P.21.
19. Draft Declaration and programme of Action for SDS: A/Conf. 166/PC/L 13, p.49, para 142.

Chapter 4

The Women's Movement in India[*]
A Hundred Year History

Maithreyi Krishnaraj

The women's movement in India has a chequered history over a hundred years. It went through many phases, from a united front to fragmentation, dispersal and now, perhaps a new hope of consolidation is in the offing. I also draw from my own experience of the movement in late 20th century. There are many books in English and in regional languages, documenting the movement through scholarly analyses and first-hand narratives of the participants. I have selected a few of those accounts which have appeared as illustrative of its non-linear history. Critical evaluation from our present context records the diversity and complexity of how the women's question was raised at different phases, in different regions, in the 19th century, and often harbouring contested relations with the left and other progressive movements. 'Perhaps less well known to Western scholars is how deeply rooted this movement was on both colonial reform and the nationalist struggles of the nineteenth century' (Kalpagam, 2000).

Preceding the national independence from colonial rule was the 'social reform movement' which made attempts to reform the conditions under which Hindu women lived. Child marriage, early widowhood and sati (the burning of a widow on the funeral pyre of the husband) were some of the oppressive conditions that high-caste Hindu women suffered from. The young widows were often children and were forced to live a life of privation. They had to tonsure their

* *Social Change* (2012), *42*(3), 325–333.

heads, wear only white, could not adorn themselves with ornaments and had to eat meagre food. They were seen as bad omen and could not take part in any festivities. Some literate women have left us records of what they went through. The reform movement was spearheaded by men who, exposed to liberal ideas, considered these conditions as an indictment of their society by colonial rulers and supported passing legislation raising the age of consent for marriage, abolition of sati practice and campaigning for widow remarriage, especially if the women had no children. They also pushed for women's education in a big way.

It is generally assumed that men were the architects of these drives towards emancipation of women, but recent research shows how the wives, daughters, sisters and followers of male leaders were equally in the forefront of the movement (Kumar, 1997). Likewise, it is generally presumed that this awakening was mainly due to colonial encounter of India under British rule and the English language which Lord Macaulay ushered into the Indian education system. His aim was to create a cadre of Indian administrators capable of replacing the British nationals in India. Ironically, these events also gave Indian leaders exposure to new ideas. The criticism of Indian cultural practices touched a raw nerve among patriotic Indians who wished to reform the system. New research has unearthed many indigenous movements much before the colonial encounter which sought to move society towards modernity. During the 17th and the 18th centuries, there were parts of India ruled by native states which were outside the British Empire, where such progressive enactments were made. Three such examples are the state of Travancore–Cochin in south-west India, the state of Mysore and the state of Baroda, where women were highly educated and were employed in many professions. There was an organization called the Brahmo Samaj in Bengal and one in north India called the Arya Samaj. They not only promoted education and autonomy for women but introduced free-choice marriages among young couples. Even martial arts were taught to women in Arya Samaj.

While the social reformers' zeal to improve the condition of high-caste women was indeed noteworthy, it was, in many ways, a limited reform insofar as women were still confined to their traditional roles as wives and mothers, and education was aimed to make them better wives and mothers, capable of being enlightened partners to their husbands. They did not envisage any public role for women. Mahatma Gandhi drew them into the national movement and legitimized their public role, but this too was mooted insofar as he extolled the essential nature of women as self-sacrificing mothers befitting them for participation in the national movement. As Sangari and Vaid contend, 'Both tradition and modernity have been in India carriers of patriarchal ideologies. As such neither is available to us in a value free and unproblematic sense, nor is either as they are conceptualised' (Sangari and Vaid, 1989: 17). The social reformers agenda did not include freedom for women outside the patriarchal baggage. Nonetheless, this limited reform paved the way for a future where women could find their own space. One cannot educate women without it leading to critical inquiry about their own lives. By 1860, many women went into professions like teaching and nursing. They became aware of themselves and their predicament. This was the period when more than a hundred autobiographies were written by women, expressing their dissatisfaction on their lack of autonomy. Some wrote of a utopia, imagining a time when women would be in charge, like the book *Sultana's Dream* (Sahkwat, 1905). Some wrote a comparison of men's lives and women's lives to demonstrate how women were denied opportunities for self-fulfilment (e.g., Ramabai, 1981; Shinde, 1975). In north India, the Indo-Gangetic plain has earned the pejorative sobriquet as the 'cow belt' to denote the ultra conservatism of the people there. Yet, in the late 19th century, there were many women who wrote in Hindi. Even though their writings, in the form of short stories and essays, evoked the image of Hindu goddesses as icons of female power, there was evident an undercurrent of desire for female autonomy and a burgeoning feminist consciousness. Thus, despite many contradictions, the reform movement was a precursor to an emerging feminist movement.

Around this time, radical voices also emerged advocating education for lower castes, and Savitribai Phule was a forerunner in opening schools for educating lower-caste women. The women's studies centre in Pune is named after her. In 1906, a social reformer Dond Keshav Karve, after visiting Japan which had a women's university, was inspired to open a similar university in India. The history of this university is itself a history of the women's movement. Karve had earlier begun a small institution to educate widows in Pune. After his visit to Japan, he converted it to a women's university offering courses in education, nursing, regional languages, Sanskrit, arts and humanities. In 1916, a mill magnate, Sir Vithaldas Thackersey, offered a handsome donation which enabled the university to expand. The Woman's University, which was the only one in India at that time, was named after his mother and continues to have the same name (Shreemati Damodar Nathibai Thackersey Women's University; in short, SNDT Women's University). By 1952, it became part of the Maharashtra state[1] university system and shifted to Bombay while retaining a wing in Pune. As a full-fledged university, it offered professional degree courses at bachelor and master's level as well as doctorate level: law, commerce, information technology, pharmacy, business management, in addition to home science and nursing, arts, commerce, humanities as before. It also acquired a new campus in Juhu. In the early 1970s, there was a symposium to decide on what the university should do for women, and thus was established the first Centre for Women's Studies at SNDT Women's University. Two more women's universities came into existence later in south India. SNDT Women's University kept in touch with the women's movement; it hosted many conferences and participated in many international conferences. It truly regarded itself as the academic arm of the women's movement. However, once women's studies became established, in many universities, women's studies had a more diverse history and, in some cases, became purely academic institutions.

Let me go back to the women's movement. During the national movement—encompassing the non-cooperation (1920–1921), civil disobedience (1930–1931) and Quit India (1942) movements—many women participated, but they were the wives, sisters or followers of male leaders. Rural women participated only during the protest against the salt tax. The movement was predominantly of the middle class. Two contradictory rationales were simultaneously espoused, namely, women's public appearance was justified as they were mothers fighting for 'mother country' and women had equal rights as men. These two contradictions were not resolved. Even today, the right-wing party uses the same rationale, while the mainstream centre party ostensibly treats women as equal to men. I guardedly say 'ostensibly' as later events will show the persistence of patriarchal resistance to women's public role. In a curious way, the national movement got entangled with the woman's question (Desai, 2006). In none of the other countries shaking off colonial bondage was there such an entwinement (Thorner and Krishnaraj, 2000).

Between 1917–1927, three major women's organizations got established: Women's India Association; All India Women's Conference (AIWC); and National Council of Women in India. At the first AIWC meeting, 7,000 women attended. The AIWC prepared a memorandum seeking right to vote for women from the British government. The AIWC was also in the forefront for reforms in marriage and property laws concerning women. All said and done, on the eve of India's independence, women were struggling to establish liberal principles with equality as the guiding principle. Unfortunately, the national movement for independence shelved the gender question to be taken later, just as it did for incorporating affirmative action for previously marginalized communities to be addressed after independence in framing a constitution.

The national movement was not as homogenous as generally believed. There were many political strands. There were subaltern groups who spoke of their oppression but they did not recognize the different levels of oppression within them. In 1958, Tara Ali Baig wrote a book on the activities of women who inherited the political mantle from men in their families. All the women's organizations and women leaders were careful to emphasize that they were not 'anti-men'. The argument of the desirability of extended space for women was assisted by women leaders' connection to male leaders and legitimized women's entry into public space, and as this was not available to all women, their participation was thus limited. What facilitated the politicization of the domestic sphere and the domestication of the public sphere was the duty of women as 'mothers' to defend 'mother country' from enslavement. The public space was seen not as flouting customary definition of women's role but a space for renegotiating the rigid rules governing women (Thapar-Björkert, 2006). There was an effort to negotiate the boundaries of identity and domesticity but the ambiguity in this new identity created paradoxes about gender equality. Despite varied motivations, women's public participation did create a precedent for future generations (Krishnaraj, 1995). A new generation of women was raised, more articulate, more politically aware and more conscious of rights.

The 1970's focus was on achieving some socio-political reforms which in no way challenged the basic gender discrimination in society. The directive principles of the national constitution had 'no discrimination on the basis of sex' as one of the clauses. This promise had created a sense of complacency that women's issues would be addressed. The publication of the report of the Committee on the Status on Women, *Towards Equality*, took the lid off this complacency. It exposed the enormous discrimination that prevailed on the basis of gender in employment, education and health, and in participation in public bodies.

Even though the number of political organizations in 1970s was more numerous than before in the women's movement, they became dormant around this time. A flexible group called the Six Sisters2 was instrumental in the Government of India ratifying the Convention Against All Sorts of Discrimination against Women passed by the United Nations. It also oversaw the setting up of a representative National Women's Commission and state-level (that is provincial) women's commissions. The plea by the women's organizations to give statutory authority to these commissions to prosecute and not just register complaints was not acceded to by the government.

During 1975–1985, progressive women's organizations began, for the first time, to identify patriarchal social structure as the cause of women's oppression. At the same time, many lower-caste and tribal women also began to organize themselves both against upper castes and against male dominance in their own communities (Rajawat, 2005; Sharma and Sharma, 2006). A kind of loose federation evolved to fight on a common front. Central to the women's engagement with politics was the realization that the Left parties did not link patriarchy and class exploitation. Two studies, *A Decade of the Women's Movement in India* (Desai, 1988; see also Desai and Patel, 1985) and *A Space within the Struggle* (Sen, 1990), give us a glimpse of the varied mass movements in which women were involved. There were student protests; textile workers' strike; railway workers strike; and fisherwomen's protest against foreign trawlers which came into our coasts to catch fish because they threatened the livelihood of traditional fishing communities; and protest against missile testing range in Odissa.[3] Throughout, in many such movements, the women's organizations appealed to the state for redress. In 1979, some incidents of custodial rape of young women by the police triggered the emergence of groups that were not affiliated to any political party. These were called autonomous organizations. A forum against rape was organized which later converted itself to forum against oppression. In 1980, a new law was passed against rape and amended in 1983, but without many recommendations of women's groups being incorporated. The basic strategy was to take recourse to law but given the strength of patriarchy, not only among the security forces but also within sections of the judiciary, and in broader society, law did not deter offences against women. Many young women, soon after marriage, were tortured or even killed or driven to suicide for non-fulfilment of dowry demands. An anti-dowry law was passed with many organizations rallying against dowry harassment by a bride's in-laws and husband. Later, when modern technology like amniocentesis was used to detect sex of the foetus and a female foetus was aborted, a central law was passed in 1990 to deter this, and medical units allowing this test were penalized. In all these events, there was a united front of women's groups.

During 1975–1985, forms and styles of action became diversified to create public awareness, to raise consciousness, to lobby, to mobilize a cross-section of society. Demonstrations, street plays, seminars, symposia, group meetings and mass parades were resorted to. Postcards, letters, telegrams, etc., were sent to the judiciary and the government. For the first time, a feminist agenda was articulated to highlight the sexual exploitation of women in conjugal relations, in inter-caste rivalries and by the police and the army in some regions. The autonomous women's groups recognized that the left's subsuming gender under class gave women no room to fight for their own needs. The All India Democratic Women's Association (AIDWA) spoke of triple oppression—class, political and gender—and many organizations like the Progressive Organisation for Women (POW) raised their voices against gender discrimination within the left. The autonomous groups were small in number, non-hierarchical, with different organizational and leadership styles, resources and different strategies of participation and intervention. They mainly worked on single issues and hence, could not address the deep-rooted gender inequality in society. Further, a divide between activists and academics fragmented the movement. Difficulties of overcoming barriers of caste and class were hurdles and the attempt to promulgate a common civil code could not succeed. This became apparent in the famous case of a Muslim woman, Shah Bano, who sought maintenance from her divorced husband under the provisions of the Indian Criminal Procedure Code (CrPC) which permits a woman to receive maintenance under the clause 'prevention of destitution'. The Muslim clerics were up in arms declaring that the provisions of the Muslim law, or sharia, are enough and the appeal under the CrPC is unnecessary and an interference with Muslim religious law. The then prime minister promptly enacted a law upholding the Muslim clerics' view. This was a major setback for the women's movement. By the 1990s, the women's movement became fractured. Many organizations became service providers and this phase is known as the non-governmental organization or NGO-ization.

The women's movement prepared an alternative document for the Beijing conference in 1995 to counter the government's version. By the 1990s, increasingly, women participated in programmes of 'gender and development' and made policy interventions. Some saw this as co-optation by the government. Perhaps it was, but it did bring in women's issues into the policy-making bodies. Though I called it fragmentation, it was more diversification, with women's groups fighting on many fronts—environment, forest-dwellers rights, against displacement of people and loss of their lands in construction of big dams and loss of agricultural land by the setting up of special economic zones to promote export industries. These oppositions arose with the advent of so-called liberalization which threw open the economy to both market forces and foreign trade.

For the first time, sexual minorities also organized themselves. There were sex workers' organizations fighting for respect and against police and pimps' harassment and by transgender people for recognition of sexual minorities. The floodgates were open for a million mutinies. The Delhi High Court has upheld the rights of sexual minorities thereby decriminalizing them, but the case has been referred to the Supreme Court. Today, there are open lesbian organizations. In a recent case of a tribal school teacher in central India, accused of being part of the revolutionary militant outfit called the Maoists, who was sexually abused by the police, women activists, academics and civil rights groups rallied to make a strong protest through the internet and appealed to the Supreme Court to ensure justice to the poor woman.

The wheel is coming to a full circle. The state is no longer the protector but conniving with the security forces under the plea of restoring 'law and order'. Corporate entities, under so-called liberalization, are flouting long fought-for labour laws and women workers are losing their rights. The National Commission for Women and the state commissions for women have not been very effective in prosecution of culprits. The Women's Reservation Bill which seeks reservation for women in legislative bodies up to 33 per cent is still pending (Akhila R. S., Ajay Anamika & Narendra Pani, 2012). Political parties also do not put up enough women candidates. The AIDWA is among the more visible parties today and some others seem to have folded up. There are still smaller organizations against 'communalism'.[4] AIDWA keeps organizing women against price raise and against violence against women. Earlier in the 1980s, many parties had come together, called the 'rolling pin' demonstration (so called because they used rolling pins struck against brass dishes, as symbolic of the kitchen), against price rises which affected the poor most. Recently, in a legislative assembly, while the session was in progress, three ministers were caught watching pornographic videos on their mobile phones. While much media outrage was voiced about the unseemly behaviour of the ministers during the sessions, AIDWA asked, whether it is ok if they watch it at home? Pornography objectivizes women as sex objects. The three offenders have been suspended. Earlier, the Left parties subsumed caste as part of class; though the two overlap they are not part of class. Similarly, earlier the left subsumed gender under class and caste but now recognize that gender is a distinct category.

There are other disquieting factors. The NGOs, which are non-party groups, have created protected niches for themselves to carry out 'women's empowerment'. Many do receive foreign grants. There are microfinance institutions sprouting all over, to lend to women worker groups called self-help groups. Much recent research is critical of this initiative as it does not promote women's autonomy.

Over the years, women's newsletters, journals, women's archives and supplements in mainstream newspapers highlighting women's issues have increased tremendously. We have a million mutinies. One way to look at it is fragmentation, but another way of seeing it is as a river that has diversified into many tributaries. This is our strength.

NOTES

1. Maharashtra is one of the provinces in western India. Provinces are now called 'states', while the central government is called union government. We have a federal system.
2. The Six Sisters consisted of: AIDWA; AIWC; Joint Women's Programme; National Federation of Indian Women; Young Women's Christian Association; and the Centre for Women's Development Studies.
3. A province in eastern India.
4. Communlism is a term used in India to denote partisan politics usually aimed against minorities like the Muslims.

REFERENCES

Akhila, R. S., Anamika, Ajay, & Pani, Narendra (2012). *Can dual member constituencies be the way forward for women's reservation?* Bangalore: National Institute of Advanced Studies.

Baig, Tara Ali (1958). *Women of India.* New Delhi: Union Ministry of Information and Broadcasting, Government of India.

Datta, Kusum (2007). *Women's studies and the women's movement in India.* Kolkata: Asiatic Society.

Desai, Neera (1988). *A decade of the women's movement.* Bombay: Himalaya Publishing House.

———. (2006). Feminism is experienced: Thoughts and narratives. Mumbai: Sparrow.

Desai, Neera, & Patel, Vibhuti (1985). *Indian women: Change and challenge in the International Women's Decade (1975–85).* Bombay: Popular Prakashan.

Kalpagam, U. (2002). Perspectives for a grassroots feminist theory. *Economic and Political Weekly,* 4686–4693.

Krishnaraj, M. (1995). Remaking Society For Women: Visions—Past and Present. Indian Association of Women's Studies, New Delhi.

Krishnaraj, Maithreyi (2000). *Remaking society for women: Visions past and present.* Background volume for the 7th National Conference of the Indian Association of Women's Studies, Hyderabad.

Kumar, Radha (1993). *History of doing. An illustrated account of the women's movement for women's rights and feminism.* New Delhi: Kali for Women.

Pandita, Ramabai (1981). *High-caste Hindu women.* Translated by Rosalind O' Hanlon (1994). Oxford University Press.

Rajawat, Mamta (2005). *Dalit women's issues and perspectives.* New Delhi: Anmol.

Sakhwat, Rokeya (1905). *Sultana's dream* (A Feminist Press Sourcebook). New Delhi: Dev Publishers & Distributors.

Sangari, K., & Vaid, S. (1989). Recasting women: An introduction. *Recasting women: Essays in colonial history,* 1-26, Zubaan: New Delhi,

Sen, Ilina (Ed.) (1990). *A space within the struggle.* New Delhi: Kali for Women.

Sharma, Seema, & Sharma, Kanta (2006). *The backwards in dalit and backward class women.* New Delhi: Anmol.

Shinde, Tarabai (1975). *Stree purosh tulna* (Marathi). Bombay: Grantha Sangrahalaya.

Thapar–Björkert, S. (2006). *Women in the national movement (1930–42).* New Delhi: SAGE Publications.

Thorner, Alice, & Krishnaraj, Maithreyi (Eds.) (2000). *Ideals, images and real lifes: Women in literature and history.* Mumbai: Orient Longman.

Section II

Women as Workers

Sectional Introduction

Ghazala Jamil

Labour studies in India originated in the colonial effort to discipline
and manage native workers and to ensure a steady supply of workers
for overseas colonies from India. As such, the most important text—
drawing from the colonial legacy—continued to be official texts
or reports of various commissions and committees appointed by
the colonial state and, after Independence, the post-colonial state (Behal
et al., 2010). In independent India, the focus did shift to producing
knowledge for aiding planned economic development which meant
industrial development for the most part. This continued for quite a few
decades and labour studies remained dominated by a labour-economics
perspective. Throughout this story, women workers were a silent
presence in literature, although the continuous decline in the women
workers' ratio in manufacturing industries over decades has remained a
subject of a lot of technical discussion and debates about the collection
of data and reporting errors (Roy, 2005). The informal sector gets some
attention as most women workers are employed in this sector and their
capacities to claim rights or to collective bargaining is severely limited
by their struggle to organize (Hensman, 2001).

When studies that were more attuned to gendered concerns began
to appear, they often narrated an account of women as (left) trade

unions activists and women economists who began using research as a tool for advocacy with the state. The gains made by their struggles are often listed in the form of legislation reforms, plan outlays and development policies and programmes. This remained the case since the 1970s to the end of the century. The articles selected in this volume pertain to this period.

The first article in this section 'National Development and Women Workers' is by Maniben Kara. The article is of great importance because of the fresh arguments it makes. Writing in 1972, she tries to sketch a portrait of women as workers as an enduring image. Although she does not make the argument about economic compensation of women's labour in the family, Kara points out the way in which women's work has always been crucial to the family's economic sustenance. She argues that the confinement of women to kitchens and only care roles was an invention by the opponents of the freedom and equality of women. Further that no society has ever been able to do without the labour of women, therefore, arguing that women had to play a crucial role in national development as workers. Population and poverty appear as one of the reasons why she saw women's numbers increase in wage work in the agriculture sector but her keen eye and experience helped her note a distinct fall in the percentage of women employed in factories, which would not be the case if only poverty and population increase were the only determinants of women workers ratio.

The article is cognizant of gender discrimination at play in skilling, training and use of technology, hiring practices and lower wages (provides important evidence from various report and surveys). But the causes she discerns are to do with regressive social attitudes prevalent in society regarding women's roles within families and their capacity to work.

While Maniben was a trade unionist, the involvement of women in the trade union movement brought the realization regarding women who worked in the non-agricultural sector but remained out of the purview of the legal regime regulation of formal paid work.

Anita Dighe's article titled 'Women's Employment in the Urban Informal Sector: Some Critical Issues' picks up the thread of these matters. Dighe performs a fine combing of data, pointing out its distortion in representing the participation of women in the economy and labour force. This article is important because, first, Dighe highlights the 'invisiblization' of workers who were engaged in the manufacturing sector but were in home-based employment. Second, she emphasises that the presence of a strong labour movement also brought into relief the situation of women workers who have no avenues to unionize. Dighe recounts how it was women workers' groups that build pressure in the UN to ask its member states to undertake an investigation on the status of women in their countries. The article is also important for flagging the challenges of theorization and developing conceptual tools in order to collect better data and for discerning a connection between informal work and urban economy.

Although women's role in the agricultural sector has long been recognized, their work in industries or in the manufacturing sector and later in the service sector was not contextualized for decades in space. In other words, although mechanization and industrialization were intrinsically processes of urbanizing spaces, a recognition of the positionality of women workers came late and did not really catch on in gender studies until very recently. The third article written by Sanghmitra Acharya is an early contribution that does this. This article is a little different from all the other articles included in this volume as it uses a statistical, data-driven, case study approach. I otherwise avoided including studies using this approach because such studies just tend to confirm certain relationships or already-held assumptions. Acharya's article, on the other hand, manages to mark a major discursive landmark by presenting tendencies in female work participation.

Through a scientific approach, Acharya establishes a set of factors that maybe impinging upon making of the 'female workforce'. Remarkably, she finds that rather than the qualification required or the desire/attitude of the person, it is the economic status and sociocultural context that define the participation of women in the labour force.

While women's work participation in wage work has remained, by and large, limited, women workers participation in the labour union movement has remained equally, if not more, dismal. Labour union movement, in general, has been in decline for reasons and with implications that are too complex to be discussed here. But one important development in this regard has been the formation of the Association of Indian Labour Historians in 1996, which is said to have 'revived' labour history as a discipline in India. It was to take another decade before labour historians also began writing social histories (Bhattacharya & Behal, 2016). Chronicling of women worker's struggles as social histories seems to suffer from the same handicap of sources. Probably to compensate for that ethnographic or narrative studies of experiences of women bidi workers, garment factory workers, domestic workers and IT workers are appearing, but by and large labour histories or labour studies appear to be, somewhat, less popular in gender studies.

REFERENCES

Roy, T. (2005). *Rethinking economic change in India: Labour and livelihood*. Routledge.

Bhattacharya, S., & Behal, R. P. (Eds.). (2016). *Vernacularization of labour politics*. Tulika Books.

Hensman, R. (2001). Organizing against the odds: Women in India's informal sector. *Socialist Register, 37*.

Behal, R., Joshi, C., & Mohapatra, P. (2010). India. In J. Allen, A. Campbell, & J. McIlroy (Eds.), *Histories of labour: National and international perspectives*. Merlin.

Chapter 5

National Development and Women Workers*

Maniben Kara

Women have all along been workers in all societies from time immemorial. Referring to the fact, Mr V. V. Giri, the President of India, wrote in his foreword to Mrs Padmini Sengupta's very informative book *Women Workers of India*:

> Every human economic system, from time immemorial has needed and utilised the work of women. From the primitive times, when men hunted animals, down to the present day, when thousands are employed in factories, women are found to stand shoulder to shoulder in all occupations.[1]

Factory industry is a comparatively new development in human affairs. Long before its emergence, women were working in fields and at home in a variety of occupations, apart from their most important occupation of looking after the household and giving birth to and looking after the children. This latter function of women, which they alone can perform, has never received from the society, more particularly its male part, its due importance. If that were done and if it were evaluated property, women would be found to be bigger producers of national wealth than men.

But women have never confined themselves only to looking after homes and bearing children. They have demanded and accepted for themselves a much wider field of activity. From time to time,

---

* *Social Change* (March 1972), *II*, 51–58.

opponents of the freedom and equality of women have advocated the confinement of women to kitchens. Hitler was the most vicious amongst them. They never had any complete success, for society could not do without the labour of women. But the thought has not died out. It has remained lurking in many minds, both male and female, and affects their attitude towards many issues.

In India, the large mass of women work on fields in agriculture. On the basis of the 1961 census, late Dr D. R. Gadgil stated the position as follows.

> In 1961, 17.7 crore women, and 18.3 crore men lived in rural areas. Further a much larger proportion of women in the countryside were at work than in towns and cities. The percentage was 31 in one case and 11 in the other; women workers in rural areas as recorded in the 1961 Census, number some what more than 5.5 crores as against a little less than 40 lakh women workers in urban areas. Of the rural women at work 4.63 crores were returned as working as either cultivators or agricultural labourers. Nearly 78 per cent of women at work in India were thus engaged in agriculture.[2]

Women work on fields as well as in a variety of other occupations of agricultural and semi-agricultural kind. They also work in village and handicraft industries as well as labourers on roads and construction sites. Mrs Sengupta has described the position as follows.

> Women in the villages are all workers, either on their own property or as hired workers, part-time and full-time. There is no choice for women but to work, because if they did not supplement the income of their husbands there would be a major economic crisis. The lower the standards of living, the harder the women have to work.[3]

The number of such women workers is increasing from year to year with the increase of the population, the fall in the standard of living and the progressive disappearance of the prejudice against women's work outside the home, which was very strong at one time amongst higher castes and richer peasants. This increase in mainly responsible for the increase in the figure of women workers in census reports. In the 10 years, 1951–1961, the percentage of women in the total working force has increased from 23.30 to 27.96.[4] The main increase was in rural areas in the category of cultivators.

Table 5.1 *Average Daily Employment of Women in Factories*[5]

Year	Number of Employees (000)	No. of Women Employees (000)	Percentage of Women to Employees
1961	3,497.0	372.3	10.64
1962	3,649.0	394.1	10.80
1963	3,864.0	400.4	10.37
1964	4,024.0	409.1	10.16
1965	4,118.0	394.5	9.57
1966	4,069.0	364.7	8.96
1967	4,071.0	380.6	9.34[5]

Turning now to the non-agricultural field, one finds that there is a distinct fall in the percentage of woman employed in factories. The actual numbers have varied from year to year. But they have not kept pace with increase of factory employees or with increase in the number of women available for employment. The following table will illustrate the trend.

The same is true of employment in mines. In 1951, the number of women workers in mines was 109,600. In 1967, it declined to 90,900 and the percentage declined from 20.1 to 13.5. The decline was particularly heavy in the case of coal mines where the percentage fell from 15.7 in 1951 to 6.6 in 1967.[6]

In the case of factory industries the decline is particularly marked in old, established, traditional industries of cotton textile and jute textile. These two industries were at one time the largest employers of women labour. The following table (5.2) giving figures from 1927 to 1950 will bear out the fact.

Later investigations have corroborated the fact that Dr Gadgil referred to as follows:

The most serious trend was the decline in proportions employed in the old and important textiles, cotton and jute. Total employment itself has declined in jute. In cotton, the proportion of women employed has declined in spite of increase in aggregate employment in the industry.[8]

Table 5.2 *Total Employment in Cotton and Jute Mills and Percentage of Women Employees*

	Cotton		Jute	
Year	Total No. of Workers	No. of Women Workers	Total No. of Workers	No. of Women Workers
1927	342,941	66,532 (19.4)	332,119	55,412 (16.7)
1932	396,523	67,756 (17.1)	263,442	41,581 (15.8)
1937	474,134	65,417 (13.8)	305,785	39,336 (12.9)
1942	611,025	69,927 (11.4)	309,962	36,859 (11.9)
1943	650,793	72,282 (11.1)	302,304	36,592 (12.1)
1944	656,613	70,464 (10.7)	288,663	37,869 (13.1)
1945	657,882	69,706 (10.6)	303,319	40,963 (13.5)
1946*	630,609	68,530 (10.9)	313,133	43,165 (13.8)
1947	637,090	64,630 (10.1)	319,302	41,872 (13.1)
1948	643,492	61,743 (9.6)	329429	41,966 (12.7)
1949	653,309	59,531 (9.1)	322,159	41,576 (12.9)
1950	622,330	52,628 (8.5)	303,364	37,531 (12.4)

Note: *The figures from 1927 to 1946 relate to pre-partition British India. The subsequent figures relate to the corresponding states of the Indian Union. Figures for 1946 exclude Punjab and NWFP. Figures in brackets denote percentage of women to total.[7]

According to the table given by Mrs Padmini Sengupta in her book, the percentage of women employed in cotton and jute textiles further declined from 12.4 to 7.8 in the case of jute.[9]

Many explanations are offered about this big fall in women's employment in cotton and jute industries. The most cogent amongst them are technological improvements which have rendered many jobs done by women redundant and prohibition of night work by woman labour which makes it, they say, more expensive for employers. It is difficult to attach much importance to this factor as, in spite of it, women workers have increased in many other industries.

There is, in recent years, a marked increase in the number of women employed in newer industries like chemical and pharmaceuticals and in industries like rice mills, tobacco curing, cashew nut and matches. Women are also employed in large numbers in plantations, *bidi* making, construction work and household and small-scale industries. The Labour Bureau of the Government of India has, in a report, given the following overall picture of women employed in industries.

In all the broad industry groups, except plantations, men constituted a majority of the working force. Women workers constituted 13.5 per cent in the factory industries group (estimated total No. of workers, 2,453,300), slightly more than 50 per cent in plantations (estimated total workers 1,874,100) and 17.0 per cent in the mining industries group (estimated total workers 505,000). Among the factory industries fewer women were employed in engineering industries, but their proportion was about 7 per cent in the textile group of industries and relatively larger in the 'Others' sub-group. They constituted a majority of the working force in a few industries like match factories, cashewnut factories, tobacco curing and tea plantations. In a few others, such as *Bidi* factories, clothing manufacture, coffee and rubber plantations and in manganese and iron ore mines they constituted more than a quarter of the labour employed. In the textile industries the proportion of women workers ranged from about 4 per cent in the jute industry to about 8 per cent in the silk industry. About 5 per cent of the working force in the cotton textile industries, and in a few other industries, such as sugar factories, petroleum refineries, printing presses, tanneries and footwear manufacture, their employment was negligible.[10]

In will be interesting to note, on the basis of this overall picture, the number of women employed in various industries. The table below gives for the year 1968 the number of women as well as the total number of workers employed in various industries.

The most significant and, at the same time, objectionable thing about the employment of women is that they are mostly employed on unskilled and low jobs. It is hardly ever that they get skilled, higher or supervisory jobs. They have to end their service usually on the wage-rate on which they started. When, through rationalization or technical development, unskilled jobs are replaced by skilled jobs, women are the first to be asked to go. Thus, larger and larger number of women are finding themselves unemployed and the number of women employees goes down progressively. The remedy against this growing evil is not to insist on the retention of those unskilled jobs but to train women to handle skilled jobs. It is necessary to women. It is also necessary to impart to them supervisory skills so that they will not be condemned

Table 5.3 *Total Employment and Women Employed in Industries—1968*

		Total Employment	Women's Employment
		.000	
1.	Processes allied to agriculture	106	46,557
2.	Food	476	106,605
3.	Beverages	11	174
4.	Tobacco	122	38,934
5.	Textiles	1,137	53,736
6.	Footwear, other wearing apparel and made-up textile goods	30	1,499
7.	Wood and cork	54	4,196
8.	Furniture and fixtures	13	106
9.	Paper and paper products	56	3,213
10.	Printing, publishing and allied work	104	1,000
11.	Leather and leather products	24	800
12.	Rubber and rubber products	57	1,318
13.	Chemical	201	19,492
14.	Products of petroleum and coal	19	548
15.	Non-metallic mineral products	194	24,154
16.	Basic metal industries	234	4,352
17.	Manufacture of metal products	172	2,579
18.	Machinery	284	2,256
19.	Electrical apparatus, machinery, appliances and supplies	150	7,065
20.	Transport equipment	400	1,526

(Continued)

(Continued)

		Total Employment	Women's Employment
21.	Miscellaneous industries	136	8,929
22.	Electricity gas and steam	47	263
23.	Water and sanitary services	7	82
24.	Recreation services (cinema studios)	2	18
25.	Personal services (laundries, dyeing and cleaning)	5	149
	Total	4,042	329,551

Note: The 1968 figures estimated by repeating figures for Jammu and Kashmir, Kerala, Mysore, Orissa, Manipur and Tripura for 1967 as returns for year 1968 were not received.[11]

to remain always at the bottom of the rung. It is only in this way that women will be able to contribute their best to the country's economic development.

Another disability from which women workers suffer is the discrimination in the matter of wages. In most cases, their wages are lower than those paid to male workers. The report of the Labour Bureau, Economic and Social Status of Women Workers in India has collected extensive information about wage rates prevailing in various industries or fixed by tribunal or under the Minimum Wages Act, which show that, in a majority of cases, wage rates for women are lower than those for men. It has stated,

The wages of women workers are usually fixed at rates lower than those for men either because the relative value and nature of work are different in the two cases or because historical developments and social and economic factors have generally made for the fixation of lower rates for women workers, irrespective of the nature of their work.[12]

It has stated further, 'Until recently the principle of equal pay for equal work was not accepted in India even in large-scale organized industries and considerable differences existed between the wages and the earning men and women.'

The position is, no doubt, changing but it is changing slowly. It is true that India is not the only country which practises this discrimination. But that is no reason why it should be continued, particularly when the constitution provides in one of the Directive Principles for the payment of 'equal pay for equal work'. One can draw little comfort from the conclusion of the National Commission on Labour, 'While generally conceding that the wages of women workers have been lower than those of men, the differences have tended to narrow down in recent years.'[13] A vigorous campaign must still be waged for the abolition of discrimination. The best plank on which it can be waged is to demand a rate for a job, whether the job is held by a man or woman.

Apart from factory and other industries, new avenues for employment have now opened out for women. They are in public service, in education, in health and medical services, in shops and establishments and in a variety of other occupations that develop in a welfare state. Women are taking advantage of these openings. In course of time, they will provide employment to a large number of women. But they may not be able to compensate for the fall in employment in factory industries and in industries like mining. If that fall continues as at present, the opening out of new avenues will not materially help women seeking employment.

The number of women seeking employment is increasing from year to year—in the first place, because of increase of population and, in the next place, because of greater desire on the part of women to seek employment owing to economic necessity, spread of education and the progressive disappearance of social taboo on women working outside their homes. Some are alarmed by this large-scale influx of women into the labour market. They are alarmed because there is already a surplus of men in the labour market and competition of women will make it far more difficult for men to get jobs.

Competition between men and women must be avoided. But at the same time, women cannot be pushed back into kitchens and homes. Pushing them back into kitchens and homes will deprive the country of a large volume of value-creating labour. Women are capable of looking after homes and bearing and rearing children as well as of doing useful and valuable work outside homes. They have done this double work throughout history and can do it now more efficiently with all the aids that modern civilization has developed for helping them in their household work. Ordinarily, women can do most work as well as men. There are only a few jobs which they are not expected to handle because of their arduousness. But, on the other hand, there are some jobs which they can do better than men. In some cases, it may be necessary to make special arrangements for women to work part-time and not far away from their homes. It is desirable to make all such arrangements in order that the valuable labour of women may not be wasted.

Women contribute materially to economic development by keeping homes clean and tidy and peaceful and looking after the health and well-being of menfolk and taking proper care of children. Over and above this, they can contribute substantially by participating actively in the nation's productive industries and services. Millions of women are already working in fields and factories and in public services like administration, education, health, medicine, transport, etc. The contribution that they are making to nation-building and to economic development is incalculable. If they are given proper opportunities, it will increase tenfold and twentyfold. The nation must give them those opportunities. It was Pandit Nehru who said many years ago that no nation which kept half its population idle or out of productive processes could ever prosper. It is the task of women's organizations and their leaders to emphasize this fact and through constant agitation and propaganda secure for women wider opportunities of employment and service on the basis of equality with men.

NOTES

1. *Women Workers of India*, Padmini Sengupta, Asia Publishing House, (1960) p. 9.
2. Women in the Working Force in Inida, D. R. Gadgil, Asia Publishing House (1965) p. 4.
3. Padmini Sengupta, p. 168.
4. Report, National Commission on Labour. p. 379.
5. Ibid p. 389.
6. Ibid p. 390.

7. Economic and Social Status of Women Workers in India Labour Bureau, Ministry of Labour (1953) p. 14.
8. D. R. Gadgil, p. 22.
9. Padmini Secgupta, p. 30.
10. D. R. Gadgil, p. 22.
11. Indian Labour Statistics, 1970 Labour Bureau, Government of India, p. 38.
12. Economic and Social Status of Women workers, p. 28.
13. Report. N.C.L. p. 382.

Chapter 6

Women's Employment in the Urban Informal Sector[*]
Some Critical Issues

Anita Dighe

INTRODUCTION

One of the characteristics of the 1970s was the deepening development crisis across the world and the growing disillusion with the 'trickle down' theory of development. Among the various groups that were seeking alternatives and were asking critical questions about reducing inequalities was a section of the women's movement which was being spearheaded in many countries of the West in mid-1960s. Pressure from these groups had resulted in the UN's decision to ask its member states to make an investigation on the status of women in their countries.

> While India shared the development crisis, there was in fact no women's movement nor any realisation of the interrelationship between women's situation and developmental trends. The women's movement which and development which had developed along with the freedom struggle had ended by the mid-fifties, with the acceptance of women's claim for complete equality in the Constitution, and the first attempt to apply this principle in Hindu Law. The organisations which had spearheaded the movement remained but had for the most part, adopted a welfare-oriented stance.[1]

---

[*] *Social Change* (June 1985), *15*, 3–6.

It was against this background of complacency that the Government of India, under constant pressure from the UN, took the decision to appoint a committee published in 1975, which became a revealing document for it showed how the process of development had, in many different ways, bypassed women almost completely. Among the various issues raised, the report noted that there was paucity of data on important social and economic indicators relating to women, and hence, a need was expressed for obtaining better data and information on women. There was an overall realization that primary data on women in the unorganized occupations (who constitute 94 per cent of working women in the country) was particularly lacking and, as such, micro studies of such women needed to be commissioned.

Consequently, some studies were brought out as series titled *Women in a Developing Economy*, on specific identifiable groups of women workers, particularly in the unorganized sector, to focus attention on the nature of problems, patterns of organization and living and working conditions of women in some of the lesser-known occupations. The studies have served to highlight the manner in which women's economic roles are being affected by the process of modernization. An attempt is made in this chapter to review some of the work done in this area and to highlight critical issues relating to women's employment in the informal sector.

WOMEN IN THE INFORMAL SECTOR—SOME CRITICAL ISSUES

The main sources of data on women are censuses, national surveys and micro-level research studies. A critical examination, particularly of census data, has revealed a distorted picture of women, particularly of their participation in economy and labour force. This is because of biases introduced by sex-based stereotypes and also because of the assumption that data collection methods which are applicable for men will automatically suit women. D'Souza notes that 'cultural and social stereotypes regarding the concept of head of household has given rise to unreliable data and serious under-reporting of the economic contribution of women in agriculture and in the informal urban sector.'[2] Singh[3] reports that in a study of self-employed women in the resettlement colonies of Delhi, a very small proportion of women

Table 6.1 Work Participation Rates (Main Workers) as per 1971 and 1981 Census

Population Category	Work Participation Rates (%)	
	1971	1981
Rural male	53.6	52.2
Rural female	13.4	16.5
Urban male	48.8	48.2
Urban female	6.7	7.6

were considered primary earners, although 81 per cent of them stated that they worked to provide basic support to their families. She points out that the dependency assumption that a woman cannot be a primary earner as long as there is an adult male in the household tends to make household surveys underestimate the economic contribution of women to the household. A look at the census data would help to highlight this point (Table 6.1).

Thus, according to the census data for main workers, women workers constituted 13.4 per cent and 16.5 per cent of the rural population in 1971 and 1981 respectively and 6.7 per cent and 7.6 per cent of the urban population in the decade span.

In terms of categorization of workers as main worker, marginal workers and non-workers, the picture that obtains for 1981 is as evident in Table 6.2.

The statistics presented in the tables show how the census definition of the 'worker' with its emphasis on 'economically productive' and full-time work tends to exclude a majority of women and regards them as non-workers.

The process of development has resulted in an 'uprooting' of rural groups and their migration to areas which provide some industrial and service sector employment. According to Singh and D'Souza, data from all major cities indicate that slum and pavement dwellers are overwhelmingly poor rural migrants, primarily from lower castes or disadvantaged communities, who migrate to cities through caste, kinship and village networks in search of better economic opportunities.

Majumdar points out that 'the urban poor are the same as those in rural areas both lying at the bottom of the social structure and suffering

Table 6.2 Total Population, Main and Marginal Workers and Non-workers—1981

India		Total Population	Main Workers % to Total Population	Marginal Workers % to Total Population	Non-workers % to Total Population
Total	Persons	658,140,676	33.4	4.1	62.4
	Male	339,895,757	51.2	2.0	47.0
	Female	318,244,919	14.4	6.4	79.1
Rural	Persons	501,952,169	34.8	4.7	60.5
	Male	256,836,180	52.2	2.1	45.7
	Female	245,115,989	16.5	7.4	76.1
Urban	Persons	156,188,507	29.2	2.3	68.6
	Male	83,059,577	48.2	1.5	50.3
	Female	73,128,930	7.6	3.1	89.4

from cumulative inequalities'.[4] The groups that are selectively absorbed in stable employment are those with some educational qualifications and those who possess the skills that are demanded by modern sector employment. Since women generally do not possess either of the two, they are pushed into the informal sector of the urban subsistence economy.

In their study of slum and pavement dwellers in Delhi, Calcutta, Bombay and Madras, Singh and D'Souza[5] found that women were invariably domestic servants, hawkers, construction workers and petty traders. Conditions of poverty had resulted in situation where women took up any kind of available occupation. As a result, occupations which involved traditional skills such as home-based production and agriculture were replaced by unskilled domestic and other kinds of manual service. Kasturi's study[6] corroborated that the process of pauperization due to the decline in handloom weaving industry in rural areas had brought women to cities for employment in domestic service and construction work. Her study also showed that some women supported unemployed or casually-employed husband. Women from such homes, to be assured of one income, were often pushed into low-status, low-paid employment and looked for better jobs or learnt a skill; the women kept the hearth going by working at whatever job was available. Studies by Singh and D'Souza[7] and Brahme[8] have shown how male absorption into the urbanizing economy has been helped by female employment in strenuous and demeaning jobs such as scavenging, sweeping, etc. Brahme's study of the Hamal Women in Pune showed that majority of the husbands of the women in her sample had moved into better paid, less arduous, skilled manual occupations. Despite this, women were principal earners in 50 per cent of the families.

Studies by Nair[9] and Mathew[10] have shown how, in order to avoid unionization and payment of minimum wages and other benefits, the cashew industry and coir industry are gradually moving units to the homes of women. Like coir industry, the cashew industry is dependent on exploitation of cheap female labour. This is facilitated by the putting out system that operates on piece-rate basis so that the workers are paid much lower than what they would be paid in factories. Mathew's study showed how women in coir industry worked long hours and under insanitary and unhealthy conditions in order to make a reasonable return. Indebtedness was endemic. Many suffered from diseases due to the work environment. Any attempt on their part to form a cooperative was thwarted by private employers who felt that better wages and conditions of work would create labour-related problems for them. Study of the women construction workers by Sinha and Ranade[11] showed that SC and ST constituted a majority of the workers and that, for similar jobs, women were paid less wages. Despite the existence of rules and regulations on wages and conditions of work, women in the Delhi survey of 150 respondents said that they were paid ₹4.50 a day against the prevailing official rate of ₹5.15. Construction work was characterized by a combination of contract labour and casual employment. This resulted in substantial differential in wage rates and those not hired by contractor on semi-permanent basis suffered far more in respect of wages and other facilities.

An important area of women's work which escapes computation is women's employment in home-based production. A substantial number are 'invisible' because they work at home, in sporadic and informal manner in paid or unpaid jobs. Largely because of cultural perceptions regarding mobility of women in public domain, women in the informal urban sector and in rural areas have decided preference for self-employment at home. Preference to work at home tends to place women outside the scope of protective social legislation and makes them vulnerable to systematic exploitation. D'Souza quotes a study of women in North India that showed that preference for tailoring at home forced women to accept much lower remuneration than tailors who sat and stitched in village shops. Thus, women literally paid for their own public 'invisibility'. According to D'Souza,

> Employment opportunities in handicrafts industry have been vigorously promoted as home industry for women in South Asia. However, there has been a failure to take into account structural determinants of employment, in handicrafts as home industry. Thus, handicrafts that are exported to developed countries are products of seated labour and though women are given employment and earn income that is useful for maintaining the family, it is the middlemen who benefit.[12]

Mies'[13] study shows how the integration of lace makers into world market has not solved but, rather, has aggravated the problems of their poverty. For the process has led to an extraordinary growth and concentration of capital in the hands of a few male merchants and exporters, while women continue to be paid low rates for their labour. Recognizing the need to provide more employment opportunities to women, the Sixth Five-Year Plan advocated self-employment for women. The main argument for advocating self-employment is the same both for men and women, namely, wage employment in the organized sector has very limited score. Also, self-employment is considered to be conducive to the development of individual initiative and entrepreneurial talent by offering greater personal freedom. In the case of women, self-employment is advocated on two additional grounds. The first is that 'it will enable women to combine their dual role of producer and home maker without stress, the assumption being that the majority of self-employed women will engage in home based productive activity'.[14] According to Sundar, the other reason, often unstated but implicitly held by the more orthodox policy makers, is that home based self-employment for women, by avoiding increased interaction between the sexes, will have a stabilizing influence of the institution of the family and, therefore, on society.

Women's employment in this sector has generally been divided into two or three categories; Jhabvala[15] distinguishes between those who are given raw materials by another person (employer) who pays them on piece-rate basis on the amount of work they produce and those who buy all their raw materials themselves and earn by selling their finished goods. According to Sundar,[16] there are three categories: (a) home-based activities which are either an extension of their household activities like dairying, poultry keeping, food processing (papad making, masala making, etc.), or which use traditional craft skills for market production (e.g., embroidery work, zari work, lace making, etc.), (b) home-based production using non-traditional and acquired skills to meet the market demand generated as a result of ancillarization of big industry. Women are engaged only in a part of the production process which is farmed out by bigger production units, for example, *beedi* rolling, matchstick making, manufacture of electronics or machinery parts, etc., and (c) retail trading and services, for example, flower and vegetable selling, old garment selling, laundering, catering of meals, etc.

There are many arguments against promoting home-based productive activity.[17] One argument is that favouring home-based production emphasizes women's roles as mothers and producers. The second argument is that, very often, domestic production means production in female appropriate areas which are low-technology and low-income roles. No improvement in the status of women results from such employment promotion because it leaves (a) the size of income small, (b) leads to no reallocation of household work and (c) leaves traditional roles unchanged. The third reason relates to the technology argument. Women working individually in home production in marginal activities cannot have access to new technologies. The fourth reason is that home-based production denies women all the benefits of collective action.

> Protective labour laws regulating wages, conditions of work, maternity leave, creches etc. cannot apply to them. Dispersed and unorganized they have no political power and no bargaining strength as they have no idea of the total numbers of women engaged in the same occupation. Finally, it becomes much more difficult to channel economic inputs (credit, technical training, marketing help), or social services (literacy training, health family planning facilities, etc.).[18]

CONCLUSIONS

At the conceptual and theoretical level, role of the urban poor in urban occupational structure is not very clear. It is only recently that the unorganized or informal sector has been recognized as an important subject of investigation by international agencies such as World Bank and International Labour Organization. At the macro level, a great deal of research remains to be done to understand how the unorganized sector articulates with the organized sector in the urban occupational structure and how the informal sector relates to the wider urban economy. Employment of women in the informal sector deserves special attention, since this is an area which has been almost totally neglected in the past and which will, in the future, be an area of special concern to those involved in policy planning and implementation of programmes for women.

NOTES

1. Veena Majumdar, The role of Research in Women's Development: a case study of the ICSSR Programme of Women's Studies, Samya Shakti, Vol. 1 No. 1, July 1983.
2. Alfred De Souza (ed), Women in Contemporary India and South Asia, Manohar Publications, New Delhi, 1980.
3. Andrea Menefee Singh and A. De Souza, The Urban Poor, Manohar Publication, New Delhi, 1980.
4. T. Majumdar, The Urban Poor and Social Change: A study of Squatter Settlements in Delhi, Social Action, 27(3), 1977.
5. A. Singh and A. De Souza, 1980, opus cited.
6. Leela Kasturi, South Indian Migrant Women in Delhi's Slums, ICSSR mimeo, 1978.
7. A. Singh and A. De Souza, Position of Women in important Bastis in Delhi, ISI mimeo. 1976
8. Sulabha Brahme, Economic Plight of Hamal Women in Pune, ICSSR mimeo, 1979.
9. K. A. Nair, Women Workers in Cashew industry in Kerala, ICSSR mimeo, 1979.
10. Molley Mathew, Women workers in unoraginsed sector or coir industry in Kerala, ICSSR memeo, 1979.
11. G. P. Sinha and S. N. Ranade, Women Construction Workers: Reports of two survey, Allied Publishers, New Delhi, 1976.
12. Alfred De Souza, 1980, Opus cited.
13. Maria Mies, The Lace Makers of Narsapur, ILO,1982.
14. Pushpa Sundar, opus cited.
15. Renana Jhabvala, The Home-based Workers, We, the Self-employed, SEWA, Ahmedabad, October 1983.
16. Sundar, oups cited.
17. Ibid.
18. Ibid.

Chapter 7

Female Workforce*
Its Contribution to Metropolitan Economy

Sanghmitra Acharya

This chapter presents trends in female work participation in four metropolitan cities of Calcutta, Bombay, Delhi and Madras during 1961–1981 and attempts to relate these trends to changes in the functional character of these cities.

I. INTRODUCTION

Participation of female population in the economic activity has a definite impact on demographic and socio-economic structure of demographic of population. Size of female workforce is governed not only by the existence of job opportunities but also by their capacity and willingness to avail them. The sociocultural set up, to a large extent, determines the size and nature of female workforce. More than the required qualification or the individual's interest, it is the economic status and the sociocultural background which decide women's participation in the labour force.

While female participation in agrarian economy has been long recognized, the recognition of its contribution in urban economy is recent. Social change ushered in by mechanization and industrialization led to rapid transformation of women's role in the post-independence era. The process of urbanization brought in changes in the functions

---

* *Social Change* (June 1992), *22*, 8–16.

of the cities and urban centres. This chapter attempts to investigate the impact of such changes on the economically active female population of the four metropolitan cities of Calcutta, Bombay, Delhi and Madras during 1961–1981.

II. OBJECTIVE

The main objective of the chapter is to identify and understand the changes in the economically active female population vis-à-vis change in the functional category of the chosen metropolitan cities.

III. RATIONALE

Transition in the social fabric over the years has ushered in various changes—desirable as well as undesirable. While there also have been factors which have caused women to participate in the economic activities, there also have been factors restraining their economic participation. On the one hand, desire, due to willingness or compulsion, to add to the family income initiated female population to work. On the other hand, general decline of handicrafts and modern industry with advanced technology deprived many of their participation.

It, therefore, becomes a matter of interest to investigate how rapid industrialization and advancement of technology in the cities have affected the participation in economic activities by the female population. The choice of the four metropolitan cities is because of marked sociocultural differences in these spatially distant cities.

IV. HYPOTHESIS

On the basis of the foregoing rationale, it has been hypothesized that the change in the functional classification of a city brings about change in the work participation rate, mainly of the female population. Interpretation and analysis, in the paragraphs to follow, attempt to test this hypothesis.

V. DATA SOURCE AND METHODOLOGY

The general population tables and the general economic tables (BII i) of the census of India for the years 1961, 1971 and 1981 are the sources of data.

The obtained data has been processed to work out the proportion of workers and the inter-censal change. The latter has been worked out by the help of a simple formula:

$$\frac{P_2 - P_1}{P_1} \times 100$$

Where P_1 is the economically active population of 'x' census year and P_2 of 'x+1' is the census year. Functional classification has been done on the basis of the methodology developed by Ashok Mitra (1974). Non-agricultural activities out of the nine industrial categories were considered for the purpose. Categories I and II did not form a part of the exercise. The workers falling in the remaining categories were clubbed together into three sectors.

1. **Industry:** Comprising of categories III to VI denoted by A
2. **Trade and Transport:** Comprising of categories VII and VIII, denoted by B
3. **Service:** Comprising of category IX, denoted by C

Proportion of workers in each sector to the total non-agricultural workers (III–IX) was worked out. The values thus obtained were plotted on the triangular coordinates of a ternary diagram to get the location of each city. The ternary diagram is an equilateral triangle with each of its arms divided into equal divisions to represent percentage values from 0–100. In this case, it is 10 equal divisions, each representing 10 per cent. Perpendiculars from the midpoint of the arms to the opposite vertices divide the triangle into six sub-triangles. These sub-triangles represent six sectors of composition of A, B and C with varying degree of intensity. Three concentric circles with the radii 6⅔, 11⅓ and 16⅔ of the base of the triangle were drawn from the point of intersection of the coordinates. The zone within the innermost circle 2 and circle 3 represent ill-balanced composition of A, B and C with predominant function accentuated. The zone outside the third circle (3) represents the composition in which one function is highly accentuated.

VI. INTERPRETATION

6.1. Inter-censal Change in the Economically Active Population

A comparison between the cities shows that Delhi experienced the maximum positive change, while Calcutta the least, recording a negative change in male population, the growth reduced by one per cent from 1961–1971 to 1971–1981. In case of female population, a remarkable increase from 2.42 per cent to 22.13 per cent was recorded.

Bombay had an increase of 30.17 per cent during 1961–1971 in male population. The change, though remained positive during 1971–1981, reduced to 27.26 per cent. Female population saw an increase from 31.93 per cent during 1961–1971 to 59.85 per cent during 1971–1981.

Delhi was the only city which showed increase in the interchange from 48.24 per cent during 1961–1971 to 62.54 during 1971–1981 in male population. Female population showed an increase of 116.39 per cent during 1971–1981, almost double of what it was during 1961–1971.

Madras, like, Calcutta and Bombay, showed a decline from 34.05 per cent change during 1961–1971 to 27.48 per cent change during 1971–1981 in male population. As regards females, it showed a sharp increase from 14.72 per cent during 1961–1971 to 71.79 per cent during 1971–1981 (Table 7.1).

Table 7.1 *Inter-censal Change in Economically Active Population*

Metropolitan Cities	1961–1971		1971–1981	
	M	F	M	F
Calcutta	−1.69	+2.42	−2.61	+22.43
Bombay	+30.17	+31.93	+27.26	+59.85
Delhi	+48.24	+69.71	+62.54	+116.39
Madras	+27.48	+34.05	+71.70	+14.72

On the whole, while the male population has been experiencing a declining growth rate of its economically active segment, female population has experienced a rise.

6.2. Work Participation Rate

As regards work participation rate, there has been a general decline in all the cities for the male population, and a negligible increase, if at all, in the female population.

Calcutta had 61.41 per cent of males recorded as workers in 1961. It declined to 56.96 per cent in 1971 and further to 55.31 per cent in 1981. However, for female population, it declined from 6.09 per cent in 1961 to 5.66 per cent in 1971, then increased to 6.17 in 1981.

Bombay recorded male work participation rate of 61.73 per cent in 1961 which declined to 57.66 in 1971 and to 54.86 in 1981. As regards female population, in 1951, 8.81 per cent participated in work, while the proportion declined to 7.12 per cent in 1971. It, however, increased to 8.57 per cent in 1981.

As regards Delhi, male work participation rate declined from 52.80 per cent in 1961 to 51.22 per cent in 1971 and then increased to 52.93 per cent in 1981. Female work participation, contrary to the male pattern, showed a rise from 4.46 per cent in 1961 to 4.83 per cent in 1971 to 6.55 per cent in 1981.

Madras recorded 52.22 per cent of work participation among the male population in 1961. It declined to 49.09 per cent in 1971 and further to 47.92 per cent in 1961 which declined to 5.08 in 1971 and then increased to 6.46 per cent in 1981 (Table 7.2).

Table 7.2 Work Participation Rate

Cities	1961		1971		1981	
	M	F	M	F	M	F
Calcutta	61.41	6.09	56.96	5.66	53.31	6.17
Bombay	61.73	8.81	57.66	7.12	54.86	8.57
Delhi	52.80	4.46	51.22	4.82	52.93	6.55
Madras	52.22	6.33	49.09	5.08	47.92	6.46

Table 7.3 Workers Engaged in Functions A, B and C and the Functional Class

Metropolitan Cities	1961				1971				1981			
	A	B	C	Functional Class	A	B	C	Functional Class	A	B	C	Functional Class
Calcutta	29.44	33.57	34.99	V11	41.21	34.31	23.46	IV2	33.26	41.26	25.41	V2
Bombay	45.16	29.36	25.49	IV2	46.46	33.32	20.32	IV3	46.02	31.91	22.07	IV2
Delhi	27.80	22.32	46.38	12	30.54	31.31	38.14	11	32.31	33.59	34.10	11
Madras	32.81	36.97	36.42	V11	36.56	40.12	23.30	V2	36.31	37.42	25.77	VI

Function 1

A—Industry

B—Trade and Transport

C—Service

Triangular Sectors 1

I Low A: Medium B: High C

II Low B: Medium A: High C

III Low B: Medium C: High A

IV Low C: Medium B: High A

V Low C: Medium A: High B

VI Low A: Medium C: High B

6.3. Functional Classification

The predominant function of Calcutta has changed while that of Bombay, Delhi and Madras have remained unchanged during 1961–1981. During 1961, Calcutta was dominated by trade and transport (B) though the composition of the three functions—A, B and C—was highly balanced. Industry (A) dominated in 1971 followed by trade and transport (B) respectively. In 1981, function B was dominant followed by A and C respectively.

6.4. Circular Zones

1. Highly balanced compositions of A, B and C
2. Moderately balanced compositions of the first-ranking function and less balanced other two
3. III balanced compositions of A, B and C with predominant function accentuated
4. One of the sectors highly accentuated

6.5. Proportion of Workers in the Functional Sectors

All the four cities show a higher proportion of women engaged in service sector and higher proportion of men in industry and trade and transport sectors.

As regards Calcutta, while the proportion of workers had increased in sectors A and B, it had declined in sector C during 1961–1981. Similar picture emerged for the proportion of female workers. In 1961, the proportion was 30.64 per cent in A for males which increased to 34.95 in 1981. sector B increased from 37.18 per cent to 43.65 per cent while sector C declined from 32.19 per cent in 1961 to 21.42 per cent in 1981. About 9.00 per cent to 12.20 per cent of female workers were engaged in A and B while their proportion declined from 81.13 per cent to 75.83 per cent during 1961–1981.

Proportion of male workers in sector A ranged between 46.27 per cent to 43.16 per cent during 1961–1981 for Bombay. Sector B engaged about 30.00 per cent and sector C about 20.00 per cent. Proportion of female workers was higher in sector A in comparison to sector B.

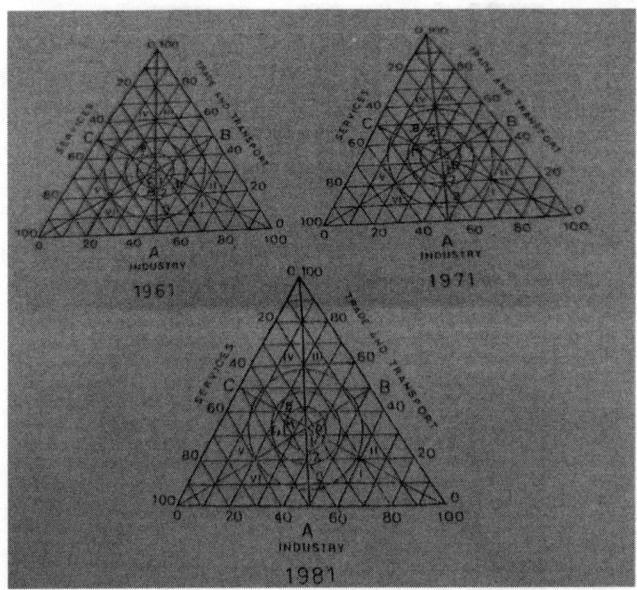

		Circle	Sector
C—Calcutta	Highly balanced	1	I–IV
B—Bombay	Moderately balanced	2	I–IV
D—Delhi	One sector accentuated	3	I–IV
M—Madras	One sector highly accentuated	Outside the circles	I–IV

Figure 7.1 *Functional Classification*

In case of Delhi, the proportion of male workers in sector A and B ranged between 28.28 per cent to 32.85 per cent during 1961–1981. In sector C, it ranged between 44.64 per cent to 35.65 per cent. While the proportions in sectors A and B have increased during the given period, sector C declined. However, in case of female workers, higher proportion has been engaged in sector A than in B.

Madras had higher proportion of male workers in trade and transport sector than in industry and the lowest in service sector. In case of female

Table 7.4 Male–Female Worker in Functions A, B and C

Metropolitan Cities		1961			1971			1981		
		A	B	C	A	B	C	A	B	C
Calcutta	Male	39.64	37.18	32.19	29.63	44.57	23.52	34.95	43.65	21.42
	Female	9.62	9.25	81.13	19.61	11.14	78.26	11.85	12.29	75.83
Bombay	Male	46.27	30.38	23.34	48.07	34.56	17.37	48.16	33.26	18.58
	Female	33.19	18.20	48.57	29.56	19.24	51.10	28.24	29.71	51.03
Delhi	Male	28.28	27.08	46.64	31.60	32.85	35.55	32.76	33.16	33.98
	Female	20.16	6.16	73.68	16.50	10.95	72.54	15.96	13.81	70.23
Madras	Male	34.19	32.76	33.06	35.20	44.91	19.88	38.54	39.44	22.01
	Female	18.18	14.68	67.14	16.29	22.75	60.96	23.05	21.30	55.59

workers, while in sector A, 18.18 per cent in 1961 increased to 23.05 per cent 1981, in sector B, about 14.68 per cent increased to 21.30 per cent from 1961 to 1981 (Table 7.4).

VII. ANALYSIS

As a city with predominant function of trade and transport, Calcutta engaged more than 80 per cent of the female workers in service sector.

The negative interchange for male workers of Calcutta speaks of the saturation point which the city has reached as far the economically active male population is concerned. Though the rate of change has increased for the female workers, only about 6 per cent of the female population is engaged in work.

Bombay, which remained an industrial city, engaged about one half of the female workers in service sector while the other half was distributed among industry and trade and transport sectors. Inter-censal growth of economically active population has shown an increase for women and a declining trend for men.

The predominant function of Delhi remained service. Inter-censal growth of workers showed a positive trend both for male and female population. This reflects upon the possible opportunity available. Entry of women in trade and transport sector is evident from the declining trend exhibited in sectors A and C.

Madras, too, like Calcutta, remained a trading city with trade and transport as predominant functions. Inter-censal growth of workers showed a declining trend for males and a positive trend for females. Though service sector engaged more than half of the female workers, a declining trend in this sector and an increasing trend in sectors A and B was observed.

When compared to the proportion of male workers in service sector and proportions of female workers in industry and trade and transport sectors, the proportion of female workers in service sector is remarkably higher. Predominance of a functional class does not exert force to aggregate higher proportion of female workers in that sector, except in case of Bombay.

Much of the female workforce has remained engaged in service sector in all the four cities. However, in case of functional shift, the industrial city of Calcutta has attracted shift in favour of trade and transport sector, while the other, that is, Madras, in favour of industry. As an industrial city, Bombay obviously had comparatively higher proportions of female worker in sector A than B. Even Delhi which remained a service city had a higher proportion of female workers in sector A than B.

VIII. CONCLUSION

It is, thus, observed that irrespective of the functional class, it is the service sector which had a higher proportion of female work participation. The second and the third-ranking functions designated as medium and low respectively, also, did not influence the shift of female workers from one sector to the other except in case of Delhi. However, the functional class of a city has influenced the shift in the male workers form one sector to the other. Remarkably low proportions of female workers in general suggest lack of incentives for their participation.

It is observed that the size of country's economically active population and its ratio to the total population reflect on the total economy of the nation. Economic activities indicate the changing conditions of demand for labour and the economic factors which determine the magnitude, character and location of opportunities of employment. In this context, various functions of the cities though, have influenced the male workers, have failed to do so in case of female workers. It is here that the preference shown by female population for service sector can be attributed to the sociocultural context in which a woman grows up. The dynamism required for entrepreneurship in not much encouraged by habit as well as by prevailing conditions. Therefore, service sector is recognized as a secure means of economic gains in comparison to other commercial activities, which, again by habit and conditions, have become man's prerogative. What probably is required to bring about a positive change in female workforce is a more rapid pace of change in sociocultural attitudes of people.

Appendix 7A.1 *Reclassification of Industrial Categories into Functions*

Industrial Categories 1961		Industrial Categories 1972		Reclassification into Functions (Ashok Mitra)
III	=	III	=	Industry
IV		IV		(A)
VI		Va		
		Vb		
VII	=	VII	=	Trade and
				(B)
IX	=	IX	=	Service
				(C)

REFERENCES

Gadgil, D. R. 1965. 'Women in the working force in India'. *Kunda Datar Memorial Lectures: 1964*, New Delhi: University Press.

Karla, B. R. 1961. 'An Analytical Note on Working Population', *Final Population Tables, Census of India*, 1961: 389–395.

Lal, A. 1959. 'Some Aspects of Functional Classification of Cities and a Proposed Scheme for Classifying Indian Cities', *National Geographical Journal of India*, Vol.5: 12–24.

Misra, R. P. 1978. *Million Cities of India*, New Delhi: Vikas Publishing House.

Mitra, A. 1974 a. *Functional Classification of India's Towns*, Delhi, Institute of Economic Growth.

Mitra, A. 1981 b. *Shifts in the Functions of Cities and towns of India 1961–1971*, New Delhi: Abhinav Publications.

Nath, K. 1965 a. 'Urban Women Workers: A Preliminary Study', *The Economic Weekly*, Vol. 37: 1405–1413.

Nath, K. 1968 b. 'Women in the Working Force', *The Economic and Political Weekly*, Vol. 13: 1205–1113.

Pethe, V. P. & V. S. Bhaduri. 1971. 'Cities of India: Functional and Locational Aspects', *Artha Vignana*, Vol. 13, No.4: 381–390.

Section III
Political Participation

Sectional Introduction

Ghazala Jamil

Writings on political participation of women often begin with an invocation of the universal suffrage given by the constitution, without mentioning the struggle by Indian women or even the important history of Indian suffragettes (Mukherjee, 2018) which remains mostly forgotten. A close reading of the early discourse of suffragettes in colonial India shows that it was not restricted to women's 'contribution to the national project' as happened in the late-colonial and early post-colonial decades. Their demand from the beginning was to contest for and hold public office. Just like the abolitionist in the USA influenced women's demands, it was the discourse on self-determination that seems to have opened up the space for women's activism in India (Sinha, 1999).

The question of party politics and women's participation/representation is important because the route to social legislation for ensuring gender equality and justice is essentially through party-based electoral contests that reach representative decision-making bodies. Over and above the question of quota, this requires that women politicians have or achieve a frame alignment with the ideology of the party. The problems of construction of 'women' as one unifying category (Menon, 2000) or a compact interest group resurface if women's affiliation to political parties is scrutinized. Members of women wings of all kinds of political parties have, historically, subsumed gender interests to ideological framing dominant in the party. This was true not only of the parties who count Muslims or Dalits or OBCs as their primary constituencies but also of the Left parties where questions of class oppression trump gender and other identity-based inequalities. While it is easy for women in all political parties to broadly agree to fix a minimum number of seats in elected bodies, to imagine women building inter-party coalitions even on questions of gender equality is an entirely different matter. The tendency in the movement has been to raise the bogey of danger to solidarities, but the questions that bear asking pertain to practices or principles that would ensure truly procedural and substantive democratic representation (Jayal, 1997) rather than the politics of presence.

The manner, experience and impact of reservation for women in elected bodies remain a contentious area of discussion which has generated passions in the movement and in polemical writing by women politicians and political theorists. With the Women's Reservation Bill not making much headway for decades, perhaps these discussions finding themselves nowhere near resolution are now fatigued. On the other hand, since the elections do happen periodically, psephologists continue to take interest in studying women voters' attitudes and behaviour.

The first article included in this section is by Usha Mehta. Titled 'Indian Women and Their Participation in Politics', it was published in *Social Change* in 1978. The article is important for containing a concise history of women's participation in organized politics. It includes a history of suffragettes in the West and other colonies of the region like Burma. Mehta notes that India has actually seen a larger number of notable women in high offices and as members of parliament than many developed countries such as the USA, Britain and France. Despite this, she concedes that representation is dismal. The author puts forward several nuanced formulations as to the low percentage of women in electoral politics and argues that democratic ideals need to be encouraged in all aspects of life and relationships for encouraging increased participation.

In her article 'Of Women, Politics and Panchayats', Farah Naqvi begins by recounting some older debates about women's participation. This article exemplifies the numerous studies on women's participation in local bodies' elections after the 73rd Amendment. In particular, Naqvi takes on the criticism of 'dummy' candidates and provides a nuanced account of what lies behind this label. Although intersectionality is not the term used in the discussion, Naqvi talks about the women from marginalized sections such as the SC/STs subjected to 'double discrimination', flagging patriarchy in the analysis. The article is also illustrative of how research became something of interest in the voluntary sector which, by this time (the late 1990s), became more organized. Voluntary organizations were not content with simple philanthropy and could also command some resources for knowledge production. In addition to individual women activists and their personal efforts, party-backed labour unions and trade unions, non-party political formations, autonomous movement organizations and international NGOs also emerge as prominent players in the movement. This was, of course, not limited to documenting gains and problems, nor to any one issue.

'Gendered Political Exclusion: Crucial Implications for Indian Democracy' is the third article in this section. Authored by Sanjay Kumar and Praveen Rai, it was published in 2007. This article belongs to a genre of research which marks the change in the nature of electoral contest as well as the perception about women voters. They could become swing voters, and so their voting patterns, motivations and attitudes about political parties and so on were of interest. They were not seen as passive voters who cast votes as directed by the men in their families. The authors show that this was mainly related to women taking interest in electoral politics, followed by media exposure, voting discretion, socio-economic background, education and employment status. This article also enumerates various barriers to women's participation in politics. Apart from giving a glimpse into women voters' motivation, in particular during the elections, the article is also important because it goes beyond merely looking for a pattern to women's political participation and attempts to show that there was such a thing as women's political interest, and whether women behaved as one class of people.

REFERENCES

Mukherjee, S. (2018). *Indian suffragettes: Female identities and transnational networks.* Oxford University Press India.

Menon, N. (2000). Elusive 'Woman': Feminism and the Women's Reservation Bill. *Economic & Political Weekly, 35*(43/44), 3835–3844.

Sinha, M. (1999). Suffragism and internationalism: The enfranchisement of British and Indian women under an imperial state. *The Indian Economic & Social History Review, 36*(4), 461–484.

Jayal, N. G. (1997). Secularism, identities and representative democracy. *Comparative Studies of South Asia, Africa and the Middle East, 17*(2), 11–20.

Chapter 8

Indian Women and Their Participation in Politics*

Usha Mehta

Centuries ago, Plato—the great philosopher, made a fervent plea to admit women to all spheres of life. Eminent thinkers and social reformers in later centuries lent a powerful support to these pleas, and yet it was only during the last century that women all over the world started demanding equal rights including the fight to vote.

The movement for granting political equality to women dates back to 1848, when Susan Anthony gave a call to women in the USA to fight for their rights. As a result, the end of the 19th century saw a small fraction of women participating in the political life of their country.

New Zealand was the first country to enfranchise its women in 1893. Then followed Australia in 1899, Finland in 1906, the Scandinavian countries in 1915, all the provinces of Canada (except Quebec) in 1916, the dominion followed in 1917, England, Soviet Union, Netherland and the Ukraines in 1918, the USA in 1920 and Switzerland as late as 1971.

In Asia, Mongolia was the first to grant franchise to its women in 1924; Ceylon followed in 1931 and Thailand in 1932. Burmese women got full right to vote only in 1935 though the country adopted women's suffrage in 1900, when it became a province of India. Philippine women got the voting right in 1937 and the Japanese women in 1956. Zanzibar, Iraq, Transjordan and Sudan still do not

* *Social Change* (September 1978), *8*, 31–40.

accept women as voters while Kenya grants only limited franchise to them.

In India, it was in the year 1917 that women started an agitation for getting franchise under the leadership of Sarojini Naidu. After heavy protests, the question was left to be decided by the provincial legislative councils. Madras granted the right in 1921, other provinces followed suit in 1926 and by 1929, they were enfranchised on the same terms as men. During the fight for freedom, women fought shoulder to shoulder with men. As a consequence, on the advent of independence, adult franchise and complete social and political equality before law became realities.

POST-INDEPENDENCE PERIOD

Since the first general elections in the country, women (despite the majority of them being illiterate) started performing their political duty religiously. This is proved by the fact that there has been an increasing trend in their voting turnout as seen in Table 8.1.

It is clear from this table that the percentage of votes cast by women has increased with the passage of time from 37.1 in 1952 to 60.00 in 1971, though once again it fell to 54.91 in 1977. Also, the difference in the percentage of votes cast by men and women has narrowed down from 17.9 in 1952 to 9.7 in 1971. Of course, once again, unfortunately the difference rose to 10.71 in 1977. While there was a sharp rise of 22.9 per cent in the number of women voters between 1952 and 1971, the increase in the case of men voters was only 14.7 per cent.

On the other hand, despite the constitutional provisions and the government having taken various legislative measures to enhance the status of women, not much was done either by the government or by voluntary organizations to create the necessary socio-economic and value structure to implement these measures. The fact is that even the modified targets for free and compulsory school education to all children, irrespective of sex set by the Education Commission of 1966, have not been realized till today and education has spread only to 19 per cent of the government. In the field of politics, voting rights have not been enabled by men. Ever since the first general elections, the numerical strength of women in neither the union nor the state legislatures has been proportionate to their total strength. In fact, it

Table 8.1 Voting Trend of Men and Women from 1952 to 1977

Year	Electorate in Millions		Votes Polled in Millions		Percentage Voted of		Difference in the Percentage of Votes Polled by Men and Women
	Men	Women	Men	Women	Men	Women	
1952	94,461	77,286	51,128	28,132	55.0	37.1	17.9
1957	99,968	89,443	55,924	35,405	56.0	39.6	16.4
1962	113,944	102,428	70,703	47,764	62.1	46.6	15.5
1967	129,569	119,434	86,460	66,264	66.7	55.5	11.2
1971	145,000	135,000	101,600	81,000	69.7	60.0	9.7
1977	167,019	154,155	109,609	84,653	65.62	54.62	10.71

has actually declined since the elections of 1967 as can be seen from Table 8.2.

The small number of women in the legislatures can be explained by the fact that a very few women come forward as candidates for the election contests.

The number and percentage of seats contested by women since the first general elections, as given in Table 8.3, show that the highest percentage was only 16.5 during the parliamentary elections in 1971 and 16.9 during the assembly elections in 1957.

In fact, women candidates were so few that they never exceeded four per cent of the total number of candidates in any of the general elections. This is certainly low compared to most of the communist countries like the U.S.S.R., China, Yogoslavia and others. However, it has to be conceded that India is better situated than some of the western democracies, which is clear from Table 8.4.

It is also worthwhile to note that long before women in some of the developed countries like the USA, England and France rose to high political office, India had a number of women in its parliament, some of them also held responsible positions including those of chief minister, governor, ambassador, high commissioner and, last but not least, president of the United Nations General Assembly. Table 8.5 shows the number of women ministers India had since the first general elections in 1952 in the Union and State Cabinets.

LOW PARTICIPATION BY WOMEN

A study of the biodata of women legislators from the first general elections to the present day reveals that a majority of them were married Hindus belonging to the middle-age group. The predominance of women belonging to this age group is attributable to the fact that they are, more or less, free from domestic duties. Also, they are less likely to be criticized for entering public life than women of the younger age group. Literacy wise, none of them was illiterate. Occupationally, the largest group came from social workers connected with several social, cultural and women's organizations.

Income wise, it was the middle-income group that was represented the best. However, it cannot be denied that women in India, as in the

Table 8.2 Numerical Strength and Percentage* of Women in the Union and State Legislatures

Year	Lok Sabha		Rajya Sabha		State Assemblies	
	Total Strength	No. of Women and Percentage	Total Strength	No. of Women and Percentage	Total Strength	No. of Women and Percentage
1952	489	23 (4.7)	214	14 (6.5)	3,641	98 (2.74)
1955	–	–	219	12 (5.9)	–	–
1957	494	27 (5.5)	232	8 (3.5)	3,284	197 (5.9)
1958	–	–	232	17 (7.3)	–	–
1960	–	–	236	14 (5.9)	–	–
1962	494	35 (6.9)	236	12 (5.1)	3,387	173 (5.1)
1964	–	–	238	17 (7.1)	–	–
1966	–	–	238	20 (8.4)	–	–
1967	520	31 (6.0)	240	17 (7.8)	3,709	134 (3.6)
1971	521	22 (4.2)	–	–	–	–
1972	–	–	243	19 (7.8)	3,697	164 (4.4)
1977	542	19 (3.5)	244	25 (10.2)	Not available	146

Note: * Given in brackets.

Table 8.3 *The Number and Percentage of Seats Contested by Women Since 1951–1952*

Year	Total No. of Seats Contested		Percentage of Seats Contested	
	Lok Sabha	State Assemblies	Lok Sabha	State Assemblies
1952	51	216	10.4	6.5
1957	70	490	14.2	16.9
1962	68	233	13.7	8.2
1967	64	230	12.3	7.7
1971	86	–	16.5	–
1972	–	351	–	9.8
1977	65	–	12.0	–

Table 8.4 *Percentage of Women Members in the Parliaments of Various Countries*

Countries	Percentage of Women Members in Parliament
Egypt	Nil
Iran	Nil
Ethiopia	Nil
Canada	0.3
Japan	1.4
France	1.6
the USA.	2.4
England	4.1
Sri Lanka	4.1
India	4.4
West Germany	6.1
Israel	6.6
Yugoslavia	20.00
Hungary	20.00

(Continued)

(Continued)

Countries	Percentage of Women Members in Parliament
Finland	5.21
Sweden	25.00
U.S.S.R.	31.00
China	40.3

other countries of the world, have been extremely under-represented in the legislatures as also in high positions in the political sphere as in other professions.

In a survey conducted amongst the women candidates contesting for 1971 parliamentary and 1972 assembly elections, an attempt was made to find out whether this low participation was due to women being afraid of violating the traditional Indian norms or because of their lacking motivation to enter the fray. A majority of them blamed the discriminatory policy of the political parties. Political parties, they complained, not only failed in encouraging them to participate in politics, but sometimes adopted positively discriminatory and discouraging attitudes. The primary object of all parties being attainment of power they tried to put up candidates having greater capacity and chances of catching votes and winning elections. Thus, other things being equal, a woman getting preference over a man was more an exception than a rule as she had to give evidence of her superior calibre and greater winning capacity before securing a party ticket. Among other reasons given by them were their domestic duties and responsibilities coming in the way of their political life, the strain of the election campaign, the atmosphere at election times not being congenial for women, especially in view of politics being a dirty game, the wide gap between sexes and the unequal social set up, and the lack of self-confidence and economic independence among women.

It must, however, be admitted that with Indira Gandhi's coming to power, the ratio of women to total candidates had increased as the Congress party then tried to give greater representation to women.

The survey also showed that though women were well aware of problems facing the country, their score on political awareness was not very commendable. Many of them were also ignorant about their duties and function as members of the legislatures. However, conducting an election campaign is a different matter. It is a challenging task everywhere and for all candidates—men and women. It is all the more so in a country like India, where a candidate is required to cover distant towns and unapproachable villages, difficult terrains and hilly tracts and especially for women, who have to conduct their campaign consistently with their duty towards the family. However, it is satisfying to note that most of the women candidates met the challenge well and creditably by organizing their campaigns effectively and facing the odds bravely. Though husbands generally assisted their wives, there were some who found no support from their family members and yet carried out their work creditably. Party leaders and workers were great assets to a majority of the candidates, yet, discrimination was found to have been shown to some in matters of granting of funds and in organizing and addressing meetings. Again, men candidates who were denied party tickets adopted a lukewarm attitude towards successful women applicants, turned indifferent and uncooperative and, at times, even hostile towards them.

However, the way women candidates organized their campaign proved that even physically women are not the weaker sex and that women with a will can work wonders.

On the whole, as far as equality in the political field is concerned, from the nonentities they once were, women have now grown into full-fledged citizens conscious of their rights and responsibilities. Though their status is not changed completely, it is in the process of being changed. The main factors that deer them from summoning enough courage to enter the political field, according to the study, are (a) traditional social norms, (b) lack of education, (c) economic dependence on men, (d) domestic duties and responsibilities, (e) political parties dominated by men desirous of perpetuating their regime and (f) hostile attitude of their male rivals some of whom do not even hesitate in indulging in character assassination.

The concept of leadership—especially of democratic leadership is changing fast. A leader in modern days is looked upon more as a teacher and an influencer relying on persuasion, goodwill and understanding rather than on assertiveness, domination and a stern attitude associated with a boss or a commander. Since these qualities are found more in women than in men, the already long list of successful women leaders who have equalled and, at times, even excelled men is bound to go up, provided they are afforded increasing opportunities to assume leadership. It is only the united effort of the political parties, the government, and women and women's organizations that can help in making this possible and improving the status of women.

POLITICAL PARTIES

1. Political parties should allocate a much higher percentage of seats contested by them for legislatures to women, than that allocated at present, the minimum being 25 per cent of the total number.
2. In order that they can play a more effective role in developing political consciousness among women and bringing them into active politics, they should organize regular campaigns to educate the electorate about their political rights and duties laying special stress on equal rights to men and women.
3. Orientation programmes meant to train aspirants for party tickets in legislative techniques will go a long way in raising the standard of public life as also in making democracy more effective. So long as this cannot be done, orientation programmes, at least for selected candidates, should be organized. In such courses, special care should be taken to see that women candidates are made well conversant with problems facing women.
4. Women's wings of the parties should concentrate more on spreading political consciousness among their members rather than on social work. They should also bring pressure on party bosses to give greater representation to women among the candidates sponsored by them for local bodies, state assemblies and the parliament as also in the executive posts in the party.

GOVERNMENT

1. The government should take positive steps to reform the electoral system and especially to bring down the expenditure involved in it so that women may not keep away from it on grounds of their economic dependence on men.

2. The principle of reservation of seats for women prevalent in some states at the level of municipalities may also be followed regarding the state assemblies, the parliament and the ministries.

3. The proposal for a coupled vote according to which every constituency will have two representatives—one man and one woman, first mooted by Bernard Shaw and later supported by many advocates of women's rights, may be given consideration and tried out on a limited scale.

4. The creation of a special ministry to look after women's problems and needs as in some of the European countries like France will go a long way in quickening the pace of women's emancipation.

VOLUNTARY WOMEN'S ORGANIZATIONS

1. Women's organizations like the All-India Women's Conference, the National Women's Council, the Women Graduates' Association and others should put in organized efforts for cultivating public opinion in favour of women getting their due share in public life and a fair representation on legislative and executive bodies.

2. They should also organize an active, national women's movement to give women a chance to develop their potential and to sensitize them of their own rights. Disorienting men and women from traditional norms and changing the prevailing social climate which looks down upon women entering public life should be the focal points of such a movement. Also, it should avoid taking an anti-male posture and the attempt of its leaders should be not to deny their sex but only to deny that it is a handicap.

However, these remedies will prove to be effective only if it is understood that the small part played by women in politics is the result of the secondary role assigned to them in the society, and that only a total revolution generating and promoting democratic values in all spheres of life will make both men and women realize that as there cannot be an inferior race or class or caste, there also cannot be an inferior sex in the world.

Chapter 9

Of Women, Politics and Panchayats*

Farah Naqvi

Consequent to the reservation of seats for women in panchayat (local government) bodies in India, there are, today, over 80,000 women who hold office in panchayats throughout the country. In the initial euphoria, there was a widespread hope, subscribed to by many NGOs and women's groups that women have the potential to bring about crucial, positive change in the political culture of panchayats. They have a nurturing disposition and are more capable of putting others before themselves; and since they themselves are subject to injustice and discrimination, they will be more sensitive to the needs for the marginalized. At the other end is a belief that women are 'inferior' and should, therefore, be kept out of the public realm. One variant of this theme is that women 'personalize' politics; they are emotional, irrational and subjective, and hence cannot understand the machinations of realpolitik, they can only be pawns in the political game. One or more of these arguments have come into play to keep women restricted to the private realm of the family and out of the public realm of politics and panchayats to the private realm of the socialization and

* *Social Change* (June–September 1998), *28*, 143–156; Volume editor's note: When originally published in *Social Change* this article authored by Farah Naqvi was attributed to voluntary organization called Nirantar. The author wishes to acknowledge that this paper was based on collective fieldwork and draws on Nirantar's experience of working with women panchayat members in Banda district, Uttar Pradesh.

preparation for adult roles reinforce this inside–outside location of men and women.

This paper takes a look at the ground realities and, more specifically, the 'spaces' within the panchayat system, or lack thereof, which make it possible or difficult for women to effectively participate. It reports on first-hand encounters with women panchayat members in Banda district, Uttar Pradesh, over the course of projects undertaken by Nirantar,[1] a centre for women's education, in collaboration with the Mahila Samakhya programme,[2] henceforth referred to as MS. Nirantar's role extended from motivating women, to helping them contest elections and working with them post-elections. Given the mandate of these two organizations, it was women from Scheduled Castes and Scheduled Tribes—Harijan and Kol women respectively—who were targeted.

The focus here will be to address some basic issues relating to women and Panchayati Raj, primarily through a series of case studies on Banda district. But first, the context.

BANDA DISTRICT

Banda is among the five most 'backward' districts in India. A significant proportion (23%) of the population is tribal and Scheduled Caste. The dominant caste group in the region are the Thakhurs, who own and control a large part of agricultural land. The mainstay of the economy is subsistence agriculture, with agricultural labour an important wage-earning activity. In some blocks, there is a high degree of dependence on the forests and minor forest produce for survival. The nexus between highly organized gangs of dacoits, the state apparatus (police, forest officials, etc.), the upper-caste landlords and political parties helps preserve the status quo and keep the lower castes subjugated. Violence is constantly manifest in this nexus. Equally routine is the violence that women have to face within their families. It is against this backdrop of poverty and violence that one has to appreciate the impact of reservations; which catapulted women from the lower castes into positions of authority in the Panchayati Raj system.

WHY DUMMY CANDIDATES?

A widely held impression is that a large proportion of women who contested elections were 'dummy candidates', who stood on behalf of their husbands and relatives, or were propped up by the powerful—the corollary being that reservations were not working, as men still ruled the (panchayat) roost. What does it mean to be a dummy candidate? It means that one is made to stand for elections by one's husband, brother, son or by someone from a powerful caste; that one is a rubber stamp, while the one who pulls the strings is the de facto occupant of one's seat. The reason why the phenomenon is so widespread in panchayat elections needs to be understood, for only then we begin to evolve corrective strategies.

The exclusion of women from the public sphere is not just due to patriarchal socialization or what some writers call their 'asychocultural disposition'. It has a material base as well, for women lack that which some writers have referred to as 'political resources', or resources which facilitate political participation (Scholzman, Burns and Verba, 1994).

Of the factors inimical to women's political participation, an important one is that along with their exclusion from the political sphere, women have been denied 'civic skills'—organizational abilities; understanding public forums; taking part in meetings; taking decisions; making a presentation and so on. Lack of education is also important. Another factor at work is lack of money. While contributing to family income, women do not have control over how it is spent. Thus, if Ramsakhi, a village-level animator in the MS programme, did not even have money to buy voters lists for her constituency, it was because she was contesting in direct opposition to her husband's wishes. Time is yet another constraint. Because of the double burden of working both inside the home and outside in the fields, women have less free time than most men in rural areas. Who, for example, will make the rotis when women are out campaigning?

Since a lack of access to 'political resources' prevents women from taking independent political action, it is not surprising that many of them are 'dummy candidates'. It is, in fact, strategic to get elected this way.

CASE STUDIES OF 'DUMMY' CANDIDATES

Chandravati, *Pradhan*, Gadhchapa

Chandravati is about 50 years old and belongs to the Thakur caste. She had little or no interest in contesting for the seal of *pradhan* (panchayat head) of Gadhchapa. She was happy single-handedly managing the family's 50 *bighas* of agricultural land, organizing labour and tending to matters on the home front. Her *jeth* (older brother-in-law) was the previous *pradhan* and her husband was an experienced politician and a member of the Congress party. Unfortunately for these two, the *pradhan's* seat, over which they had acquired a hold, was declared reserved for a woman candidate. Family pressure was brought to bear on Chandravati, until she relented and agreed to contest. She did not do any campaigning, but still managed to win, albeit by a slim margin of 37 votes. Although disinterested in elections, she was happy when she won.

At the time of writing, it had been over a year since Chandravati became *pradhan* of Gadhchapa. In that period of one year, she had been to the block for at least six meeting, each time accompanied by her husband, of course. She was extremely well informed about government schemes and the functioning of the panchayat. ₹50,000 came in the last Jawahar Rozgar Yojana (JRY) instalment and plans were afoot to use the money to construct pucca roads. It is incumbent on the *pradhan* also to decide who gets houses under Indira Awas. But Chandravati still had not learnt how to manage panchayat paperwork. All the paperwork was done by her husband and she would just sign on the dotted line. She often wished her husband would go without her to the block meetings, but he would say it was very embarrassing when she is the *pradhan* and he lands up alone. Chandravati is among the few women *pradhans* who actually attended these meetings, at which she would feel uncomfortable and isolated. She is aware she should have regular meetings with panchayat members, but so far has had only two such meetings. She (and her husband) have also held two gram sabha (village assembly) meetings.

Chandravati has been educated up to class eight, and can read newspapers, which she scans for news on panchayats. It was through the papers that she learnt that, in the neighbouring State of Madhya

Pradesh, *pradhans* get ₹500 a month as honorarium. She thinks it is extremely unfair that in Uttar Pradesh, *pradhans* get noting.

Rani, Panchayat Member

Rani, a Kol woman in her mid-20s, is married to Nandlal, a man who is not only educated but is also extremely well informed and articulate. When panchayat elections were announced, he was dying to stand for any post. But the panchayat samithi seat that covered his village from where he was in a position to muster electoral support, was declared reserved for a woman candidate, as was the panchayat member seat that likewise lay in this sphere of influence.[3] Nandlal decided that his mother and wife would contest for the panchayat samithi and panchayat member seats respectively.

Rani is illiterate and by nature quiet, shy and reticent. Nandlal has taught her nothing about panchayat procedures and rural schemes. He did teach her to sign her name, which she does without understanding on papers he reads and approves. Nandlal is a little resentful of the fact that he himself is not in the panchayat. He has a lot of grouses against the functioning of the *pradhan* (corruption in panchayat finances, lack of accountability, not following procedures, no information sharing with the other panchayat members, no meetings), but has no locus standi to do anything about it.

We ask Rani if she knows anything about the other women panchayat members. Nandlal replies on her behalf: 'There are three women members'. Rani corrects him gently, saying, 'No, there are four', and proceeds to tell us their names and castes. Rani has only one son. Her earlier children died in infancy, and she is loathed to leave her son even for a second. Rani knows nothing about the functioning of the panchayat and has never heard the word *yojana* (planning).

What was it like to stand for elections, we asked Rani. 'I loved the '*bhaag daud*' (running around) and flurry of activity during the elections', she says, 'We roamed about here and there, met people, filled forms. But all that has stopped now. When there is no work to do, where shall I roam about? '*Man to laagta hai ki jayeen, par kahan jaayen?*' She replies caustically, with a smile: 'Yes become a member and sit at home!'

Chandravati and Rani are just two among many, many women who were ostensibly 'dummy' candidates. Chandravati has the advantage of education and, therefore, some independent access to information. Also, by virtue of her upper-caste status in a predominantly Harijan gram sabha, she is able to wield power with greater ease. Since her election, her exposure and awareness levels have increased dramatically.

Rani, although completely subjugated by her husband, has begun to articulate some resentment at being made to just sit in the house. Was her candidature a waste of time and money? Perhaps not entirely. She has, for the first time in her life, experienced moments of power and mobility. Would both of them be more independent of their husbands in the next elections? We have to wait and see.

We clearly have to reassess our perceptions of the so called 'dummy' candidates. If we look for dramatic signs of change (like women independently holding gram sabha meetings of discontent) we might see some potential. Slow, cumulative political experience will add up to greater gender equity in politics.

WOMEN WHO CHOOSE TO FIGHT INDEPENDENTLY

The elections also saw a sprinkling of women who made an active and independent choice to contest elections. While they did not necessarily win, they provide an insight into the kind of women who consciously sought the political space provided by reservations.

Sonia, Candidate for the Post of *Pradhan*, Gram Sabha—Nihi

Sonia, a woman from the Scheduled Caste Kol community, in a village that is extremely feudal in land relations and social structure, contested for a *pradhan* seat reserved, with the powerful Brahmin landlords on the one side and on the other, the landless Kols, who worked virtually as bonded labour. If the Kols were captive labour on Brahmin lands, it was because there was no other work to be found for miles around. It was in a feudal village like Nihi that a *pradhan*'s post was reserved for a Scheduled Caste candidate, and that too, a woman.

To make matters worse, Sonia had been embroiled in a long-standing conflict with one of the major Brahmin landlords of Nihi,

Hem Narain Tripathi. The story is that Hem Narain illegally took out huge government loans under the Integrated Rural Development Programme in the names of about 20 Kol families after having procured their thumb prints under some pretext. He paid off a few rural bank managers and helped himself to the money. When the time came for loan repayment and the Kols defaulted, they were repeatedly harassed. Sonia, then a village-level worker with MS, took up the issue and fought a year-long battle. This became a case of open rebellion by the otherwise oppressed Kols. It was also the beginning of Sonia's enmity with Hem Narain.

Hem Narain owned most of the land in and around Nihi. Sonia and about 50 other Kol families used to live on his land and work on his fields. This was not an easy situation to break away form; the choice was either to bear repression and stay put or move out. The Kols decided to move out, no matter what the cost. After much running around and struggle, Sonia, along with about 40 Kol families, managed to get some government land to live on, and about five *bighas* each to farm. No matter that the shift meant a move further into the interior of the forest, a place with no ready water supply; at least they were free from the clutches of Hem Narain. In another hamlet of Nihi—Govarhaai, there lived one Mishra, a former *pradhan*, who happened to be at loggerheads with Hem Narain. Mishra was also a powerful landlord with many Kol labourers dependent on him. Once, Sonia and the others had agitated against him for a wage increase. They went to the extent of forcibly preventing outside labour from working on Mishra's fields. All these minor struggles, whether against Hem Narin, Mishra, or any other landlord, have been going on for the past three years and are hopeful signs of a change in the normally subservient, opposed Kols. Sonia is burning with awareness of her rights both as a woman and as a Kol. But were the Kols ready to field a candidate as *pradhan* of Nihi?

Apart from Sonia, there were two other Kol women who stood for elections—Surji and Suakali. Behind each was a dramatically different story. Sonia stood for all the reasons a Kol woman should have. She is aware, articulate, strong, definitely a leader, someone who represents the best that could emerge from the reservations policy. But Surji was Mishra's nominee for the post of *pradhan*. He paid her and made her stand as a 'dummy' candidate. Suakali was Hem Narain's candidate.

Soon Sonia contested and campaigned as she could, saying, *'Mein bas chin batati hoon. Mere paas daaduon ka sahara nahin hai'*. (I just show people my election symbol. I have no landlords backing me). She had no wherewithal to distribute largess; hers was a low-cost campaign, almost dramatic in its simplicity. There were no huge crowds accompanying her on her rounds, no big banners, no loudspeakers—none of the usual electioneering paraphernalia. She often went about on her own, chatting with people on village roads and cutting a strangely lonely figure against the rocky terrain of Nihi. Sonia showed people her election symbol but made no promises. She just said, 'We'll solve our problems together.' Meanwhile, the two other candidates, propped up by Brahmin money, were promising to hand out free saris.

In addition to being a wealthy and powerful landlord, Hem Narain also resorted to strong arm tactics to elicit support for his candidate, Suakali. To this end, he struck a deal with one Dauda, the most dreaded dacoit leader in an area notorious for its dacoit gangs, whose word was a *fatwa* to be disregarded only at great risk to one's life. The rumour that Dauda was backing Suakali unnerved Sonia, but being the gutsy woman she was, she did not back down.

Come election day, Nihi was a sight to be seen. Hem Narain and his gun-toting thugs were present in the vicinity of the polling booth and there was silent terror in the air. The morning passed with hardly any Kols coming out to vote. The MS team, present in Nihi to give Sonia moral support, went house to house, asking the Kols not to be afraid. 'Come out and vote', they said. 'Don't vote for Sonia if you don't want to, but please vote.' By midday, people gradually emerged from their homes and did just that—they voted, but not for Sonia. Even the Kols from the hamlet of Koradia, who had broken away from Hem Narain in an open rebellion some years ago, did not vote for her. They said: 'We have just settled down to living somewhat peacefully. We don't want to risk aggravating the landlords any more. We want peace at all costs.'

Sonia lost the elections by a huge margin. Today, Suakali is the *pradhan* of Nihi. She also washes dirty dishes in Hem Narain's house, and slaves on his fields for five *pauwas* a day.

Sonia's experience underscores a fundamental point in rural politics—it is caste based. It is complete subjugation of the Kols by the upper castes that forced them to vote for Hem Narain's candidate. In fact, upper-caste women are often better placed based in the village. There are no gender-based constituencies to which women can appeal.

WOMEN CONTESTING FROM OPEN SEATS

In Uttar Pradesh, elections were announced twice, before they were finally held in April 1995. After each announcement, there was a great deal of discussion in village about reservations for women, which had happened for the first time. Women, hesitant at first, started coming forward gradually. '*Agar seat pakki hi hai to hum bhi khada honge.*' (If the seat is certain, I will also stand). When they were asked why they wanted to contest, many were unable to articulate their motivations. It remained at the level of barely recognized desire to come forward. MS and Nirantar did a lot of information sharing, motivating, explaining the concept of reservations, the modalities of elections and so on.

It was not clear until just before the elections were finally held as to which seats were going to be reserved. In many cases, women who had mentally prepared themselves and were not reserved, decided to contest nonetheless. For them, there was no going back. The idea of reservations had provided the initial spark, made panchayats seem accessible and allowed them to come forward to claim a space in public life. Many of them had to convince their husbands, families and communities to let them contest, and now, they were going to do so, even if the seats they sought were not reserved. Thus, the phenomenon of women contesting from open seats was a fallout of the reservations policy.

Ramsakhi, Candidate for the Post of *Pradhan*, Gram Sabha—Churehkaseruwa

Ramsakhi, who stood for the post of *pradhan* from a Scheduled Caste seat, had, in the past, been very active in getting hand pumps installed in the village to solve its acute water problem. When the issue of reservations was discussed and women were being motivated to come forward, Ramsakhi was one of the first to express her desire to contest. Subsequently, the *pradhan*'s seat in the village was declared reserved for a Scheduled Caste candidate, who could be a man or a woman. Even though this gram sabha was dominated by Kols and other Harijans, the previous *pradhan* had been a Brahmin. Now for the first time, the downtrodden would have their moment of power. A large number declared their candidacy, among them was Ramsakhi. She did this without the approval of her husband, who supported another candidate. He tried to dissuade her, but she was adamant. Her motivation was straightforward—she wanted to contest because she felt women should be allowed to do so. Her husband was furious. On the day of the nominations, when all of us were busy helping women fill out forms, he landed up at the block office. Before we knew what was happening, he started abusing and beating up his wife in front of a hundred staring people. But because Mahila Smakhya was there in full force, he was forced to back down. Ramsakhi fought the elections but she had neither village support nor money. She lost.

WOMEN AND POLITICAL SPACE: A BARRIER BROKEN

The case of both Sonia and Ramsakhi illustrates one crucial fact—reservations have not only had a quantifiable impact (800,000 women entering panchayats), it has fundamentally altered rural women's relationship to politics and their perception of the political realm. With the joining of words 'women' and 'political participation', a psychological barrier was broken—and there was no going back. If one were to stop reservations in subsequent years, we may not have many women winning seats, but one would certainly have many more women contesting because, for rural women, as a social category, a *Laxman rekha* dividing the private from the public has been crossed. Reservations have forced both men and women to accept the 'political' as a credible, valid and contested space for women.

This is borne out by the fact that a large number of women panchayat members, who have had extremely disempowering experiences in the last year, still want to stand for the next elections—some of them are so called 'dummy' candidates, and some are simply ordinary women members of panchayats. This, despite the fact that they are being kept out of meetings, denied information and have gained nothing in concrete terms. What then motivates them? Perhaps, the same impulses that made them stand in the first place.

Among these is the need for an identity other than that of wife and mother. All the women members enjoy being known as *sadasyi* (panchayat member) even if they do little with their position. It is an identity that, to some extent, legitimizes their existence and mobility outside of the family. Even attendance at a panchayat meeting is enough to give them that new sense of self. Consider the case of Sundi, a Chamar member from gram sabha Laudhwara. Although her role in the panchayat is very limited, her position as a member has spilled over into other areas of community life. People come to her with various types of problems and for resolving disputes. Sometimes, they come to her to say she should ask the *pradhan* to start employment-generating construction work. Even though Sundi herself, along with the other members, has little power to prevail over the panchayat or its *pradhan*, she still feels an enhanced power in being the message carrier.

The fact is that a lot of women members, and indeed the general rural population, do not perceive panchayats as institutions of local self-governance. They perceive the panchayat merely as one route through which to make contact with a nebulous but all-powerful entity known as sarkar. This includes the entire rural administration. We asked Janki, a spunky member of the Ranipur Bhatt panchayat, what she liked about being a member. Why did she want to contest again when the *pradhan* did not deign to include her in any aspect of panchayat functioning? Her reply was, *'Achcha lagta hai. Gaon sab janat ki hum sadasyi hain. Yahan gaon mein nahin sunege to sarkar mein to sunwai hogi'*. (It feels good. Everyone in the village knows I am a panchayat member. Even if they do not listen to me here, at least I get to be heard by the government).

WOMEN CAN FUNCTION ONLY IF THE SYSTEM DOES

It is commonly assumed that it is primarily a patriarchal social structure which militates against women functioning effectively in panchayats. Much of the planning and discussion on women's training needs, over the last few years, have focused on these effects of patriarchy, namely—as women, they lack the experience it takes to function in a public realm; they lack knowledge about the structures of governance; and above all, centuries of patriarchal conditioning has robbed them of the confidence that they can function effectively. These 'weaknesses' of women as political actors have been the subject of scrutiny and strategizing.

All that is undeniable. But it is not the whole story. The other part of the story lies in the nature of the system itself, for any actor needs some sort of functional stage and same minimal props in order to play their role. The panchayat system is not only patriarchal, it is undemocratic, highly centralized, bureaucratic and corrupt. In one sentence—it simply does not work.

That panchayats are plagued by undemocratic norms of functioning is clear. It is rare to find a village in which regular panchayat meeting takes place. Ideal gram sabhas are definitely in the realm of fantasy. The old, familiar scenario of the *pradhan* and gram secretary taking all the decisions and sending pieces of paper to members houses for their signatures continues. This happens despite grand legislative promises to the contrary.

One reason for the disempowering experiences of many panchayat members in this past year is that they are women. But equally important is the fact that it is a highly pradhan-centered system, in which the position of panchayat member is weak in itself. This is clearly born out of the fact that male panchayat members express equal helplessness, especially if they belong to a lower caste.

The stranglehold of the bureaucracy is something else to be contended with. The members of the local bureaucracy—the gram sevak, the junior engineer, the assistant development officer, the block development officer (BDO)—have the most information, not about how the system and schemes should ideally function but how they actually do function. They extremely loathe to part with this knowledge, for their power lies in being able to manipulate processes and procedures so that other contenders for power are kept from breaking in.

CORRUPTION AND WOMEN IN PANCHAVATS

Little needs be said about the ethos of corruption that pervades the system. But how have women panchayat members performed on his front? As mentioned at the beginning of this paper, when reservations were introduced, the faith so often articulated by a wide cross section, from conservative quarters to feminists, was that women will not fall into the quagmire of corruption. This faith stemmed from different sources. There were some who believed that women are innately pure and, therefore, more honest and that women are motivated by a sense of commitment to the community and not to self-interest. There were other who did not glorify women in any way but felt women's own experience of oppression would mean greater sensitivity towards other forms of injustice.

Budhilia, *Pradhan* of Mangawan

Budhilia is a Kol woman who won an election to the post for *pradhan* from a reserved seat. She was a village-level worker with MS and had been through numerous trainings on gender empowerment. When she won, everyone was euphoric. She had every potential to be a model woman *pradhan*. Initially, she used to turn to MS for all her information about rules and procedures. When she first became *pradhan*, she did not even recognize a JRY cheque which the BDO had given her; she kept complaining that her panchayat had not received funds! Thinking the cheque was a piece of paper, she had crumpled it and tucked it away in the folds of her sari. About six months after she became *pradhan*, we started noticing signs of change. Budhilia slowly started refusing to give information about government schemes and money. Once, we discovered that she was paying lower wages to women labourers on a construction site. It went against every principle of gender equality she had been taught. In time, her irritability turned into open hostility. Budhilia gradually got sucked into the system of corruption, as have many other women *pradhans*. But are the women as bad as their erstwhile male counterparts? The answer is no, not because they are innately nay less susceptible to corruption, but simply because they have not been in the public realm and, therefore, have less experience of corruption. Also, as women, they are more vulnerable and, therefore, less likely to be corrupt with impunity. After all, it is much easier to point a finger at a woman in power than at a man in a similar situation. Shortly after winning elections, many women were eager to do what they had promised during their campaigns, not because they had a greater conscience, but because they were scared that the villagers would call them to account if they didn't. Also, some women naively believe that their work performance will affect their chances of re-election. Thus, Sitali, a Harijan member said, when asked if she would contest again: 'I want to, but who will vote for me? I have done nothing'.

WHICH WAY FORWARD?

In the context of centralization, undemocratic norms of functioning, corruption and caste hierarchies there are no easy answers as to what strategies can be adopted for women members. There is, however, a need to recognize the limitations of some of the strategies which we have been adopting and to learn from efforts to grapple with the basic issues of government like transparency, accountability and people's right to information.

Does Information Equal Power?

Information, they say, is power. Hence, the solution to corrupt and undemocratic functioning is to arm members with information about how the system ought to function; teach them about rules and regulations; tell them that it is mandatory for the *pradhan* to call a meeting of the panchayat every month; that beneficiaries of housing schemes are to be selected in an open gram sabha meeting; that the amount sanctioned for JRY should be displayed in a public place. We told women members all that and more. The result was not what one had expected. Janki of gram sabha Ranipur Bhatt, after a training programme on the rules of the Panchayati Raj Act, marched off to the *pradhan* and told him he was obligated to hold a gram sabha meeting at least once every six months. He turned around and told her: 'Your information is completely wrong. You must have studied the wrong law!' Janki came back, tail between the legs. Clearly, as this case illustrates, it is not information which gives power; it is the authority and power of a person that panchayats and they should have it. But much more important is the question of their power base and alternative support mechanisms.

Panchayats and NGOs

Where is the alternative power base for rural women? Over the years, the work of NGOs and women's programmes has necessitated interaction with panchayats or rather *pradhans* and panchayat secretaries. However, little has been done in terms of trying to impact upon the functioning of the panchayats. For instance, even those NGOs who have been doing extremely valuable work for a number of years have not made efforts towards ensuring that gram sabhas meet. That NGOs are not familiar or comfortable with the realpolitik of the gram panchayats was evident during the elections. Even NGOs who have been working in the field for long were unprepared for the dynamics play. Complex kinship and caste alliances corroded the honesty and commitment of candidates supported by the NGOs. Despite the fact that much about the panchayat elections is bewildering and disheartening, for helping women panchayat members play an effective role in panchayats necessitates an understanding and direct engagement with panchayat politics.

Sanghas

Sitalia, a member from gram sabha Ghipni, like many other women in the area, belongs to a women's sangha (society or group) while also being a panchayat member. While the sangha is no more than an informal group of 5 or 10 women, the panchayat is ostensibly a formal institution of local self-government. But which does Sitalia derive greater strength from? She is unequivocal—the sangha is the source of her power. Her sangha membership, moreover, adds to her power in the panchayat. It not only gives her an alternative source of information but, also, the authority to validate the information she has.

Alternative Strategies: The Right to Information Campaign

The Mazdoor Kisan Shakti Sangathan (MKSS), based in Beawar in Rajasthan, has evolved a strategy to make the system more accountable. Over the past two years, MKSS has organized a series of *jan sunvais* (public hearings). Each hearing focused on a local issue relating to development expenditure or the use of community resources. Sangathan activists managed to procure government paperwork (bills, vouchers, muster rolls) related to a particular development expenditure. They also built enough strength and confidence in the people so as to get them to speak out the corruption in the government machinery, which is clearly exposed in public forums as individual after individual shares first-hand experiences. Bills, vouchers and muster rolls with the names of people who worked on construction sites, etc., are shown to be fraudulent. One speaker said he was not even in the village when his name was put on the muster roll. Other said only 10 bags of cement were used to repair the school wall, not 50 as shown in the official bills. In this process, the entire village collectively either validate or reject the official story through first-hand personal testimonies.

This experience of corruption led to the demand that the guilty be brought to book and 'stolen' returned to the community. Although there are many demands that have still to be met, a number of local officials have returned money they had stolen, payments long overdue have been made, corrupt contractors have completed structures that had been abandoned. But most importantly, there has been an increasing realization on the part of people in the area that they have a right to monitor the way public money is spent.

Given the crucial role of information in any social audit, the *jan sunvais* have led to the demand that any person should have the right to photocopy bills, voucher and other records relating to development works. That the demand has tremendous implications is clear. After the third hearing itself, the Ajmer district gram sevak union went on strike, stating they would not be subject to a social audit and would agree only to an official financial audit. Despite tremendous pressure, the Rajasthan Government is still to give an official sanction. The issue of right to information is now assuming the dimensions of a national-level campaign that demands transparency of functioning and the accountability of all public institutions.

At the core of *jan sunvais* and the campaign for right to information are the issues of transparency, social audit and accountability. And it is these very issues that are fundamental to a move towards democratic decentralization.

CONCLUSION

Clearly, women entering panchayats through reservation is a long-overdue corrective. Whether they function better or worse than men, they have a right to be there, simply in the interest of social justice. It is also undeniable that they do need special inputs to enable them to function. But efforts so far have focused on 'women' as an isolated group of actors, not as actors embedded in a fundamentally flawed system. Any effort to help women function better has to first take cognizance of the system in which they are embedded and plan inputs accordingly. Also, it has to be a multi-pronged attack—working with women has to occur alongside working with the community, to make it more democratically oriented and working to 'clean up the system.' Telling them about how JRY is meant to function in not good enough. One has to give 'critical' information, tell them why JRY does not function, where the loopholes are and provide support structures, because the only existing ones are steeped in the ways of secrecy and corruption.

NOTES

1. Nirantar, a Delhi-based resource group, has been actively providing inputs to NGOs in the field. It has been associating with its field-based partners in planning, training, documentation and material creation.
2. Mahila samakhya is a Central government programme of the Department of Education. It was launched in 1989 in the states of Karnataka, Gujarat and Uttar Pradesh in pursuance of the National Policy on Education 1986, which was the first policy-level expression of the belief that education can bring about a change in the status of women.
3. Panchayat member seat refers to the panchayat at the lowest tier. Panchayat samithi refers to the next higher tier of Panchayati Raj in the state.

REFERENCE

Scholzman, Burns and Verba. 1994. 'Gender and the Pathways to Participation: The Role of Resources'. *The Journal of Politics*. 54(4).

Chapter 10

Gendered Political Exclusion[*]
Crucial Implications for Indian Democracy

Sanjav Kumar and Praveen Rai

INTRODUCTION

The political status of women in any society can be defined not only as equality and freedom with which they share power with men, but also the value society places on the role of women in politics. It is an important indicator of the working and functioning of true democracy in any country. The Constitution of free India promulgated in 1950 promised 'to secure to all its citizens justice, social, economic and political' and 'equality of status and of opportunity' (Basu, 1998, p. 21), and yet women, despite their constituting nearly half of the population, continue to be grossly under-represented in parliament and the state assemblies. Statistics available show that women's representation in the Lok Sabha has not yet reached the world average of 10 per cent representation of women in the House of Representatives, failing thus to acquire the 'critical mass' required for influencing decision-making at the top legislative and executive levels. Similarly, women continue to be marginalized in most of the prominent political parties in the country, not only in terms of seat allotments in elections but also within the party structure and hierarchy. This could be attributed to a large extent to India's democratic process that is fraught with inherent dynamics and contradictions that exclude women from sharing power

---

[*] *Social Change* (December 2007), *37*(4), 180–201.

as equals with men. In contrast to women's poor participation rates as candidates in the electoral fray and within party ranks and file, women's participation as voters has seen a remarkable upsurge in the late 1990s, as voter turnout figures of general elections held in this decade clearly reveal.

Overall, the political participation of women in India is a contested issue and opinion is quite varied and divergent. There are competing arguments about the levels and patterns of women's participation in the political process in the country. On one hand, some theorize that the democratic process is fraught with inherent dynamics and contradictions that exclude women from sharing power as equals with men. That is, the lack of political voice and poor representation of women in parliament is a result of exclusions on gender basis (Agarwal, 2006). On the other hand, we have theorists who feel that the growing political participation of women over the years and sharing of political power by women at various levels reflects that politics in India is not gender exclusive but rather inclusive. They argue that due to the strength and determination of women's movements across India, as well as government-regulated quotas, women's presence in the political arena is increasing, particularly in terms of women's voting patterns and decision-making power, as well as in women's access to positions in public office (Ahern et al., 2000; Banerjee, 2003; Vyasulu and Vyasulu, 1999).

It is within this framework that the ensuing analysis, based on primary and secondary sources, will try to ascertain the underlying patterns and themes of women's political participation and their levels of inclusion or exclusion from the political process. The chapter is divided into six sections which are as follows: Section I provides the definition and indicators of women's political participation; Section II assesses gender exclusion in political participation from a historical perspective to map the beginning of women's participation in political activities and stages of exclusion or inclusion with the passage of time; Section III is about the trends and temporal patterns in political participation of women since the first general elections as voters, representation in the Lok Sabha (Lower House of Parliament), as candidates of political parties and their levels of exclusion. For a comparative analysis, this section also focuses on the political participation of women in the

Indian parliament vis-à-vis women in parliament of other countries of South Asia. Section IV is the most important section of the chapter as it tries to find out the main determinants of women's participation in the electoral process quantitatively. It also attempts to ascertain which are the best indicators of women's participation and their levels in formal politics. Section V tries to qualitatively analyse the impact of women's exclusion from politics on women and the future of Indian democracy. Section VI is the last section that concludes the chapter and suggests the way ahead for women's enhanced participation in the political process and their political empowerment.

DEFINITION AND INDICATORS OF WOMEN'S POLITICAL PARTICIPATION

The definition of political participation of women in broad terms entails a wide range of activities such as participating in trade unions, cooperatives, women's collectives, and informal and formal political processes. Political participation has been defined as a citizen's active involvement with public institutions, which may include voting, candidacy, campaigning, occupying political office and/or lobbying individually or through membership in a group (Arora, 1999; Gleason, 2001). However, in this chapter it is used in a much narrower sense to include women's participation only in formal/electoral politics at the levels of state legislatures and parliament. Women's participation at grassroots level of Panchayati Raj Institutions (PRIs) have not been delved into as affirmative action for providing reservations to them and has corrected the gender exclusions and disparity to a large extent. The political status and empowerment of women in India and the efficacy of the instrument of political rights in achieving the general equality of status will be evaluated and assessed on the following parameters.

1. **Participation in the political process:** The turnout of women voters, the number of women candidates in general elections held in independent India with special emphasis on general elections 2004 based on data from Election Commission of India.
2. **Political attitudes and behaviour:** The level of political awareness, commitment and involvement of women participating in politics,

their autonomy and independence in political behaviour and preferences and as active campaigners during elections. As discussed in the relevant section, the data for this analysis are drawn from the Centre for the Study of Developing Societies (CSDS) Data Unit.

3. **Impact of women in the political process:** The assessment of women's views of their own roles and efficiency in the political process and society's attitude to new political roles of women. This is indicated by the success of the women candidates at elections, the efficiency of women's pressure groups, the nature of leadership and women elected in government and political parties and the effectiveness of campaigns for women's mobilization, particularly on issues that directly concern them. Since quantitative data is not available to gauge the impact of women in the political process, it will be more qualitative and based on gender analysis.

It may be pointed out that empirical data for women's participation in India are mostly available for state and national-level elections. The CSDS data is, therefore, used to capture the grassroots participation in a qualitative manner, so as to provide a more comprehensive picture about women's levels and patterns of political participation and exclusion.

GENDERED EXCLUSION IN POLITICAL PARTICIPATION: AN OVERVIEW

This section provides a brief sketch of the historical background of women's participation in politics as a backdrop, both chronologically and thematically, for subsequent discussion.

It may, perhaps, be argued that the British rule marks the formal recognition and beginning of change in the pathetic status of women in India vis-à-vis society and nation, when James Mill observed, in 1817, that the condition of women in a society is an index of its place in civilization (Mill, 1817)—writing 'women' into the project of modernity and modern history in India. Overall, the roots of women's participation in politics can be traced back to the 19th century reform movement in which several eminent women reformers participated (Chattopadhyaya, 1983). Their activities not only gave momentum to women's participation in public spaces, but also highlighted their entry into the independence struggle and political domain in the long run. The Swadeshi movement in Bengal (1905–1908) marked the beginning of women's participation in nationalist activities, although initially, a large number of women were from families involved in nationalist politics. The base broadened with middle-class women's entry into the movement as they took active part in the boycott of foreign goods and in revolutionary activities during this period. The movement for independence also gave rise to the question of women's suffrage and voting rights. During the same period, several all-India women's associations came into existence (mostly called *Mahila Samitis)* for the purpose of women's upliftment and advancement (Chattopadhyaya, 1983). From the 1920s, the Indian National Congress began to forge links with women's organizations in order to demonstrate its mass support to the British Government. The partition of Bengal (1905) also attracted women in large numbers including uneducated rural women into its fold.

Mahatma Gandhi extended the logic of the feminist mode of protest to the nationalist movement. His emphasis on *satyagraha* and passive resistance in which women participated in large numbers created spaces for women, and thousands of women joined in Mahatma Gandhi's salt Satyagraha that could be termed as the first mass movement of Indian women in the independence struggle (Kumar, 1997). The active participation of women in the political struggles for independence eventually resulted in framing of a constitution based on the principles of equality and guaranteeing universal suffrage to both men and women in 1947. Though the foundation for political participation of women was laid down during the freedom movement, post-independence did not witness much concerted or united effort to create inclusive political spaces for women. By and large, women's participation after independence was constrained by social norms shaping not only opportunities for, but also perceptions of, women's involvement in politics—perceptions that were, sometimes, unique to men, at times shared by women (Arora, 1999; Gleason, 2001; Nair, 1996). Overall, the mass participation of women in the political field during the freedom struggle seemed to decline after independence. Their involvement in politics became confined to familial connections rather than based on interest and societal encouragement to actively participate in politics. Also, political parties that were reflecting the prevailing societal ethos failed to address and systematically excluded women from political participation (Baseline Report, 1998). However, as tokens for their contribution in the struggle for India's independence, political parties allotted them a few seats in general elections. This becomes evident from the first Lok Sabha Elections held in 1952, where women could win and occupy a paltry 4.4 per cent of the total seats in the lower house. Even now, despite the constitutional provisions guaranteeing equality of sexes, political participation of women, in terms of legislative or decision-making bodies, is quite low and they continue to remain marginalized and under-represented. The demand for greater representation of women in political institutions in India was taken up seriously after the Committee on the Status of Women in India (CSWI) published its report in 1976. The CSWI report suggested that women's representation in political institutions especially at the grassroots level needed to be increased through a policy of reservation of seats for women. In 1988, the National Perspective Plan for Women also suggested that a 30 per cent quota for women be introduced at all levels of elective bodies. Women's groups and gender politics strictly insisted that reservation be restricted to the panchayat level to encourage grassroots participation in politics. The national consensus around this demand resulted in the adoption of the 73rd and 74th amendments to the Indian Constitution in 1993 that introduced 33 per cent reservation for women in institutions of local governance. In 1995, the question of affirmative action for women was raised again, but this time the focus was on reservations for women in parliament. Initially, most political parties agreed in principle to this demand, but soon discord and dissensions surfaced. When the bill addressing this issue was introduced in the eleventh parliament in 1997, several parties and groups raised objections. The objections focused around two main issues: First, the issue of overlapping quotas for women in general and those for women of the lower castes; and second, the issue of elitism. The proposed bill is still gathering dust and is yet to be passed by parliament.

The following section delves into the issues more specifically.

TRENDS IN POLITICAL PARTICIPATION OF WOMEN AND THEIR LEVELS OF EXCLUSION

Prior to analysing trends in Indian polity, it would be of interest to see how Indian women fare as compared with women in other countries of Asia. A look at Table 10.1 reveals that India figures at the bottom of the table among South Asian countries, ahead of Sri Lanka only in terms of women's representation in the lower house of parliament. The representation of women in the lower house of Afghanistan is the highest (27%) among the countries of the region that witnessed its first parliamentary elections after the downfall of Taliban rule in the country. Apart from Afghanistan, only Iraq (25.45%) and Pakistan (21.35%) are the two countries in the region where women representatives occupy more than 20 per cent seats in the lower house of the parliament. The reason for higher representation of women in the lower house of parliament in Afghanistan and countries ranked higher than India is mainly due to reservation of seats for women. Thus, India and Sri Lanka are the two countries in the region where women's representation in the parliament is below the world average of 10 per cent representation of women in the House of Representatives.

An analysis of political participation of women in the Indian elections both as candidates in the electoral fray in terms of their winnability vis-à-vis men and as voters and campaigners for political

Table 10.1 *Representation of Women Members in Lower House in South Asia, 2006*

Country	Total Seats	Won by Women	%
Afghanistan	249	68	27.31
Pakistan	342	73	21.35
Nepal	329	57	17.33
Bangladesh	345	51	14.78
India	545	48	8.26
Sri Lanka	225	11	4.89

Source: Website of Bangladesh Government.

parties will reveal participatory trends and their exclusion from the political process. Accordingly, Tables 10.2 and 10.3 provide women's participation in formal politics, both as candidates and voters and also patterns of women's participation during election campaign.

Table 10.2 *Turnout of Women in General Elections—1st to 14th Lok Sabha*

General Elections	Total Turnout	Men's Turnout	Women's Turnout	Difference in Turnout
First (1952)	44.8	–	–	–
Second (1957)	45.4	–	–	–
Third (1962)	55.4	62.0	46.6	15.4
Fourth (1967)	61.3	66.7	55.5	11.2
Fifth (1971)	55.3	60.9	49.1	11.8
Sixth (1977)	60.5	66.6	54.9	11.7
Seventh (1980)	56.9	62.2	51.2	11.0
Eighth (1984)	64.0	68.4	59.2	9.2
Ninth (1989)	62.0	66.1	56.9	9.2
Tenth (1991)	61.0	61.6	51.4	10.2
Eleventh (1996)	57.9	62.1	53.4	8.7
Twelfth (1998)	62.0	66.2	57.9	8.3
Thirteenth (1999)	60.4	64.0	55.6	8.4
Fourteenth (2004)	58.3	61.9	53.5	8.4

Source: Election Commission of India, New Delhi.

Table 10.3 *Representation of Women Members in Lower House—1st to 14th Lok Sabha*

Lok Sabha	Total No. of Seats (Elections Held)	No. of Women Members Who Won	% of the Total
First (1952)	489	22	4.4
Second (1957)	494	27	5.4
Third (1962)	494	34	6.7
Fourth (1967)	523	31	5.9
Fifth (1971)	521	22	4.2
Sixth (1977)	544	19	3.4
Seventh (1980)	544	28	5.1
Eighth (1984)	544	44	8.1
Ninth (1989)	529	28	5.3
Tenth (1991)	509	36	7.0
Eleventh (1996)	54 1	40*	7.4
Twelfth (1998)	545	44*	8.0
Thirteenth (1999)	543	48*	8.8
Fourteenth (2004)	543	45*	8.1

Source: Election Commission of India, New Delhi.
Note: * Including one nominated member.

An assessment of women's participation in the political process as voters reveals that it has been low in all general elections held till now as compared to men. However, their participation over the years has steadily increased from 46.6 per cent in 1962 to 53.5 per cent in the year 2004. The difference in voter turnout between men and women that was as high as 15.4 per cent in 1962 has narrowed down to 8.4 per cent in 2004. Despite the difference remaining significant, there was not only a definite participatory upsurge among Indian woman in the 1990s but also in their turnout (Yadav, 2000). In fact, the general elections in 1998 had witnessed the highest voter turnout among women.

What are the reasons for the upsurge of women's participation as voters in the general elections held in 1990s? The reasons could be: Firstly, the liberalization of the economy in the 1990s witnessed a proliferation of electronic media creating awareness and educating women about their political and electoral rights. This proposition, however, needs to be empirically researched. Secondly, civil society and women's group awareness campaigns and advocacy at grassroots levels encouraged and educated women about their voting rights and importance of vote in electing the right candidates and political parties. Thirdly, Election Commission of India's initiatives in conducting free, fair and violence-free elections may have contributed in larger women turnout as it inculcated a sense of safety and security among them. The reservation of 33 per cent seats for women at the PRIs in the 1990s gave women in the country a sense of sharing power with men equally. It may have acted as a catalyst and resulted in the upsurge of women's political participation as voters. Finally, the dominant perception (Vissandjee et al., 2006) that women generally think that politics is a dirty word and tend to stay away from it also saw a meltdown in this period as a result of women's reservation and participation in large numbers at the grassroots level (PRIs). The success stories of women in panchayats dispelled, to some extent, the perception among women that politics is dirty.

As seen, over years, a large proportion of women have turned up to vote to reduce the gender gap to less than 10 per cent in the 1990s from almost 20 per cent in 1971. Yet, women are still not well represented in political life as members in parliament and in state legislative assemblies that would require them to be active in the public sphere (Chhibber, 2002). Women's representation in the Lok Sabha since the first general elections reveals that they continue to be grossly excluded even after so many years of independence. In 1952, they constituted 4.4 per cent of the total seats in the lower house; by 2004, their share doubled to 8 per cent and stabilized at that in the last 3 Lok Sabhas—still below the world average of 10 per cent representation of women in the House of Representatives.

The question as to what the reasons for under-representation of Indian women in the lower house of the parliament are, by itself and also in comparison with other countries in South Asia, is an intriguing one. Though there are many factors that act as barriers for women's political participation leading to poor representation in parliament and state legislatures, the main factors could be attributed to (a) socio-historic forces inherited from nationalist movements, current social policies and the gendered nature of citizenship in hampering women's political participation in government structures, elections and community organizations (Vissandjee et al., 2006); (b) absence of legislation to reserve seats for women in the parliament and state legislatures; (c) the lack of national consensus and willingness among political parties to give more tickets to women in elections (Basu, 1992); and (d) perpetuation of patriarchal political structure together with class, caste and gender subordination acting as strong deterrents for women to contest elections (Baseline Report, 1998). Finally, the lack of awareness and knowledge of electoral politics combined with lack of support from family and political parties in terms of resources severely affects women's chances to contest and win elections. The complete lack of support to women by political parties is corroborated by Kishwar, who states,

> In our country, even the best of women parliamentarians feel side-lined and powerless within the party. The few women leaders have not been able to facilitate the entry of a greater number of women in electoral and party politics, and so remain an ineffective minority. (Kishwar, 1996, p. 2871)

She recommends that in allocating tickets for elections, parties should be compelled to give at least one-third of their tickets to women through amending the Representation of People Act.

A collective outcome of these hindrances and deterrents becomes evident by numerical analysis of the number of seats allotted to women in general elections (Table 10.4). It can be seen that although the number of women candidates who contested the elections increased from 274 in general elections held in 1999 to 355 in general elections 2004, the number of women candidates fielded by national parties has remained almost stagnant during this intervening period. Thus, national parties have followed an exclusionist policy for women in allotment of seats in elections for the Lok Sabha over the years for one reason or other. The policy of exclusion of women in granting seats at national and state-level election is not only being done by national parties alone But, also, by regional political parties of all hues and shades in the country.

Table 10.4 Women's Exclusion from Electoral Participation by National Parties

National Parties	General Elections 1998		General Elections 1999		General Elections 2004	
	Contested	Won	Contested	Won	Contested	Won
All India	274	43	284	49	355	45
Congress	38	10	51	41	45	12
BJP	32	15	25	15	30	10
CPI	6	2	4	1	2	–
CPM	8	3	5	3	8	5

Source: Election Commission of India, New Delhi.

It has been suggested that women's lack of 'winnability' (Deshpande, 2004) often influence such political decisions. However, an analysis of success rates of women candidates as compared to men reveals that it has been higher in the last three general elections. For example, in 1999, national hustings women's success rate was 17 per cent as compared with men's success rate at 11 per cent—higher by six percentage points, suggesting apprehensions on the part of political parties rather unfounded.

In formal politics, election campaign forms an integral part of the electoral process. Political parties in India now heavily rely on both print and electronic media to put forward their agenda among the voters during the time of elections. But still, traditional campaign methods like holding rallies and meetings, door to door canvassing by party workers and supporters and road shows by party leaders remain the more-popular means.

Women's participation in election campaigns is an important indicator. For analysing the trends of women's political participation as campaigners in the last two general elections, a political participation index is based on following variables: attended election meetings, participated in rallies, door-to-door canvassing, donations to parties and distributing party agenda leaflets has been calculated.

Table 10.5 *Increasing Participation of Women in Election Campaigns*

Levels of Participation	NES 1999	NES 2004	Increase/ Decrease (%)
Low	91	80	−11
Medium	6	13	+7
High	3	7	+4

Source: National Election Study (NES) 1999, 2004, CSDS Data Unit, Delhi.

Table 10.5 indicates that incidence of low participation of women in campaign activities has, in fact, dropped by 11 percentage points in general elections of the year 2004, as compared to the general elections of 1999.

On the other hand, however, the number of women with high levels of participation in election campaign increased from 3 per cent in 1999 general elections to 7 per cent in the 2004 national hustings. This suggests that, relatively, more women are now actively participating in electoral politics during campaign activities and political parties are mobilizing their support in large numbers. It seems that political parties are quite keen and enthusiastic in treating women as constituencies and campaigners but run shy in allotting adequate number of seats to them in elections and in sharing political power (Kishwar, 1996).

KEY DETERMINANTS OF WOMEN'S PARTICIPATION IN THE ELECTORAL PROCESS

As is clear from the earlier discussion, women's participation in formal politics is determined by many factors, some of which are universal in nature while some are specific and localized to some countries. In India and elsewhere, it has been suggested that women's participation is, generally, lower either because they have been socialized differently, especially as far as marriage, motherhood, employment, ownership are concerned or because they have fewer resources (Burns et al., 2001). Similarly, socio-economic demographics of women and gender-specific reasons have been mostly cited in researches as factors that determine their level of participation in the political process.

Once again, this section uses the political participation index based on the CSDS data in order to assess the main determinants of women's level of participation in formal politics. It is to be reiterated that political participation is restricted to women's participation in election campaign activities during the general elections of 2004. The key questions that need to be probed and addressed in this section are:

1. What are the key determinants that promote or act as hindrances in women's participation in the electoral process during elections?
2. Is it the patriarchal social structure and the freedom enjoyed by women that determines their levels of participation in formal politics?
3. Or is it the propagation of stereotypes that politics is not the domain of women or does not interest them that keeps them away from the political process?
4. Or are there deeper underlying determinants like their socio-economic background and psychography of women that plays a key role in their levels of participation and exclusion from the political process?
5. To what extent does women's interest in politics and exposure to media determine their participatory levels in formal politics?

One of the key factors that determine their high level of participation is women's interest in politics. Table 10.6 shows that women with interest in politics are also those who participate actively in the political process, that is, about 18 per cent of women who had interest in politics also had high levels of political participation in the 2004 general elections as compared with those who did not have interest in politics in general (3%). Conversely, 89 per cent of women who were not interested in politics (apart from elections) reported low participation in the election campaigns. The findings are corroborated by earlier researches arriving at similar outcomes (Burns et al., 2001). Thus, we can assume that women's interest in politics is a prerequisite in encouraging higher participation of women in formal politics.

Individual socio-demographics including education and income, social–cultural norms and caste are also associated with women's opportunities for political participation (Agarwal, 1997; Banerjee, 2003; Gleason, 2001). Women's level of participation in electoral politics depends upon their societal background and the levels of liberty and freedom enjoyed by them. Thus, women who exercise their own discretion in deciding whom to vote for have a higher level of participation in electoral politics than those whose decisions are influenced by family and friends. Accordingly, women who decided whom to vote for on their own had three-percentage points higher political participation than women whose decisions were influenced by others.

It is well acknowledged that more educated women, those who are employed, women of higher social standing (social class) and urban women are more likely to be interested as well as more active in politics (Chhibber, 2002). Observations in Table 10.6 support this as women who are employed have higher participation in election campaigns (9%) as compared with women who are not working (6%). Similarly, women who are educated (9%) have higher participation in election campaigns than those who are uneducated (6%). The findings are supported by earlier reports as in India, women have less education than men and since they are also less likely to be in the workforce, women may be

Table 10.6 *Key Determinants of Participation of Women in Elections*

Categories	Political Participation (%)		
	Low	Medium	High
Interest in politics	59	23	18
No interest in politics	89	9	3
Own voting decisions	77	14	9
Voting decisions influenced by others	82	12	6
Working	78	13	9
Housewives	81	13	6
Educated	76	15	9
Uneducated	84	10	6

Source: NES 2004, CSDS Data Unit, Delhi.

less politically active than men (Gleason, 2001). Although in some cases, differences are not very significant, they are suggestive of the potential roles that the demographic background of women can play in political participation of women in the electoral process.

In a pluralistic society like India, media is the major means for political and social groups to reach their audiences and build a rapport with them. Thus, media has come to occupy a significant role in our society in creating political and electoral awareness. The increased participation of women as voters and in election activities could be attributed to Indian media to some extent as data in Table 10.7 reveals. The success stories of women in grassroots politics, after reservations of seats for them, played a key role in participatory upsurge witnessed in the last decade of the 20th century. Media has been vociferous in campaigning for affirmative action for women not only at the grassroots level but also in parliament and state legislatures.

How far does media exposure of women lead to their increased participation in the electoral process and to what extent it determines their levels of participation in election campaigns are the questions to which authors turn now. Media Exposure Index 2 is a combination of newspaper reading habits, listening to news on radio and television. According to Table 10.7, women who had high exposure to media also had higher political participation levels (13%) as compared with women who have no exposure to media (5%). It is because women exposed to media are more aware about their political and electoral rights and are more willing to participate in the electoral process (CSDS Data Unit).

Table 10.7 *Media Exposure Increases Women's Participation in Elections*

	Political Participation (%)		
Levels of Media Exposure	Low	Medium	High
No exposure	85	10	5
Low exposure	77	14	9
Medium exposure	75	15	10
High exposure	70	17	13

Source: NES 2004, CSDS Data Unit, Delhi.

Thus, we see that there are a host of determinants like media exposure, interest in politics, voting discretion and socio-economic background that determine the levels of political participation among women. Which among these are the most important determinants of women's participation in the political process? A regression of political participation of women by determinants like media exposure, locality, occupation, interest in politics, influence in voting decisions, education and economic class reveals that 'interest in politics' is one of the best predictors of their levels of participation (b = 0.412, Sig. = 0.000). This implies that women who have interest in politics also have the highest levels of participation in electoral activities. This is supported by findings earlier reported that women with political interest are more likely to be politically active (Chhibber, 2002).

Apart from 'interest in politics' being a strong predictor, media exposure is the second-best predictor of political participation of women in elections (b = 0.051, Sig. = 0.000). This indicates that women with high levels of exposure to media have high participation in the political process. Interestingly, the locality where women reside has a negative relation with political participation among women (b = −0.084). That is, women living in urban areas were found to be participating less in electoral politics as compared with women living in rural areas. The reasons could be manifold, but low participation in

Table 10.8 *Result of Regression on Political Participation of Women*

Independent Variables	Beta	Sig.
Media exposure	0.051	0.000
Locality	−0.084	0.000
Occupation	0.045	0.000
Interest in politics	0.412	0.000
Influence on voting decisions	−0.018	0.083
Education	0.020	0.089
Economic class	0.021	0.000
	R2: 0.129; Constant: 0.617	

Source: NES 2004, CSDS Data Unit, Delhi.

electoral politics is a common phenomenon among urban voters in India and urban women are no exception (Chhibber, 2002).

The occupation and economic class of women both have a positive relationship with political participation with $b = 0.045$ and 0.021, respectively. Women who have a life outside the household are more interested in politics and more politically active (Chhibber, 2002). This means working women who are more exposed to public life participate more in election campaigns than non-working women housewives. But in case of economic class, the findings show the women from the poor economic class participate more in electoral politics than women from the rich class. Higher economic class apathy towards political participation reflects that there is no gender divide among the affluent class. In case of educational background and influence on women's voting decisions, our analysis reveals that they have an insignificant relation with political participation, that is, 0.089 and 0.083 respectively. Thus, we can conclude that apart from women's interest in politics as a strong predictor of their increased participation in electoral process, media exposure is the best predictor of political participation of Indian women. So, we can fairly say that women's interest in politics is a key factor that determines their high level of participation in electoral politics; media exposure is an equally strong determinant of gender participation and their degree of participation in formal politics.

IMPACT OF WOMEN'S POLITICAL EXCLUSION ON WOMEN AND THE FUTURE OF DEMOCRACY

Despite the Constitution's guarantee for equal rights to both men and women to participate in political activities with universal franchise, the existing societal value system, the private–public divide in terms of domain identification and male preponderance in political institutions restrict women from exercising and enjoying their political rights. These factors also act as deterrents and hindrances in the larger issue of women's advancement as a whole. The lack of representation of women in key decision-making positions results in women's agenda not getting reflected and addressed in public policies and programmes (Baseline Report, 1998).

The public agenda of elected men and women as people's representatives are quite different and their priority of public works undertaken is also not similar. While women representatives addressed issues of long-term benefits such as education, health, violence against women and basic amenities that affect community, men concentrated on issues that needed immediate attention such as roads, community and commercial centres, tanks, bridges, etc. (Interim Narrative Report, 2002–2003). Thus, men's agenda of public work tends to neglect women's issues and is detrimental towards women's advancement and progress in the larger interest of the society.

It may be argued that if there were a significant number of women representatives in the parliament, they could have played a crucial and concerted role in getting the Bill to introduce 33 per cent reservation for women in state legislature and parliament passed and enacted, cutting across party lines and divide. On one hand, the absence of critical mass of such women representatives reduces their bargaining and negotiating power during the allotment of key cabinet berths such as finance, home, defence, health, etc., which are generally allotted to men and considered heavyweight ministries. On the other, women are mostly allotted ministries during cabinet formation which are not only termed as 'feminine' ministries like women and children, information and culture, social welfare, etc., but which are perceived as relatively less important with fewer resources and reach among the people. To this extent, women seem to have failed in breaking the glass ceiling and relegated to the fringes in power sharing at the top level, which in turn has an adverse impact on their overall political status in the country.

A low proportion of women in the inner party structure further erodes women's efforts to lobby and garner resources and support for nurturing and building their political constituencies as well as mobilizing financial and human resources required to meet the demands and aspirations of their constituencies, which inevitably results in women being perceived as weak representatives—generally unaccepted as political leaders by people in their constituency. At times, being in insignificant numbers may put them in a vulnerable position resulting in seeking alliances along caste, religion and regional identities rather than along common gendered interests (Baseline Report, 1998). Thus, women in public life as people's representatives often become co-opted in the men-centric structure of development agendas. At the grassroots levels of PRIs, there have been strong roadblocks to women's entry into politics and a backlash of violence to keep them away from politics (Baseline Report, 1998).

The absence of affirmative action for 33 per cent reservation of seats for women in state legislatures and parliament is having a negative impact on women's share in the institutions of representations. However, having said that, it must be noted that treating women as a blanket category for the benefits of reservation would further complicate the issue of women's representation because such benefits would largely be appropriated by those women who belong to the upper stratum of society or by those having a political background. Hence, women from the lower economic strata, backward castes and from marginalized groups would get further excluded from contesting elections and sharing political power.

Thus, it is likely that the disadvantaged sections among the women who have already been denied their political rights to participate in elections as candidates arising out of their situational deficiencies and lack of political connections are further relegated to the background. And yet, the absence of proportionate and qualitative representation of women in top legislative and decision-making bodies is leading to a lopsided working of democracy in the country. Thus, for democracy to become successful at the ground level, men and women should get a free and proportionate chance to enjoy and exercise their political rights and participation. The inclusion of women in the political structure and their proportionate participation will not only correct the existing gender gaps but also bring gender issues to the forefront leading to women's empowerment and advancement in the society.

CONCLUSION AND WAY AHEAD

A balance sheet of gender participation in formal politics reveals that there has been a marked increase in voting turnout and election campaigning among women. While there have been significant gains among women in these areas of political participation, they continue to be excluded from legislative bodies at national and state level and deprived from key decision-making positions in government and political parties. The under-representation of women in Lok Sabha and state assemblies and from crucial decision-making positions like important cabinet berths are clear pointers of their systematic exclusion from power sharing on gender basis. Though women head a significant number of national and state-level political parties as party leaders, their representation within the rank and file of prominent political parties are not in significant numbers. Women who have made their presence felt in inner party structures are also relegated to second rung leadership and have failed to break the 'glass ceiling'. They rarely play any role in formulating policies and strategies in political parties and are assigned the job of keeping an eye on 'women's issues' that could bring electoral benefits and dividends for the party in future hustings.

However, the silver lining in dark clouds over women's participation in politics is a participatory upsurge witnessed among women as voters in the 1990s. Women's participation as voters has steadily increased in the few decades from 46.6 per cent in 1962 to around 53.5 per cent in 2004. The difference in voter turnout among men and women that was as high as 15.4 per cent in general elections held in 1952 has narrowed down to 8.4 per cent in 2004. The difference in voting based on gender remains significant, but it clearly points out that the participation of women as voters is on the upswing at the national level as more and more women have started exercising their electoral rights. Similarly, women's participation in formal politics has also increased in campaign activities during the election. A comparative analysis of the last two general elections revealed that low participation of women in election campaigning, which was as high as 91 per cent during general elections 1999, dropped by 11 percentage points to 80 per cent in general elections held in the year 2004. Thus, political participation of women in electoral politics and activities connected with it is witnessing a definite upswing as is quite evident from their increased participatory trends.

The levels of political participation among women are governed by an array of factors as revealed by the NES 2004 such as exposure to media, interest in politics, voting discretion and demographics like educational attainments, economic class and employment status. A regression analysis of key determinants of women's participation revealed that 'interest in politics' is one of the best predictors of their levels of participation. This finding is substantiated by earlier researches which have shown that women with interest in politics are likely to be politically more active than those who have no interest in politics. Among the other factors that determine the intensity of women's political participation, 'media exposure' is a strong determinant of political participation of women in India as women with high exposure to media have higher participation rates in electoral politics. Thus, women's interest in politics and media exposure—proxy for awareness creation—are the key determinants of gender participation and their degree of participation in formal politics.

Women's movement and gender politics in the country is currently divided over the question of affirmative action for women in parliament and state legislatures which centres around two main issues: First, the issue of overlapping quotas for women in general and those for women of the lower castes and, second, the issue of elitism. These are difficult issues to resolve. However, given the dismal representation of women as a whole in the political arena, it may be argued that affirmative action for women in legislative bodies is the need of the hour, which would go a long way in bridging the existing gap in the democratic political set-up and make it gender inclusive.

The key areas that need to be addressed for improving political participation of women and inclusion in the political process apart from affirmative action are more representation of women in political parties, including them in the decision-making bodies of political parties and providing them key cabinet berths in government at the centre and state level. Women should be promoted and encouraged by concerted effort of government in partnership with civil society for enhanced and quality participation in formal politics. An increased political participation by women in all spheres of political life will not only ensure political parity and equality with men but would also serve the larger issues concerning women, that is, upliftment and empowerment of Indian women.

NOTES

1. Political Participation Index was created from women who participated in the following activities in NES 2004 data set: women, who attended election meetings, participated in election rallies and meetings, door-to-door

canvassing, donations to parties and distributing party agenda leaflets. The participation level of women in election campaigns were indexed into three categories: Low, women who participated in any one activity; medium, women who participated in two or three activities; and high, women who participated in three or more activities.

2. Media Exposure Index was created from women's exposure to the following media from NES 2004 data sets: newspaper reading habits, listening to news on radio and watching news on television. Women's exposure to media were indexed into three categories: Low, women who were sometimes exposed to any one medium and never in rest; medium, women who were sometimes exposed to two or three medium; and high, women who were mostly exposed to three or more mediums.

REFERENCES

Agarwal, Bina. (1997). 'Editorial: Re-sounding the Alert-Gender, Resources and Community Action', *World Development*, 25(9): 1373–1380.

Agarwal, Bina. (2006). 'Social Exclusion' *Plenary Comments*, Asia 2015, March 2006.

Ahern, P., P. Nutti and J. M. Masterson. (2000). 'Equity in the Democratic Process: Women's Paths to Political Participation and Decision-making' Washington, DC: International centre for Research on Women, and Washington, DC: Centre for Development and Population Activities.

Akerkar, S. (1995). 'Theory and Practice of Women's Movement in India: A Discourse Analysis'. *Economic and Political Weekly*, Vol. xxx, No. 27, 1995. pp. WS-2–WS-22.

Arora, Banarsi. (1999). 'Women in Politics: Governance in Patriarchal and Non-participatory Culture', *Guru Nanak Journal of Sociology*, 20(1–2): 111–118.

Banerjee, Sikata. (2003). 'Gender and Nationalism: The Masculinisation of Hinduism and Female Political Participation in India', *Women's Studies International Forum*, 26(2): 167–179.

Baseline Report. (1998). 'Women and Political Participation in India' Prepared by NIAS et al. and coordinated by IWRAW Asia Pacific Advanced Unedited Version.

Basu, Amrita. (1992). *Two Faces of Protest: Contrasting Modes of Women's Activism in India*. Berkeley: University of California Press.

Basu, Durga Das. (1998). *Introduction to the Constitution of India:* Prentice-Hall of India, New Delhi.

Burns, Nancy, Kay Lehman Scholzman, and Sidney Verba. (2001). *The Private Roots of Public Action: Gender, Equality, and Political Participation*. Cambridge, Harvard University Press.

Chattopadhyaya, Kamaladevi. (1983). *Indian Women's Battle for Freedom*. New Delhi: Abhinav Press.

Chhibber, Pradeep. (2002). 'Why Are Women Politically Active? The Household, Public Space, and Political Participation in India', *www.worldvauesurvey.org*

Country Report. (1995). *Fourth World Conference on Women: Beijing.*

CWDS. (1994). *Confronting Myriad Oppressions: The Western Regional Experience,* New Delhi.

CWDS. (1995). *'Towards Beijing: A Perspective from the Indian Women's Movement'* New Delhi.

Department of Women and Child Development (DWCD). (1988). *National Perspective Plan for Women 1988–2000,* New Delhi.

Deshpande, Rajeshwari. (2004). 'How Gendered was Women's Participation Women in Election 2004' *Economic and Political Weekly,* Vol. 39 (51), pp.5431–5436.

Gleason, Suzanne. (2001). 'Female Political Participation and Health in India', *Annals AAPPS,* 573: 105–126.

Gopalan, Sarla. (2002). *Towards Equality - The Unfinished Agenda - Status of Women in India—2001,* National Commission for Women, Government of India.

Interim Narrative Report. (2002–2003). *Gender Studies Unit, National Institute of Advanced Studies,* Bangalore.

Kishwar, Madhu. (1996). 'Women and Politics: Beyond Quotas' *Economic and Political Weekly. XXXI,* Number 43, p. 2871.

Kumar, Radha. (1997). *The History of Doing: An Illustrated Account of Movements for Women's Rights and Feminism in India 1800-1990,* Kali for Women, New Delhi.

Liddle, J. and R. Joshi. (1986). *Daughters of Independence,* New Delhi: Kali for Women.

Mill, James. (1817). *The History of British India,* with notes by H. H. Wilson, London, James Madden, 5th Ed. (1840).

Mukherjee, Geeta. (1997). 'Unite and Support of One-Third Reservation for Women', National Federation of Indian Women, New Delhi.

Narasimhan, Sakuntala. (1999). 'An Overview of Past State Initiatives' *Empowering Women: An Alternative Strategy from Rural India,* SAGE Publications, New Delhi.

Nair, Janaki. (1996). *Women and Law in Colonial India—A Social History,* New Delhi: Kali for Women.

National Centre for Advocacy Studies. (1998). 'Lok Sabha Election 1998' *Info Pack Issue* No. 2 May–August.

Rajan, Rajeshwari Sunder. (1999). *The Scandal of the State: Women, Law, and Citizenship in Post Colonial India,* Delhi, Permanent Black.

Sarkar, T. and U. Butalia (eds.). (1995). *Women and Right-Wing Movements: Indian Experiences,* London, Zed Press.

Shah, Nandita and Nandita Gandhi, (1991). 'Do we need reservations? *The Quota Question: Women and Electoral Sears,* Akshara Publications, Mumbai.

Sen, Samita. (2003). The Indian Women's Movement in Historical Perspective in Karin Kapadia (eds.), *The Violence of Development: The Politics of Identity, Gender and Social Inequalities in India,* New Delhi, Kali for Women.

Swarup, H. L., Niroj Sinha, Chitra Ghosh, Pam Rajput. (1994). 'Women's Political Engagement in India', In B. Nelson and N. Chowdhury (eds.), *Women and Politics Worldwide,* London: Yale University Press.

Yadav, Yogendra. (2000). 'Understanding the Second Democratic Upsurge' in Francine R Frankel, Zoya Hassan, Rajeev Bhargava and Balbeer Arora (eds.) *Transforming India,* Oxford.

Vissandjee, B., S. Abdool, A. Apale, and S. Dupéré. (2006). 'Women's Political Participation in Rural India: Discerning Discrepancies Through a Gender Lens' *Indian Journal of Gender Studies,* 2006; 13; 425.

Vyasulu, P and V. Vyasulu. (1999). 'Women in Panchayati Raj: Grassroots Democracy in India, Experience in Malgudi' *Background Paper No. 4,* New Delhi, United Nations Development Programme.

Section IV

Culture and Identity

Sectional Introduction

Ghazala Jamil

Wrestling with the issues of sustenance, systemic discrimination and violence, scholars in the movement must have found the simplistic explanation of 'backward attitudes' of Indian citizenry limiting. As is wont, newer resources had to be found. In the developed Western world, social science research experienced a narrative or a linguistic turn in the late 1970s. Feminists began to utilize the tools of literary criticism to study how gender ideology is encoded in the formal structures of cultural texts. In India, historians appear to have taken the lead in using these tools to recover lost narratives of women from historical texts and sources, and to gain a historical understanding of the patriarchal social phenomenon (Sangari & Vaid, 1990).

Although in the Indian discourse on women's rights, it was not new to hark back to religious and mythical texts, a systematic study of narrative structures within a text to discern how gender is culturally constructed was certainly new when it took root in the 1990s. Another genre created by this narrative turn paid attention to self-expression or authorial voices of women—especially those forgotten, misread or not accorded the value they deserved. Several strategies were used to bring them to the fore, through offering a fresh critique by translating a text or transcribing oral testimonies into textual form. The works of Sharmila Rege (2014) on Dalit women's narratives and Urvashi Butalia (2000) on women's experience of Partition violence have been landmark entrants in this regard.

Methodologically, too, the narrative turn was empowering because it created a space within the movement for the voices of women who hitherto appeared, if at all, through representations by other women. The redistribution versus recognition debate manifested itself in India as a question of difference in articulation (Guru, 1995) and of the possibility of an assumable standpoint (Rege, 1998). In a way, it is a reverberation of the debates around the demand for quota within quota in the women's reservation matter. While intersecting disadvantaged identities have produced quite a bit of feminist literature in India, the disquieting gap in gender studies, in this regard, is writing that displays self-reflexivity regarding intersectional privileges.

The three articles included in this volume are examples of this contested history of women's studies and contestation for articulation within the movement.

In their article 'The Family in Ancient India: Ideal and Reality', historians Uma Chakravarti and Kumkum Roy discuss how the discourse around family structures has emerged with time to suit societal needs. While women's place/role in family has been an enduring concern in women's rights scholarship, the authors note that it was not considered as an area of serious investigation among historians. Utilizing, what they call a cross-disciplinary approach, they excavate family as a site of violence and conflict and not just as a site of love and care. The article veers a bit away from history to establish that the range of family types vary according to region and caste, and not just across time and history. The article argues that the normative family was a construction designed to 'reproduce both itself and caste hierarchy'. It also contains a discussion of kinship through well-known episodes in epics and Hindu mythology in an attempt to offer resolutions to issues raised in constructing 'ideal' family relations. The article is an interesting example of challenging the mythical family which fixed a woman's place in society, simultaneously subservient and divine. But what is also interesting is that even this challenge was mounted from within the Hindu mythology and religious discourse and went so far as to problematize simplistic readings.

The theme of mythology or historical epics continues to be explored in the next article in this section. Sujata Mukherjee shows how the style of popular Hindi films are influenced by the great myths of Indian history, the two great epics—the Ramayana and the Mahabharata—and to some degree, folk traditions, mythologies, Parsi theatre and the Vedas. It could be argued that these end up being used repeatedly as sources of popular narratives that could be translated in films and conveyed easily to the audience during the early days of the medium because of an existing ubiquity of these narratives in popular or collective consciousness in India. In this article, Mukherjee tries to deconstruct past orientations towards gender, feminism, modernity and so on, all connected with the portrayal of the female character in moving Indian images. The author's notion of woman—be it the mother, the daughter, the partner, the antagonist, the conspirator, the seducer, the murderer—those conceptions focused on 'mythical' and 'Indian psychology' that have been incorporated into Indian film narratives. But more importantly, analysing a wide range of films, the author discerns a change from portraying the woman as an object to patriarchal essentialism or as a biological force designed to give man and agent sexual gratification in the reproduction of mankind, to a complex, almost ephemeral, force within a cultural force-field of cinema, where she too can have dreams, fantasies and sexualities. The article is a landmark in *Social Change* because it argues that postmodernism has replaced the hierarchical top-down style of early cinema with the bottom-up style, bringing a psychoanalytical twist to the woman's portrait.

Rupturing this narrative of better representation of women in media is the last article in this section. Vivek Kumar, in the article 'Locating Dalit Women in the Indian Caste System, Media and Women's Movement', seeks not only 'to locate' Dalit women in media but further comments on the positionality of Dalit women vis-à-vis women's movement and, also, within the caste system. The article makes a few fundamental and necessary moves before this. It establishes the threefold exploitation of Dalit women due to gender, poverty and caste discrimination, that is, their structural location, occupations they are forced to perform and the treatment meted out to them by the society. Within this framework, Kumar defines the term Dalit and argues that suffering from humiliation, stigmatization, social and occupational exclusion in the society makes for a unique consciousness that they construct for themselves. Dalit women were seen as objects for sexual consumption by upper-caste men in various historical institutions and practices like *devdasis* or more blatant and explicitly brutal sexual violence meant as caste atrocity. Kumar argues that this violence was not just physical violence but inflicted as a right by upper-caste men and served to prevent any consciousness or uprising taking place in the Dalit community. The evidence put forth by the author and the issues addressed are of prime concern and importance in the article.

Almost the entire latter half of the article is dedicated to exploring the construction of a Dalit woman through the imagery of the Dalit politician, Kumari Mayawati. Kumar discusses the casteist character of the hostility and humiliation that Mayawati is subjected to by rival politicians and in media narratives and calls out the women's movement for failing to defend her. The question he asks is whether this failure in the feminist field of vision is a manifestation of latent casteism in the movement.

REFERENCES

Butalia, U. (2000). *The other side of silence: Voices from the partition of India*. Duke University Press.

Guru, G. (1995). Dalit women talk differently. *Economic & Political Weekly*, *30*(41–42), 2548–2550.

Rege, S. (1998). Dalit women talk differently: A critique of 'difference' and towards a Dalit feminist standpoint position. *Economic & Political Weekly*, *33*(44), WS39–WS46.

Rege, S. (2014). *Writing caste/writing gender: Narrating Dalit women's testimonies*. Zubaan.

Sangari, K., & Vaid, S. (Eds.). (1990). *Recasting women: Essays in Indian colonial history*. Rutgers University Press.

Chapter 11

The Family in Ancient India*
Ideal and Reality

Uma Chakravarti and Kumkum Roy

History as a discipline, especially in the Indian context, has tended to ignore the family as an area of investigation. This is one reason why we do not have a really large body of writing on the family as an institution, from a historical perspective. It is only in recent years that one can see the beginning of some kind of concern with the family among historians. This may tie in with the fact that the traditional focus of history has shifted. There has been a questioning of history as focusing on the arena of public politics and the scope of the discipline has been widened to open up new areas of investigation. More specifically, there is now a serious interest in the history of hitherto marginalized groups, implicit in subaltern studies and women's studies, for instance. This concern with new questions, and with those who have been powerless and hence ignored in histories which have reflected the concerns of dominant social groups, has opened up the way for studies of the family, amongst other institutions. At another level, this interest in the family is also a positive fall out of the cross-disciplinary approach which has been, more or less, systematically encouraged in both history and in other disciplines in recent years. Apart from enrichment in terms of methodologies, those engaged in research in a specific discipline have tended to investigate the subject and themes, or even questions raised in other disciplines as well. The family has been an important area of investigation within anthropology for a very long time, and

* *Social Change* (June 1996), *26*, 26–33.

with the attenuation of boundaries between disciplines, the possibility of shared interests, or the interests of one area spilling into another, has grown.

Yet, at one level, it is surprising that the family, as a subject of historical interest, has come so late in the day, given that the conventional sources of early Indian history, in particular, are so rich in data pertaining to the institution and that the social history of early India has attracted attention for a number of decades. Moreover, while these sources lend themselves to the study of the family, their incorporation within historical studies has been very limited. Indological treatments rarely raise the issue of relations within the family and, by and large, even when the family figures in historical writings, there has been a tendency to treat it as a homogeneous unit in relation to other more or less identical units, without exploring its internal complexities. Thus, while Indologists have, in a sense, worked around the family, they have not raised certain basic questions. What comes to mind are the kinds of issues raised by Hans Medick's work on *Interest and Emotion*, which explores the possibility of conflicting interests coexisting within the family, as well as the fact that it functions as a centre for emotional bonding. The possibility, and indeed the likelihood, that similar contradictions may have existed in the Indian situation needs to be kept in mind.

If one of the dimensions of the family that is not normally addressed is that it is as much the locus of conflict as any other institution in society, this is because of the fostering of the ideology of the family, which constructs it as a no conflict zone, ideally characterized by love and/or duty. However, while there is mutual emotional and physical sustenance of members in many families, power is not equally shared by all. As such, the disjuncture between the ideological model and the real conflicts over material and other resources amongst members of any family generate a great deal of stress and tension, while they are expressed in a number of ways.

Not surprisingly, such conflicts figure in the epics. These raise issues of ideal familial relations. And what are regarded as threats to this and offer possible resolutions through narratives, which have been disseminated through the centuries in a variety of forms. A classic example of this is represented by the characterization of Kaikeyi in the Ramayana. At one level, she is explicitly villainized and held responsible for disrupting the harmony and indeed the existence of the family; she is depicted as selfish and brings about the death of her husband by insisting on Rama's banishment and the installation of her son Bharata as crown prince. Yet the entire episode can be read differently. As the favourite wife of Dasaratha is the rejected senior wife who does not please the king in the same way. When Kaikeyi discovers Rama's impending enthronement, she fears that it is Kausalya, as the mother of the future king, who will now wield power, while she herself will be marginalized. The normal conflicts in a household between brothers or between mother-in-law and daughters-in-law are intensified here in a polygamous situation, but the need to uphold the ideology of the family which requires an insistence on unquestioning obedience to the head who is expected to work for the well-being of the subordinate members of the family means that the depiction of Kaikeyi as insubordinate and scheming obscures the central issue, which is that the power or security women have within the family is entirely derivative, depending on their relationship with the dominant male heads of the household or his representative, and hence, women's influence within the household is tenuous in nature.

On the subject of kinship terminology, there is the issue of Dravidian or South Indian kinship and terms such as *mama*. While the word is used in North Indian languages as well, the Sanskrit equivalent, *matula*, occurs only in the later-Vedic and post-Vedic texts. Moreover, while *mama* in the South Indian context is a single generic term with a number of different connotations, in the North Indian context, the term has single meaning, that of mother's brother. In the South Indian situation, *mama*, apart from meaning mother's brother, can also refer to the father-in-law, because cross-cousin marriages are permitted. Besides, the *mama* may be a potential husband, because the mother's brother is regarded as the first partner for the girl. Therefore, a single term holds within it the possibility of three distinct relationships which could be engaged in by a single person.

The fact that *mama* can have different meanings in different situations illustrates that we have a range of family types, varying according to region and caste, apart from changing over time, so that, effectively, there is no single type which we can regard as the epitome of the Indian family. Nevertheless, what is significant is that some family types have tended to be viewed or portrayed as variations from the norm, or even deviant, depending on their location in terms of region and caste. It is difficult to specify when this begins, but there is a process whereby certain family forms are regarded as more acceptable than others.

Part of this process can be discerned in epics like the Mahabharata, where there are descriptions of different family forms. The tensions of incorporating them within a single narrative structure are apparent. This is especially true in the case of the polyandrous family way and its existence and suggest that despite its obvious differences and distinctive features, it conforms to the normative structure, which was defined as both patrilineal and patriarchal, with a strong emphasis on marriage to a single man. The normative family is also linked to rituals which complete and sanctify a marriage and which vary according to caste. Ideally, according to the textual traditions, the normative family was established through the performance of rituals. In the context of marriage, such rituals ensured that the bride was transferred from the father to the husband. The unit was ideally envisaged as patrilineal in terms of kinship and property relations.

ASSIMILATION INTO THE NORMATIVE MODEL

The normative family, thus defined, was designed to reproduce both itself and the caste hierarchy. This required a strict adherence to endogamy, that is, marrying within the caste. At the same time, there is a concern with and insistence on exogamy as well, which seems to be a typical feature of all cultures which define certain relationships which may be so categorized and are obviously culture specific. The combination of endogamy and exogamy means that the field of relationships within which legitimate marriages can be contracted has tended to be defined rather strictly, at least in principle. This is reflected in legal texts, where law-givers were rather preoccupied with ensuring that the ideal marriage took place within a single-caste category. Yet this ideal was not always realized. Therefore, both precept and practice had to take into account variations, which were defined as aberrations. These included hypergamy and hypogamy. The former, which involved the marriage of a high-caste woman, was endorsed and accepted, whereas the latter, that is, the marriage of a high-caste woman to a low status man was viewed with horror. This ideal, tight structure has had major consequences for both caste and gender relations, and given that marriages which conformed to the requirements of the caste hierarchy were accorded legitimacy, the norm has proved influential not only for the upper castes but all down the line. At the same time, the fact that caste and family structure were so loosely connected has led to a situation where certain kinds of practices generated within the kinship structure have been accorded legitimation even when they do not literally conform to the normative code.

This has endowed the normative model with a certain degree of flexibility, which has probably ensured its survival. We find that those who constructed the normative model tend to adopt two strategies. One is to recognize and legitimize what were perceived to be aberrant structures. An example is the recognition accorded to cross-cousin marriages as a practice peculiar to and acceptable in the southern part of the subcontinent, in spite of the fact that it ran counter to the ideal exogamous system. While this extended the range of the normative code as it incorporated alternative practices, it also diluted the preoccupation with a single model to some extent.

This is true also of the other method by which the scope of the normative model has been widened—fabricating of lineages in cases where the purity of the lineage was actually in doubt. The strategy has been used consistently by ruling families which acquire power and prestige and then require social legitimacy, which is achieved through the construction of fictitious ties with legendary lineages, such as the Suryavamsa and the Chandravamsa, the lineages of the heroes of the Ramayana and the Mahabharata respectively. Not surprisingly, lineage recorders have been very much in demand in different parts of the country, especially when relatively unknown groups have acquired social, economic and political power, and/or when access to such power has been contested by rivals. Lineage recorders very often blend fact with fiction, recoding significant marital alliances as well as genealogies.

What is important is that the preoccupation with establishing the normative pattern as what is indeed prevalent leads to a tendency to obscure the fact that what are regarded as variations may have a certain logic and validity of their own. For instance, the importance of polyandry as an aspect of family systems in the entire Himalayan belt may be linked to the fact that relatively small plots of land are available for cultivation. In such a situation, polyandry, far from being anomalous, may be an effective means preventing the fragmentation of holdings.

However, in practice, there is a sort of stigma attached to polyandry, while polygyny is naturalized. As we have just seen, this is evident in the treatment of polyandry in the Mahabharata, for instance. Given the pervasive influence of such narratives, and the insistence on the norm through prescriptive texts, people tend to try to conform to the normative pattern. As we have seen while discussing the narrative of the Ramayana, polygamous households may be extremely prone to tension, as the logic of transferring property becomes complex, and women see themselves as deriving power from those who are in control of property-related transactions. As such, there is intense competition within households, given that polygamy has been confined to propertied and/or elite groups in most historical situations. We find that such elite households tend to be fraught with tension, and the threat to such households is perceived as lurking within rather than being generated by extraneous problems.

MATRILINY AND THE 'MAINSTREAM'

Another familial structure that has a very important place is the matrilineal household. Two such systems have been documented fairly exhaustively—the matrilineal households in Kerala, lined to the caste system, and the households of the Khasis, a situation where we find that women function as a conduit for the transference of property without exercising direct and independent control over resources. What this implies is that, in certain situations, in spite of the existence of matriliny, women are not necessarily empowered in terms of larger social relations. In the case of the Nayars of Kerala, for instance, the manager of the property of the household is also clearly in the hands of men. In spite of these qualifications, it is extremely important to bear in mind that matriliny has crucial consequence for gender relations. What is possibly most significant is that the woman has a firm place in her own house and is not someone who lives at the mercy of her male kinsfolk. In fact, matriliny cannot exist without the household being uxorilocal, that is, where the wife's residence is the seat of conjugality.

The debate on the significance of metronyms in early Indian history is of interest here. As is well known, rulers such as the Satavahanas were designated by metronyms, such as Gautamiputra, that is, the son Gautami. While some historians have argued that this is a pointer of a matrilineal situation, others have suggested that the use of metronyms may have been necessary in a polygynous situation, where princes born to different queens may have been identified in terms of their mothers. If matriliny can coexist with a patriarchal situation, we can think of exploring such instances in terms that are less-sharply polarized and more nuanced.

It needs to be pointed out also that matriliny need not be seen as too radical a departure from the patrilineal 'mainstream'. Even within patrilineal systems, there are certain institutions that mitigate the situation as far as women are concerned. For example, women have a better deal within Dravidian kinship structures owing to the system of cross-cousin marriage. This renders the kinship structure relatively more bilateral, as both the mother's and the father's kinsfolk are regarded as important. Besides, given that marital kin may be relatives, the young daughter-in-law is less vulnerable than she would have been in a purely patrilineal situation, where women are ideally married outside the boundaries of the village and into families which are explicitly beyond her kinship networks. This ensures that the bride is a complete outsider among her in-laws, without any support from kinsfolk or neighbours.

EVOLUTION OF FAMILY STRUCTURES

Some of the earliest references, from the Rig Veda, suggest that there were no distinct terms for kinsmen and women belonging to different generations or lineages. What we have are broad, generic terms such as *pitr* (father), *matr* (mother), etc. In later Vedic texts, we have separate terms for the father, paternal grandfather, and great grand-father. It is likely that the usage of distinct terms is related to different family structures; while both the Rig Vedic and the later Vedic evidence points to the existence of patriarchal and patrilineal families, there were important differences in degree.

Attempts have been made to argue that these variations in kinship terminology and family structures are related to the role of the family in terms of organizing production and determining access to productive resources. It seems that the Rig Vedic economy was predominantly pastoral, and cattle were owned by the household. In the later Vedic situation, settled agriculture grew more important and, in this context, access to cultivable land acquired importance. Hence, kinship ties acquired new significance, as these were regarded as a means of claiming access to land. As such, patrilineal genealogies seem to have been maintained with greater care than in the earlier situation.

Somewhat later, in the early Buddhist period, different terms were used to designate distinct elements which constituted crucial aspects of family relationships. For instance, two terms which are repeatedly used are *jnati* and *kula*. It is unclear whether *kula* meant an extended family, although it does seem to be distinct from *varna* and *jati*. *Jati* has meant to provide an alternative to worldly society, the Buddha recognized that monks and nuns could continue to have obligations towards their *jnati* even after renouncing the world. Besides, the Buddha realized the importance of kinship bonds, symbolized by the ties amongst *jnati* and attempted to create an identical support structure within the framework of the *samgha* or monastic order. What is also interesting is that although the *jnati* does not seem to have been patrilineal, it seems to have been an important element of family relationships. The fact that the *jnati* were not related to one another patrilineally may account for the fact that the Brahmanical texts recognize the existence of *jnati* and provide for their presence on a number of ritual occasions but, at the same time, tend to treat the *jnati* as relatively less important than the patrilineal kin group. Similarly, while the *kula* is recognized, as its dharma or specific customs and practices, these are not valorised in the same way as the dharma prescribed for different *varnas*, for instance.

ALTERNATIVES TO THE FAMILY

It is worth drawing attention to the fact that alternatives to the family as well as alternative family structures also have a long history, that there have been alternatives to it as an institution for controlling property, transmitting it to the next generation and consequently, controlling reproduction and recruiting members. In fact, there have been experiments with alternatives to the family from the early historical period onwards. These seem to have arisen out of a situation of renouncing the family and its obligations, especially those of reproduction. At the same time, experiments were undertaken to create alternative bonds amongst communities of people who were boned to one another through ties which were often modelled on but distinct from those of kinship. For example, in the sixth century EF, many men and women opted out of the family to adopt the life of the renouncer, to devote themselves to the pursuit of what was termed the higher life. While some men and women chose a solitary existence, others built alternative communities such as the Buddhist *samgha*. The *samgha* denied conventional social hierarchies, denied conventional social hierarchies, attempted to regulate material possessions, which were perceived as a source of conflict, and ensured both physical and emotional support for its members. However, despite the attempt to dissolve power relations by working through consensus, the *samgha* did not erase the gender hierarchy, since the *bhikkunis* or nuns were placed under the authority of the monks.

While such alternatives have existed in different forms throughout the centuries, we can see a different kind of questioning of the family today. If we recall the issue of interest and emotion which we raised earlier, it is interesting that we find attempts to create alternative familiar relationships, shared interests. Such families are potentially more flexible in terms of membership; they can incorporate members of a single sex or both. One does not know whether such experiments will succeed, but they are important in suggesting that the family is not static but is open to redefinition over time and space.

REFERENCES

Duby, Georges. (1983). *The Knight, the Lady and the Priest: The Making of Modern Marriage in Medieval France.* Middlesex: Penguin Books.
Goody, Jack. (1990). *The Oriental, the Ancient and the Primitive: Systems of Marriage and the Family in the Pre-Industrial of Societies of Eurasia.* Cambridge: Cambridge University Press.
Mediek, Hans and David Warren Sabean. (1984). *Interest and Emotion,* Cambridge: Cambridge University Press.
Oberoi, Patricia. (Ed.) (1993). *Family, Kinship and Marriage in India.* Delhi: Oxford University Press.

Chapter 12

The Female Character in Indian Moving Images*

Sujata Mukherjee

The process of de-colonialization, the rise of transnational cultures and the spurt in satellite communications has compressed the world and, at the same time, given rise to a highly complex, global situation, where the local is as important as the global, and there is no static standpoint as to where power actually resides. The intermingling of cultures across continents has created such a bricolage of hybrid identities that the boundaries among nation states have diffused. This hybridization process has led to the emergence of the 'global ecumene'[1] signified as a cultural flow, where there is the coexistence of cultural homogeneity and cultural disorder, the spilling of cultures across boundaries, moving in non-linear and 'non-isomorphic paths'. It is this question of the hybrid that is now the buzzword of contemporary social and philosophical circles. The hybridization of the masses of the developing countries has redefined popular culture, concepts of gender, historicity and sense of time and space, traces of which have spilled over to their mode of communication. The greatest influence of this has been reflected in contemporary cinema and film narratives. In fact, Third World film aesthetics, which is a direct corollary of this newly found hybridity, and the situation and identification of women in this hybridity paradigm is what this present essay will deal with.

* *Social Change* (March 2004), *34*(1), 1–9.

By deconstructing the myth of the female prototype, as has been propagated by our pre-colonial grand narratives, I will try to locate the woman of today, who has surpassed the boundaries of modernism and has entered the realm of the postmodern, transcending the non-essential and blurred boundaries of male versus female stereotypes. By drawing from the representations of women in contemporary Hindi films and other moving images, by deconstructing the monolithic function, situation and identity of women as portrayed in modern Hindi films, I will 'try' to disengage the reader from their habitual orientation.

Before I embark upon the present-day representations, it is important to analyse the specific historicity of our culture that has depicted women in a particular manner. Like in all cultures, our notion of the 'woman', be it the mother, the daughter, the wife, the villain, the conspirator, the seducer, the destroyer, has descended from the grand narratives—the Ramayana and the Mahabharata, Indian folk elements, the Parsi Theatre, etc. The concept of the mother, whose duty is to sacrifice her life for the betterment of her husband and children, has been heralded from the character of Kunti, or from Kaushalya, and the notion of the chaste and devoted wife has been brought down from the character of Sita who, in spite of repeated proposals from Ravana, did not forget her husband, due to which the entire battle between Rama and Ravana ensued (though the virgin lady was ultimately abandoned by Rama). Sita also embodies the concept of the responsible and loving sister-in-law to Laxman. Concepts like piety and chastity of motherhood are all intermingled in the threads of the *Ramayana*. The *Mahabharata,* on the other hand, exemplifies the duties of the wife towards her husbands—even if she is married to five men to honour the word of the mother and, later, staked by the eldest as a prize in a game of dice. The *Mahabharata* highlights the role of Kunti, who altruistically sacrifices her son Karna, and it brings the spotlight to play or the platonic and, perhaps, ethereal friendship, devoid of any sexual overtones, between Kunti's daughter-in-law, Draupadi, and Lord Krishna.

The notions of womanhood in the Indian culture are derived also as a juxtaposition of the grand narratives with the feudal economic system in later years (let's not forget that Lord Krishna was himself a product of the agrarian, feudal social structure of Mathura).

Briefly, these are the notions, steeped in our traditional mooring, which entered into mainstream Hindi films. In this context, it is significant to state that this fusion of the grand narratives along with the forces of feudal agrarian setup was essentially opposed to any modernization agenda, thereby giving rise to the traditional/modernity binary. Thus, the formations of the status of the woman was unilinear in pattern—comprising of the woman who was a doting daughter, dutiful towards her father and brothers, a responsible and chaste wife, who consummates her relationship to the husband by never questioning his authority (and his promiscuity), who never fantasises about any men except her husband and who, as a mother, again, is inserted into an asexual role, where her only aim is to see to the betterment of her children and make all possible sacrifices to ensure their happiness. This is the basic 'mythical' and 'Indian psyche' based interpretations that have been woven into the narratives of the Indian films, for example, the traditional wife of *Ghar Ek Mandir;* or of Nargis in *Mother India*[2] who, despite extreme poverty, her children being hungry without food, goes on to protect her chastity from the local landlord Sukhilal; or the mother of *Ram Lakhan,* who preserves her husband's honour by not bowing to the feudal lord and by sending her two sons to fight him and restore order. What is interesting in these films is that they are covert adaptations of the same grand narratives. The wife's role in *Ghar Ek Mandir* reminds us of the calmness and femininity of Sita. Nargis reminds us of the ultimate mother figure of Kunti who sacrifices her son Karna because he belonged to the enemy camp of the Kauravas; and the mother in *Ram Lakhan* (played by Rakhee) is reminiscent of Kaushalya, who virtually sent her two sons, Rama and Laxman to fight Ravana.

This influence of the folklores and the grand narratives can also be seen in the recent film *Mohra.* Here, Raveena Tandon plays the role of a journalist, who has set out to do a story on the inmates of a jail. In the process, she meets Akshay Kumar, who is police officer, and seduces him into a sexual relationship with her. The rain song in the film shows her in wet clothes, thereby enhancing her sexuality. However, after they are married, she is the ever-devoted wife and wears the *mangalsutra*[3] as a token of her love for her husband. What is remarkable (and perhaps contradictory) is that soon after the marriage, the lyrics of the songs change from *Paani ne aggan lagayee* (the water has ignited the fire) to *Mujhe pyar karo* (love me), a much more subtler feeling proper to a loving wife. By displaying her *mangalsutra* within a few seconds of her appearance, she makes the audience understand how she relates to the hero. Interestingly, after this, her image is transformed from a common girl to that of Sita. In another scene, when she is going around the jail and is attacked by one of its inmates who wants to rape her, she is rescued by Vishaal (Sunil Shetty), who is himself serving a life sentence in the jail.

Vishaal draws a line which if anyone trespasses, he will kill. (This directly bears resemblance to the *Laxman Rekha*[4] drawn by *Laxman* to protect his sister-in-law—Sita—from the clutches of Ravana). After establishing this relationship, we are made to understand that there is now no possibility of a sexual relation between them. By doing so, the film reconfirms the feudal notion that a woman can only be safe under the protection of a man who is either her husband, or her brother, or anyone who bears a chaste relationship with her.

The feudal family romance has also been portrayed in Hindi films with great clan. Describing a typical romantic film, Madhava Prasad says:

> The romance was typically a tale of love and adventure, in which a high born figure, usually a Prince, underwent trials that tested his courage and at the end of which he would return to inherit his father's position and to marry. This narrative structure occurs, not in its original form, but in the form that it acquired in popular theatre, where the entertainment programme would include the narrative interspersed with other elements like the comic routine, music and dance, etc.

It is necessary to add that this feudal structure that was so judiciously followed in Hindi films demarcated a boundary pertaining to the portrayal of female characters. Any character who crossed this feudal boundary of ethics was considered taboo. This is why the girl characters that were raped had to head for the quarter of the prostitute, because she had lost her chastity and was ostracized from her village. Again, if it was in the urban setup, the raped girl, under patriarchy, became a vamp, more commonly known as the *tawaif*.

Theoretically speaking, most of the narrative patterns of Hindi films are essentialist in nature. Thus, the locale of the female prototype was restricted within the patriarchal essentialism of the 'Indian' ethos of womanhood, perpetually vacillating between the boundaries of tradition and modernity. Modernity is framed by the grand narratives by big ideas such as womanhood, morality, tradition, God and history. According to postmodernists, on the other hand, meanings are a social and cultural construction and cannot be ruled by essentialism. Thus, if the notion of fixities is challenged, then the distinctions between the binary of the virtuous woman/the hooker or sexually aggressive woman/subdued woman, get blurred.

To put this by way of an example, the female character of the film *Jism*, played by Bipasha Basu, had no fixity to her character. The postmodern element in her role is the fact that unlike earlier films like *Dil Apna Aur Preet Parayee* where Meena Kumari, in spite of being allured by her ex-fiancé at a very crucial juncture of the film, does not desert her sick husband, *Jism* not only shows the wife inviting the 'other' man through sex, it shows a lot of intimate moments between her and the other man and makes her the conspirator to the husband's murder. Hence, the feudal myth of the woman is fragmented—she is shown as a wife, a seducer, a murderer and a selfish slut who seduces men to get her job done. There are various shades to the character, thereby there is no fixity of meaning; the role of the loving wife, seducer, murderer and nurse (her profession)—all get blurred.

Then there is the interplay of the binary of tradition and modernity. Earlier (and even now), Hindi films consisted of what is theoretically known as 'simple hegemony', where the forces of patriarchy, suppression and subversion were the dominating force against the currents of modernity. It was thought that a girl from a good and honourable family married according to the wishes of her parents, who never dreamt about premarital sex and this was considered the counter to modernity. In *Rajanigandha*, the character of Vidya Sinha depicted a typical middle-class Indian girl, traditional in her lookout, who does not show much of the signs of modernity. However, in the recent blockbuster *Kuch Na Kaho*, starring Aishwarya Rai and Abhishek Bachchan, the female character was also a middle-class girl, who had traditional values (she had a kid) but was extremely modern in her attitude towards life, that is, she could lead her life independently even after her divorce and give vent to her latent sexuality when she meets Abhishek Bachchan. Hence, in postmodern parlance, the female role played by Aishwarya does not comply into any structure of binarity—that she is traditional or modern. There are both the elements of tradition and modernity in her; she hugs her child with as much gracefulness as she handles the western clothes that she wears. She is as efficient as a professional as she is feminine in charming the hero. This blend is of the tradition and the modern, where neither opposes the other or seeks dominance. Viewed alternatively, in a synthetic space, modernism contains an overlap of tradition and vice-versa. Their identities are incomplete, open and negotiable.

We can also trace the character of the female in Hindi films from a feminist postmodern angle. Feminist postmodernism has it that there is no fixed meaning of masculinity and femininity, and locating the position of women from such a constricted angle creates a myopic representation of her. Some feminist thinkers, for example, say that the very notion of the 'woman' is a fiction that can lead to a lot of negative connotations. The film *Bandit Queen* directed by Shekhar Kapur shows how a 'woman' goes on to assume the role of a 'man', saving innocent village women from being raped and, ultimately, becoming a woman gangster. Her manly attire, use of filthy language, and the gun she carried (symbolic of the phallus) disillusions our erstwhile notion of the feudal woman. On the other hand, the film *Akele Hum Akele Tum* shows the father bringing up the child whose mother deserts him. There are scenes where the father is shown to be cooking a meal, taking the child to school, crying when he scolds the child for a particular fault and even getting hysterical at times—qualities that are generally said to be possessed by mothers.

The poststructuralist thinkers not only believe that there can be no binarity between men and women, but they also believe 'masculinity' and 'femininity' are qualities present in every human being. It is not correct to slap the character into a stereotype, because the character of a woman can never be static. No woman is the same and there are not only differences between women themselves but also within themselves. The endeavour of the poststructuralists is that no referent has any fixed signifier.

To help to understand this fully, I will now give two examples from the Indian moving images—one from the hugely popular tele-serial *Kusum* and the other from the hit film *Pyaar Tune Kya Kiya*. The first example shows how the simple, middle-class girl Kusum is brought up with the values and morality of her family, specially her mother, to whom she turns to in any crisis. Then it goes on to show how her intelligence (nobody thought that a simple, middle-class girl would marry the managing director of the company she works in) brings her in the limelight. She rescues her boss every time he is in the midst of a financial crisis, marries him, divorces him, marries another man (Siddharth) who, ultimately, dies in an accident, goes on to remarry her ex-husband, finds out that it was he who had killed Siddharth, reconciliates with him again, magically helps her husband to recover from brain tumour, then rescues another girl after she is raped by a cousin, suffers injuries, is unable to become a mother, brings in a surrogate mother, then suddenly becomes pregnant, gets suspicious of her husband and again leaves him.... The interesting fact is that one cannot establish Kusum's character with particular signifiers.

The referent being Kusum, the signifiers starting from the beginning of the serial ultimately lead nowhere as the audience cannot give a fixed attribute to her character. The signifiers change perspectives often—once she is the devoted daughter, tending to all the crises in the family with courage and dignity of a son, whereas on the other side, she is a traditional wife, an entrepreneur who has immense business acumen and an angry woman who fights against the torment of rape. At one point, it gets so diffused that the significance of the referent (that is Kusum) becomes fuzzy. There are so many singularities in the same woman that all forms of structure are lost and her character becomes 'differed' one or there is 'difference'.

The next example, *Pyaar Tune Kya Kiya,* shows a model (portrayed by Urmila Matondkar) who is attracted to Fardeen Khan. However, the shades in her character, transforming her from an aspiring model lost in her fantasies of the man to a psychotic and possessive voyeur, who portrays negative emotions of love, the contradictions in her behaviour, the trauma and the chaos in her mind and her neurotic attitude is devoid of any signifiers. The last scene which shows her days at the mental asylum, void of any emotions, brings the audience to a fix. The initial signifier that they had, regarding a model, gets fragmented and unstructured. Her role starting off from a legible background becomes decentred, and, ultimately, the woman is no longer important in the filmic narrative, only her overpowering desire for the man becomes important, his wife becomes important, and the fact that the phone goes on ringing and he is unavailable becomes important to the narrative.

Coming back to the question of the 'tradition–modernity binary',[5] it is not always true that the Hindi film has never tried to do anything different. The Indian popular culture has not only established feudal values through its filmic genres, it has also countered feudal values, however, retaining the boundaries of the feudal hierarchy. This is a typical postcolonial syndrome, where the subaltern remains within the imperialist framework (in this case feudalism), and is a part of it in the sense that it earns its wages within its economic framework and, at the same time, caricatures its inherent fallacies, pokes fun at the feudal chieftains and mimics its prevalent norms. When we place the portrayal of women characters within this conditional framework, what emerges is the hybrid individual, who is nurtured within an ideological framework, but who also in turn voices her protest against the system by way of 'the Carnival' or 'mimicry'. The realm of postcolonial theory emphasizes this very concept of hybridity—which has its ethos in films like *Dilwale Dulhaniya Le Jayenge* , *Mirch Masala* and *Daman*.

Dilwale Dulhaniya Le Jayenge shows the crisis in a Punjabi family when the daughter falls 'in love' with a man the father disapproves of. Apart from showing the values inherent in the Indian familial structure, it also points out to the hypocrisies and the double standards of people in the name of social sanctity. Hence, itself being constituted by a feudal background, the film pokes fun at some of the idiosyncrasies that are practised in the name of preserving heritage.

Daman, on the other hand, shows the transformation of a subdued woman into an icon of courage when she sees her own daughter undergo the trauma and the social stigma that once she had to face from her husband and in-laws. The film has a brilliant performance by Raveena Tandon, who represents a woman victimized by the sexual perversions of her husband, marital rape and child abuse, where her daughter (born out of marital rape) is aggressed upon by her own father. She ultimately assumes the role of Durga and kills her husband, much like the manner in which Durga killed asura.[6] The film is the depiction of a system whose by-product (Raveena) demolishes the system itself. It was the feudal setup that had constructed her identity, femininity, subdued sexuality, forbidden attraction for her brother-in-law, acute vulnerability, but in the end, she ridiculed the entire system and brought an end to it.

The example of *Daman* not only emphasizes the concept of mimicry of traditions that are so much a part of postcoloniality, it also shows the transformation from the real to the unreal, that is, from reality to myth—in such a way that ultimately the myth becomes more believable than the reality. In this case, the real character of Raveena is transformed into Durga[7]—the slayer of the devil, with its numerous connotations. People watching the movie are, however, so dawn to its cinematic appeal that the boundaries of the real and the simulation collapse and become the same. Meyrowitz uses the term 'implosion'[8] to refer to this process, whereby the character becomes a woman and the goddess at the same time.

The location of the woman in the entire narrative of the Hindi filmic mode has, in fact, undergone a metamorphosis[9] in the sense that compared to the earlier films, contemporary films are not predictable. Initially, the narrative pattern was unilinear, predictable and moved towards restoration of the order. Thus, in the female characters in *Seeta Aur Geeta, Chaalbaaz* or *Damini* we see that the theme is a fluid one resembling a bell-shaped graph. There is the simple, happy family, the appearance of the villain, misunderstandings between siblings, unfolding of the 'real' villain, the arrival of police and restoration of order. If I may dissect the narrative according to the norms of deconstruction, the postmodern narrative of some of the recent Hindi films does not follow any predictable structure of narration, neither is the end predictable. In fact, there is no cinematic closure and the conclusion is often open ended.

In the words of Madhava Prasad,[10] 'The post independence Bombay films aesthetic has often been traced to the structuring of the film text around a single linear strand of narrative with one dominant effect—pathos, comedy, action, mystery, music romance, horror'. The essence of postmodern narrative[11] is that there is no structuration, no sequence, no cause and no effect. The scenes are sorted together in a non-symmetrical manner- so much so that any scene cut from the middle put in the beginning will serve just as good. There are no superbly planted gardens (meaning coherence of ideas) and often there is the reign of chaos, diaspora, absurdity, and boundary crossing. A brilliant example of this is the film *Gaj Gamini* by the painter M. F. Hussain. In his words, it is a collage. We see the female character, played by Madhuri Dixit, in different roles, at different locations and in different space and time. She is inserted into the role of Eve, of the painter's muse, of Mona Lisa, of Goddess Saraswati—aptly drawing on the chaotic and the absurd. Another example could be character of Priety Zinta in *Dil Se* directed by Mani Ratnam. Here, Priety transgresses the boundaries of womanhood when she asks the hero (Shah Rukh Khan) whether he is a virgin. This sort of double entendre has a tendency towards transgressing boundaries. She is shown to be a well-dressed and poised woman, who likes and intends to marry the hero but asks about his virginity and, at the time of their marriage, calls the 'other' woman (Manisha Koirala)—who she knows her husband loves—and asks her to participate in the wedding rituals. Her character literally sits on the fence—between logic, rationality, reason on one side and dark emotions, absurdity, and trauma on the other.

This overwhelming aggressive tendency of the woman is something that opposes the discourse of the folk traditions and mythical religiosity of the Indian orientation of womanhood. There is a shift in focus from situating the woman as victim of patriarchal essentialism, as a biological entity, meant for giving sexual pleasure to man and an agent in the reproduction of mankind, to a fluid, almost ephemeral, entity who is a cultural construction and has multiple selves. She too has desires, sexualities and fantasies. The authoritative, top-down approach of erstwhile cinema has been replaced by postmodern thinkers by the bottom-up approach—giving a psychoanalytical twist to the image of the woman.

NOTES

1. Muller, Bob 'Seeing Things' (Routledge) pp. 44–46.
2. *Mother India* is heralded as a new episode in the genre of Hindi films in India. It was a huge success, and it portrayed the Indian woman as a strong and decisive character, something that was not known before.

3. The *mangalsutra* is a necklace, worn by the Indian woman after she gets married. It is considered that every virtuous wife should protect her *mangalsutra*, as it is considered to be like a lifeline for her husband. No woman takes it off unless she is really in a sorry state.

4. The *Laxamn Rekha* is believed to be the line of demarcation drawn by Laxman, the brother of Rama, to protect Sita from the hands of Ravana. It signified the demarcation, trespassing which Ravana had to lose his life, if Sita had to lose her virtue.

5. Trivedi, Harish & Mukherjee, Meenakshi ed. 'Interrogating Postcolonialism' IIAS, (2000) pg. 14.

6. Asura is the incarnation of the Evil, according to Hindu philosophy, who battled against Durga and was slayed by her.

7. The goddess Durga, according to Hindu philosophy is the mother goddess, who is said to be the guiding force in truth, crushing falsity and good against the evil.

8. Meyrowitz, J. 'No Sense of Place' New York: Oxford University Press. pp. 29–30.

9. Cook, David A. 'A history of narrative Film' 2nd Edition, New York: W.W Norton, 1990.

10. Prasad, Madhava 'Ideology of the Hindi Film' (Oxford) pg. 47.

11. Kapur, Geeta 'Mythical Material in Indian Cinema' Journal of Arts and Ideas 23/24 (January 1993): 79–108.

Chapter 13

Locating Dalit Women in the Indian Caste System, Media and Women's Movement*

Vivek Kumar

Caste prejudices and discrimination against Dalits are a social fact of Indian society. Dalits have suffered social exclusion based on caste since time immemorial. Because of prejudice and social exclusion, they have not been allocated a legitimate place in the Hindu social order and have been reduced as an appendage to the Hindu society. Even today, Dalits suffer from crude forms of humiliation, stigmatization and exclusion, specifically in the villages of India. This is evident from the number of facts. For instance, they still live in their separate settlements, perform defiling and stigmatized occupations, are addressed contemptuously, abused and ridiculed routinely, and suffer from numerous types of physical atrocities. Although the social exclusion is not absent in urban India, its intensity and nature is different. It is subtle and sophisticated and a detailed inquiry of such types of exclusions is long pending.

When Dalits, in general, are treated in such a contemptuous manner, then the women of the Dalit community are naturally more vulnerable. That is why it has been argued that Dalit women are triply exploited, that is, on the basis of caste, class and gender. It is in this context of Indian society that we have tried, in this chapter, to evaluate

---

* *Social Change* (March 2009), *39*(1), 64–84.

the structural location and treatment meted out to Dalit women in general. This chapter tries to understand the existing prejudice in the society against Dalit women which, in a way, is articulated by the atrocities committed on them by the so-called upper castes. This prejudice got manifested also in the way casteist remarks were hurled by the leader of a dominant caste at Mayawati—who is emerging as a Dalit icon in spite of existing structural hurdles in a hierarchically arranged society. We have analysed this issue in detail in the chapter. The chapter also deals with the facts and events because of which Mayawati has successfully become an icon of the Dalit society. Further, we have explored how she has deconstructed many established images of Dalit and general caste women.

At the end, this chapter raises three main issues. One, why at all a leader of a dominant caste ridiculed Mayawati with casteist remarks who is now recognized as one of the most powerful women of the world? Second, we have tried to understand why the Indian media has failed to appreciate her achievements in full glory. Third, why does the Indian women's movement not accept Mayawati as part and parcel of the Indian women's movement and defend her from the onslaughts of media and prejudices of caste in the male-dominated society?

Before we come to the main theme of the chapter, let us understand in what sense the term Dalit has been used.

DEFINING THE TERM DALIT

Lots of confusion prevails regarding definition of the term Dalits in the sociological literature. Therefore, it is necessary to define the term at the outset. The Dalits, in the annals of Indian history, were addressed with different nomenclatures like Chundulus, Avurnas, Achhuts, Numashudru, Purihas, Adi-Dravidu, Ad-Dharmis, Depressed Classes, Oppressed Hindus, Harijans, etc., at different points in time. But especially after the emergence of the Dalit Panthers movement in the 1970s in Maharashtra, they preferred to be called Dalits. The definition of Dalits as propounded by Dalit Panthers was a class definition as they included members of Scheduled Castes (SCs), Scheduled Tribes (STs), the landless and poor peasants, women and all those who were exploited politically, economically and in the name of religion (Murugkar 1991: 237). The term has both a negative and positive connotation. Some Dalits associate themselves with a negative and more objective situation of the Dalits, that is, of an exploited and excluded community. On the other hand, many Dalits have asserted that the term Dalit is a symbol of assertion and 'Dalitness' is a source of confrontation. It is a matter of appreciating the probability of one's total being (Murugkar 1991: 54). Here, a point should be noted that it was political compulsion of the Panthers that forced them to propound such a definition of a group, which never existed before, as they wanted to forge an alliance between these aforesaid groups, so that they can get maximum support from these groups. But sociologically, this definition cannot be sustained, as each group, that is, SCs, STs, landless, poor peasants and women is different from the other.

Therefore, the word Dalit has been strictly used for ex-untouchables of Indian society who have occupied a unique structural location in it. Here, the term structure has been used in terms of the pattern of interrelated roles and statuses, which the actors of a specific society occupy in the spheres of rights and obligations. Nadel (1969) argues, 'We arrive at the structure of a society through abstracting from the concrete population and its behaviour the pattern or network (or 'system') of relationships existing between actors and in their capacity of playing roles to one another.' One can infer from the above what structural position Dalits occupied and still occupy in the Indian society, which in turn resulted in their social exclusion. In this context, the term 'social exclusion' can be defined as,

> A multi-dimensional process, in which various forms of exclusion are combined: participation in decision-making and political processes, access to employment and material resources, and integration into the common cultural process. When combined, they create an acute form of exclusion that find a spatial manifestation in particular neighbourhoods. (Madanipour et al., 1998: 22)

However, in the Indian context, as far as social exclusion of Dalits is concerned, we have to add to the elements of religious justification of such exclusion based on dharma and karma. Moreover, social exclusion for Dalits is ascriptive in nature. The structural location of the Dalits and the process of their social exclusion, as discussed before, results in construction of unique consciousness of Dalits, which is depicted through their worldview, and their orientation towards life and nature. This consciousness cuts across the boundaries of different castes found among the Dalits and, hence, unites them in spite of their regional and language differences.

Therefore, sociologically, the Dalits can be defined on the basis of three social characteristics.

1. Their structural location in Indian society
2. Social exclusion they suffer in the society
3. Their unique construction of consciousness, which is anchored in their structural location and social exclusion.

Based on the above elements of structural location, social exclusion and construction of consciousness, we can argue that the Dalits are different from STs, women and poor persons belonging to caste Hindus that were included in the definition of the Dalits given by the Dalit Panthers.

The logical question then would be how are Dalits different from other groups? At the outset, an economically poor person is different from the Dalits because he (or the group of economically poor persons) may be deprived in economic spheres especially in terms of income necessary to participate in the economy. But he may not be necessarily deprived in social and cultural spheres, that is, he may not face the same type of exclusion in the social and cultural life either in his neighbourhood or in the society at large as Dalits face. For instance, penury-stricken Brahmins, Kshatriyas, Vaishyas or Shudras are never forced to live outside the boundaries of the main village. They interact within themselves at least in secular realms on more or less equal terms. Contrary to this, the Dalits were excluded from the main residential areas of the village and were also kept outside the interaction pattern of social life. Similarly, although a penury-stricken Brahmin begs but has power to give blessings. Richest of rich may go to Kashi and Haridwar and bow down at the feet of poorest of the poor Brahmin. On the other hand, although a Dalit with his hard labour cleans shoes, lifts dead animals or cleans toilets, yet he is looked down upon. Hence, we can argue that a poor person may be economically or politically deprived or may be both, but he is never excluded from the social and cultural spheres. But an ex-untouchable is deprived in all the three—social, economic and political realms. And therefore, Oommen has rightly pointed out, 'If proletarian consciousness is essentially rooted in material deprivations ....Dalit consciousness is a complex and compound consciousness which encapsulates deprivations stemming from inhuman conditions of material existence, powerlessness and ideological hegemony' (Oommen 1990: 256).

The social exclusion of an ex-untouchable is so overpowering that even though he attains economic and political mobility or even goes beyond the national boundaries through his hard labour, he is not accepted by the castes located higher up in the caste hierarchy as an equal. His social identity remains stigmatized and his achievements are basically associated with that social identity. Few examples in this regard can make the fact clearer. One, it is a fact that as soon K. R. Narayanan became the President of India, in spite of his high educational achievements and political experience, everyone tried to evaluate his ascendance to the presidential post only on the basis of his caste identity. Most of them argued that Narayanan was elevated to the post of president because he belonged to the Dalit community (Kumar 2007b). Second, if we take the Dalit diaspora as another example, the issue of social exclusion of Dalits becomes further clear. It is true that amongst the Indian diaspora, 'that caste was increasingly an aspect of culture rather than social stratification per se ... [however] the stigma of caste did not die out completely' (Jain 2003: 74). Jain makes amply clear how the caste stigma exists with the Dalits even though they have transcended the national boundaries. In his own words, 'Women of high caste married to low caste men ... looked down upon their husbands ... and even told their children how their fathers were of a lower caste than them' (ibid). The caste stigma and consciousness haunt the Dalits in the diaspora in spite of their economic mobility, whenever they visit their ancestral village. The villagers still despise them.

Another impact of social exclusion on Dalits is the loss of 'social capital' that could give them the potential to develop consciousness and motivation for their amelioration. Moreover, because of lack of this consciousness, they could not revolt against the existing unequal Hindu social order for long. Their cultural co-option in the Hindu social order, even though they were formally not part of the *varna* hierarchy, was affected by the artificial consensus. The artificial consensus was, of course, part of Hindu hegemony legitimized by the karma theory, which makes people believe in the deeds of previous births determining one's status in the present.

Further, who can deny the differences between Dalits (ex-untouchables) and tribals? Tribals are not a part of the Hindu social order, although few sociologists have tried to include tribes in the Hindu social order, by calling them backward Hindus (Ghurye 1963). Moreover, the theory of the tribe-caste continuum argues that there are certain castes and tribes which have substantially retained some attributes or characteristics of tribes and vice versa (Ram 2007: 23–24). However, it is difficult to accept both these explanations because the traits or characteristics commonly present in them may be because of diffusion not because of any continuum. There is no shared life situation and interaction between tribes and Dalits and there is no consciousness of presence of each other. Therefore, the mere presence of common traits between the two groups does not make them members of the same society. That is why it is difficult to accept the tribals as a part of Dalits. As the tribes have their own independent social system with its stratification, deity, family, kinship, etc., they did not face the same type of social exclusion, atrocities and violence as the Dalits. Their exclusion was more because of their geographical location in the hilly or forested terrain. On the whole, tribals differed from Dalits in political, religious, economic and psychological aspects. These aspects have kept them away from the Hindu hegemony in terms of their status in the caste hierarchy, occupation, commensality, etc. In addition, this differentiation from the Hindu social order has resulted in a different type of construction of consciousness among the tribals and, therefore, unlike the Dalits, they revolted against their exploiters a number of times in the past. Consequently, because of differences in their structural location, social exclusion and construction of consciousness from the Dalits, we cannot include them in defining the Dalits.

Women also cannot form a part of the category of Dalits as propounded by the Dalit Panthers. The reasons are very clear. One, women in Indian society, undoubtedly exploited on the gender and class basis, do not constitute a monolithic whole. There is differentiation among the Indian women on caste lines as well. For instance, the women belonging to the castes located in the upper echelons of the caste hierarchy have the same attitude towards the Dalits as their male counterparts. They practise untouchability in the same manner, as any caste Hindu male would do. Secondly, general caste women have never revolted or organized any movement against the exploitation of the Dalit women and men by Hindu caste men. Not only that, they have also not launched a decisive movement against the exploitative Hindu religious sanctions for them. On the contrary, most of the so-called upper-caste women feel proud of their structural location and cultural heritage. Hence, how can we differentiate caste Hindu women with Hindu men and include them in the category of Dalits (Kumar 2005, Kumar 2007b)?

Based on the afore-discussed social facts, the term Dalit can be used for ex-untouchables in the contemporary social science parlance. Now, here a paradoxical situation emerges. The paradox is that the Dalits who were never accepted by the caste Hindus as part of their society, at least in the 'book view' are now being accepted by the caste Hindus as a part of them.

Caste Hindus justification that Dalits are part of the Hindu social order arises only from the fact that there are a number of cultural traits which are common to both Dalits and caste Hindus. However, this proposition is not sustainable. As Ambedkar has emphasized long ago that the cultural traits found in two different communities may be because of the process of diffusionism and not necessarily as a part of each other. On the other hand, the Dalits claim an independent status of a separate community from Hinduism. Consequently, Dalits can claim their separate and independent status from the Hindu social order on the basis of three characteristics, namely, structural location, social exclusion and unique construction of consciousness. In this social exclusion of the Dalits, it assumes more significance than economic and political exclusion, as we have seen earlier. This sociological conceptualization of the Dalits is necessary because only then can we draw the exact contours of a social group that is useful for analytical purposes, in researches, without confusing it with other social groups.

STRUCTURAL LOCATION AND STATUS OF DALIT WOMEN

At the outset, Dalit women are located at the lowest ebb of the caste hierarchy. That is why she is triply exploited in terms of caste, class and gender. It is because of this structural location that Dalit women were accorded statuses such as *devadasi, dai* (midwife), *dayan* (witch), etc. It will be worth mentioning the wretched condition of the Dalit women in different aspects of the Indian society here.

Analysing the exploited situation of Dalit women, Omvedt argues that,

> The Dalit girls were dedicated to the goddess Yellama/Renuka [...] Following this 'marriage to the god' most of the girls remained in their own village; they were considered accessible to any men but at the same time not bound to or polluted by sexual relations[...] These girls were as 'Murali' and among Mahars, 'Matangi' among the Madigas and 'Basavi' among Holeyas[...] whatever the 'matriarchal' or 'matrilineal' remnants that can be seen in the custom, by late feudal times it also helped to institutionalize the sexual accessibility of the Dalit women for higher caste men. (Omvedt 1994: 72)

Vijayashree (2004) explains the prevalence of the devadasi custom among Dalits. She argues that because of the existential condition of devadasis—Sule/Sami—customs in the Telugu-speaking area, Jogin or Basavi in Andhra and Karnataka calls them 'outcaste sacred prostitutes'. There was no ritual space for them and marginalization was more starkly signified through the imposition of beginning as they were not granted land rights, she opines. Further, she explains that outcaste devadasis were forced to dance during funeral processions and were forced into prostitution as they had no alternative way of earning once they were out of their youth.

Bhriggs has also highlighted the vulnerable condition of Dalit women in his study of Chamars—an untouchable caste of North India. He wrote in the 1920s,

> There are other social customs, more or less objected to but often allowed and not considered wrong, which are gradually disappearing under modern conditions. Such are the jus prima noctics of landlords

and gurus. The zamindar often takes liberties with the Chamar's wife in consideration of his payments to the Chamar. The Sais's wife gives immoral services where her husband is employed in the towns or cities. (Briggs 1920: 43)

Further in Tamil Nadu, Rudolph and Rudolph (1987: 39) have also revealed the pathetic condition of Shanan women in the area. They argued that a riot broke out in 1858 when Shanan women attempted to cover their breasts like the locally dominant Nair caste. The next year, Sir Charles Trevelyan, the Governor of Madras, granted them permission to wear a cloth over their breasts and shoulders. The hegemony of the Dalit women has been so overpowering that even as late as 2002, Arun (2007)—while doing his fieldwork among the Paraiyars, a Dalit caste of Tamil Nadu—reported that the older Paraiyar women do not wear blouses and sandals in the presence of higher castes of the village.

Apart from this look at the occupations of the Dalit women, from cleaning of human excreta to helping women of every caste in her delivery, she performs unique occupations which women of other castes do not perform. For instance, at every household birth, especially in the villages, the Dalit women perform the role of *dai* (midwife). According to Pinto (2006: 214),

This work...involves tasks which others (including, usually, the persons who delivered the baby) do not perform: cutting the umbilical cord, removing trash and offal, rubbing the baby with dirt, massaging the baby and mother, and bathing the infant.... These women remove pollution from home by removal of trash.

In certain areas, the Dalit women clean human excreta just for a few chapatis a day or she collects the *joothan* (leftovers) from some party organized at her client's house (Valmiki 2003).

Along with the aforesaid exploitation and discrimination of the Dalit women, she is also the victim of societal ridicule in the society at large. Look at the following examples:

Bitiya Chamar Ki, Nam Rajraniya
(Daughter of Chamar with the name of Rajrani (chief queen)!!)
Manifestly, the saying represents a paradox that a girl belonging to Chamar caste, who is economically poor with low–caste status, cannot

become a queen. But the latent meaning of this saying is that how can a Chamar give his daughter a sophisticated name? There is a case of role distancing. Such is the stigma attached to this saying that it is often used by the caste Hindus to ridicule their own girls who are somewhat extrovert. Similarly,

Chappat par Chamain Chale, Sandal Par Dhobiniya
Hai Mor Rama Badal Gail Duniya
(The Chamarin [woman of the Chamar] walks in slippers and *dhobinya* (washerwoman) in sandals, Oh my Rama! The world has changed.) This means that the Dalit women should not wear even slippers because traditionally they were not allowed to do so, and if they have started doing so, then the times have changed.

UNDERSTANDING THE MEANING OF ATROCITIES ON DALIT WOMEN

The Dalit woman has a unique position in the society not only because of her stigmatized occupation and ridicule heaped on her by larger society but also because of atrocities committed on her by so-called upper castes. Specifically, if we analyse the rape of Dalit women by the caste Hindus this fact becomes clearer. It is a fact that a rape of any woman is a heinous crime and a punishable act under the law of every society and also in India. But rape of Dalit women is qualitatively different. It is not only a sexual violation of Dalit women but assumes caste or communitarian atrocity. The process of sexual assault on Dalit women by the so-called upper castes assumes the nature of caste atrocity because of three reasons. One, in number of cases, the rape of Dalit women is not committed by an individual. It is usually in the form of gang rape. The case of Madhya Pradesh is a case in point. A report presented in the Madhya Pradesh Legislative Assembly revealed that in 2005 there have been approximately 1,217 cases of gang rapes (*samuhik balatatkar*) with Dalit women, out of which 726 rapes were with Dalit girls under 18 years (Singh 2007: 28). The Khairlanji Massacre of Maharashtra on 26 September 2006 is also a case in point.

The second reason is that had the rape been only a sexual act, the victims (in this case, the Dalit women) would have been left alone. But it has been reported in several cases that the so-called upper

Table 13.1 Table Depicting the Number of Rapes of Dalit Women

Years	1981	1982	1983	1984	1985	1986	1987	1995	1996	1997	1998
Number of rape cases	604	635	640	640	692	700	727	837	949	1002	1000

Source: Collated from different Annual Reports of Commission for Scheduled Castes and Scheduled Tribes, New Delhi.

castes deliberately desecrate the private parts of the Dalit women. The third reason to describe the rape of the Dalit women as a caste atrocity is that, since time immemorial, the caste atrocities on Dalits by the caste Hindus are often directed through Dalit women. In a normal struggle with the Dalits, the castes located higher up in the caste hierarchy try to teach a lesson to the Dalits by assaulting their women. Thereby the whole community is terrorized, and they try to suppress the emerging consciousness and assertion among Dalits. Hence, the process of sexual assault on Dalit women assumes the nature of caste or communitarian atrocity. Therefore, the point which I am trying to make here is that the atrocities on the Dalits have a social structural basis of caste prejudice.

The aforesaid established status of Dalits is self-explanatory that how much Dalit women are exploited. Therefore, on the basis of her structural location, the type of occupation she is forced to perform, the stigmatization and ridicule she suffers, etc., we can safely argue that the construction of consciousness of Dalit women is different from the women in general. That is why her existence has been denied in society in general and Dalit society in particular. And hence, the Dalit woman is triply exploited on the basis of her caste, class and gender. Therefore, one can imagine how much effort Mayawati had to make to come to this level where she is being even hailed by international media.

DECONSTRUCTING THE ESTABLISHED IMAGE OF DALIT WOMEN AND THE MAKING OF MAYAWATI

First of all, Mayawati has broken the aforesaid established image of a Dalit woman. What is astonishing today is that against the established image of Dalit women—namely, devdasi, dai or dayan—Mayawati is revered as *Bahenji* (sister), which is not a mean achievement. *Bahenji*, of not traditional Indian society, who is suppressed and remains within herself tight-lipped and with the shackles of tradition and customs. Mayawati's construction of *Bahenji* is different. She is considered a hard taskmaster who cannot be taken for granted and with whom nobody can take liberties. She means business-deliver or be ready for punishment is the moral lesson she has taught to her followers and subordinate officers. She commands respect and loves discipline.

But this has not happened in a day. There is a history behind this construction.

Like every conscious Dalit youth or Dalit individual, Mayawati started identifying herself with the Dalit community through Babasaheb Ambedkar's life and mission. She was motivated by Babasaheb's achievements. Babasaheb's story was narrated to her by her father. When she was in class 8 one day, she expressed her desire to her father that, 'If I work like Babasaheb Dr Ambedkar then will people celebrate my anniversary after my death as they celebrate Babasaheb Dr Ambedkar's anniversary?' (Mayawati 2006: 10). Her father answered in the affirmative and she resolved to achieve that end. Mayawati accepts that she is 'a stubborn type of girl' (Mayawati 2006), and that is why, in 1972, she could pass classes 9, 10 and 11 in one year. Born on 15 January 1956, in Delhi, Mayawati after doing her graduation from Delhi started preparing for the civil services exams. In the meantime, she got a job of teaching in the department of education in Delhi. She also pursued a law degree from the University of Delhi. Then came Manyavar Kanshi Ram who changed her life and motivated her to join the social reform movement instead of joining the civil services. Mayawati (2006: 5–6) eloquently observes,

> But because of coming into contact with Manyavar Kanshi Ramji, via BAMCEF, my thoughts, ideas and aspiration to do something got a new shape, new dimension and a new height. Appreciating my thoughts, Manyavar Kanshi Ramji had told me that 'you can become not only a collector but a good leader too and then many officers like collectors will be behind you holding files and flattering, with their help you can serve and uplift the exploited-suffering Bahujan Samaj in the real sense of the term'. In this way Manyavar Kanshi Ramji showed a dream, a path.

And since then, Mayawati has been with the Bahujan movement.

From 1977 to 1984 Mayawati worked as a Delhi government employee and also as a social worker first in Backward and Minority Communities Employees Federation (BAMCEF) and then in Dalit Shoshit Samaj Sangharsh Samiti which were established in 1978 and 1981 respectively. This proves that she was committed to a cause without any certain future, as nobody was convinced that the Bahujan movement would succeed. It was only in 1984, when the Bahujan Samaj Party (BSP) was launched, that she joined full time politics. Mayawati had to face lots of hardship to achieve today's status. She had to face resistance from her father who was against her joining politics and thought that she could do more for Dalit uplift if she joined Civil Services. Her father threatened her, that if she did not leave Kanshi Ram's company he would throw her out from the family. Mayawati has written, 'He (her father) knew that where will this young girl go leaving home and therefore he was exerting pressure on me, but I did not listen to my father' (Mayawati 2006: 11).

Further, she explains that she left her house for creating awareness among Bahujan society with her elder brother as he had similar ideology. She did have her seven years earnings. But there were more problems to follow her. When she started living with her brother in a separate room rented by Kanshi Ram then, '... some mean minded and selfish people started spreading rumours about me and Manyavar Kanshi Ram' (Mayawati 2006). In the end, she bought a separate house out of her saved money and started living alone. But Mayawati's problems were not over. Kanshi Ram himself had accepted that when she entered the political fray, she had to face many problems. He argued,

I feel the toughness appears to be the result of the initial opposition during her launch as a leader.... Initially her father opposed her joining the BSP movement .... Keeping in mind the opposition of her father, I decided to give her more and more opportunities to exhibit her talents. This was not liked by the seniors in the movement. They started opposing her. This opposition created problems for her .... They tried to put pressure on me, to curtail the opportunities, I was giving her. On refusal, most of the seniors left the BSP. (Mayawati 2006:73)

Apart from this, when Mayawati was about to become UP'S Chief Minister in June 1995, she was attacked by the goons of the Samajwadi Party in the Lucknow state guest house. In this context, Mayawati herself has written, '... because of his criminal mentality...Mulayam... with the help of police and criminals not only kidnapped BSP legislators but tried his level best to kill me in the State guest house in front of the public and media.' (Mayawati 206: 548). But Mayawati survived the criminal onslaught.

Hence, facing several challenges from within the family, within the party and society at large, Mayawati has risen from the grassroots by establishing a chord with the masses. She has not been imposed from above and neither has she had any political connections or patronage of society or media. Neither did she have a high parentage. But what a pity people only see her crown, gold and diamond necklace and birthday celebrations. They could not see her sufferings, sacrifices and torn ankles. The way she used to travel for hours on feet or on the back of the bicycle to mobilize the Bahujan Samaj. The way she spent days and nights in the Dalit *bustees* in different seasons. Sleeping on straw and eating with the villagers. Why have the masses in general and Indian media in particular not noticed it?

PORTRAYING A CONTRAST WITH SAVARNA WOMEN IN INDIAN POLITICS

Mayawati's attire and mannerisms presented a contrast to the so-called upper-caste women in Indian politics. We can observe ourselves that most upper-caste women in Indian politics, who have some stature, carry a typical image of the Indian women wearing a sari. Indira Gandhi, Vijeraje Sindhia, Sonia Gandhi, Jayalalita, Vasundhara Raje Sindhia, Sushma Swaraj, Brinda Karat, Pratibha Patil to name just a few. All these women wore saris in public. Further, barring a few, most of them use their *palh* to cover their heads in deference to elders in society. Moreover, all the aforesaid women used a docile and polite way of conversation prescribed specifically in Hindu culture where raising one's voice while talking to elders and with male counterparts is considered disrespectful.

Against this, Mayawati never wore a sari and wears a *shalwar-kurta* with *dupatta* wrapped around her neck. This suggests that there is no preferred code of dress for Indian women in Indian politics where patriarchy is still strong. Similarly, instead of a polite tone, she uses rough and aggressive speech in public. She has a commanding voice. There is a challenge and assertion simultaneously in her speech. This aggressive tone and tenor of her speech reveals her structural location of the people she has to handle. On the one hand, she had to fight with the society at large and to train the illiterate and rustic masses for political mobilization. So, it is natural for her to raise her voice. She has created a climate of fear to motivate her party cadres and officials to work to her agenda.

MAYAWATI: BECOMING OF AN ICON

Although Indian media, academia, intelligentsia and different political parties have tried every trick to project and portray her negatively, her followers adore her state craftmanship and upright attitude. Her style of functioning is readily accepted by the masses which were exploited for generations. It was even accepted by her mentor Manyavar Kanshi Ram who gave her title 'Iron Lady' suitable for her style of functioning. That is why we can safely argue that she has become an icon of Dalits in general and Dalit women in particular. We can observe the young Dalit girls wrapping their *duppatas* round their necks and calling themselves Mayawati in different localities where Dalits and OBCs live. Another fact that proves her iconic status is that Dalits have named their girls after her name—Mayawati. The words of a woman sweeping the Lucknow roads in the morning depict the social change in the society even better, 'She has not given me gold and silver nor has she raised my pay but now my supervisor speaks to me politely. He used to be very hostile and rude.'

Mayawati has now developed an appeal cutting across the caste and religious line as she has established herself as an able administrator and hard taskmaster. She is considered to be the first political boss of the state to teach bureaucrats a lesson that they are the servants and not the masters. She also taught an over-due lesson to self-styled aristocrats of Kunda and other mafias to prove the point that no one is above the law. As far as commitment to her ideology is concerned, by pursuing the Ambedkar Village Scheme, effective implementation of Anti SC/ST Atrocities Act, constructing cultural and historical symbols for the Dalits and Bhaujans, communal riot-free, three regimes in 1995, 1997, 2003, she has justified her commitment to Dalits, minorities and other marginalized sections of the state. And now, she has given the slogan of Sarvajan. In August 2008, when United Progressive Alliance government was seeking a vote of trust, Mayawati became the fulcrum of an alternative political coalition. The oft-quoted rhetoric *'Dalit ki beti'* took a seat and she acted like a stateswoman while addressing the nation on the nuclear deal with the US. Almost 10 parties from left to centre were ready to join hands with her, the prominent ones being Communist Party of India (Marxist), Communist Party of India, Telugu Desam Party, Telangana Rashtra Samithi, Revolutionary Socialist Party, Indian National Lok Dal, etc. (Kumar 2008: 9). When will the whole nation celebrate her achievement as it celebrates the achievement of any other daughter of the country?

CASTEIST REMARKS AGAINST MAYAWATI AND SILENCE OF THE INDIAN MEDIA AND WOMEN'S MOVEMENT

The existing caste prejudice against Dalit women became public once again in Uttar Pradesh (UP) when a leader of the dominant caste Mahendra Singh Tikait used abusive language against Mayawati—the UP Chief Minster and the President of BSP. One would dismiss these vulgar and casteist remarks as ridiculous (the remark is so un-parliamentary that it cannot be reproduced here) and can argue that it was a statement of the illiterate and unsophisticated Jat leader of the fading Bhartiya Kisan Union (BKU). Hence, it should not be given any credence whatsoever. However, if we evaluate the socio-political context in which Tikait has uttered this obnoxious statement, we will be able to argue that it is not just a cliched remark but it has its roots in history and sociology of Indian society, the structure of caste and the relations which emerge on the basis of the caste system. That means Tikait's remark on Mayawati is born out of a deep sense of pride and prejudice with which Jats—a dominant caste of west UP—live.

Tiakait belongs to the Jat community who are an intermediary but dominant caste in west UP. According to Gupta (1997: 49),

> Tikait believes that his clan, the Baliyan *khap*, came to prominence when his forefathers helped Emperor Harshvardhan (AD 606–647) in a very difficult battle. Impressed by their valour the Emperor applied a *tika* of his blood on the forehead of the clan *chaudhury*. From then on their family was called Tikait.

Similarly, each Jat *Khap* (sub-grouping among Jats) have an exalting story of their origin. The pride and prejudice of Jats is further highlighted by their claim of a warrior past and, hence, a belief that they can bow to no one, and are, therefore, best suited in times of peace to an agricultural occupation where a Jat can be his own master in fields (Gupta 1997). The Jats proudly claim that they are 'number two Hindus'. The number one Hindus are Brahmins and Baniyas. Furthermore, for traditional Jats in the villages, freedom means the liberty to follow their traditions, lifestyles and customs without hindrance from outside. This Jat pride and prejudice is also reflected every time the state government does something offensive and coercive. The BKU leaders used to be quite pleased every time when the officials from the state department were locked up by Jat youth (Gupta 1997: 88–89). In the same vein, 'every time a Tikait cocks a snook at journalists, at politicians ... .or irrigation officials, the Jats enjoy it highly. It is like a live demonstration of their pride and dignity and their willingness to take on anyone regardless of power and wealth' (Gupta 1997: 99).

If this was the level of Jat pride and prejudice for the general masses, one can imagine their treatment of Dalits. It is interesting to note that the Jats do not practise untouchability in its most overt form; however, they hold the Dalits in open contempt. The contempt is evident in how Jats address Dalits in villages. For instance, Bhangis and Chamars do not want to be called by their names for these names were derogatory in character. The Jats, however, still address them with these pejorative terms. It is an established fact that the Dalits are addressed in a contemptuous manner in the Indian villages whether in the north or south, east or west. The ridicule and disrespect of Dalits is openly displayed while they are addressed by their specific caste names, which already has a stigma, attached to it in the local area. Or when Dalits are addressed by their first names with a stress at the end of the name with 're' or 'ri'.

The existing domination of Jats was also visible in the manner in which they paid wages to other castes. Jats seldom paid Dalits their wages; even if they paid, they were never in time. Although the Dalits feel like revolting, they were subdued because of the dominant presence of Jats in the village, police and in the local political structure. It is because of this socio-political background, contempt of everyone

180 | Vivek Kumar

in general and Dalits in particular by the Jats that the Tikait hurled abuse on Ms Mayawati—a Dalit woman but presently the Chief Minister of UP. This abusive language of the Tikait against Mayawati is testimony to the existing mindset with which the Jats have been living in these areas. Probably, in his arrogance and celebration of past glory, the Tikait did not realize that socio-political reality has changed. The Dalits for whom the Jats had contempt and ridicule have reached a level where they are not prepared to take things lying. With the state power and power of the movement, Dalits can repay the Jats in the same currency. There is no doubt that over the years, the BSP has created self-confidence among the Dalits. With the formation of four governments, it has led to a structural change in the caste-ridden UP (Kumar 2003, 2007a). Even then, the caste pride in Tikait was so entrenched that it took 10,000 policemen, the whole administrative machinery and local Dalit population to make him realize that he had committed a crime against one of the most powerful women, not only of the state but of the world.

However, what is astonishing to note here is that the whole Indian women's movement, which cries for the dignity and respect for the Indian women, did not come forward to condemn or criticize the statement made by Tikait. Not even one women's organization—left, right or centre—came forward to react against the vulgar statement of Tikait hurled at Mayawati. Hence, a question emerges that whether Mayawati comes under the sisterhood of Indian women or is she so powerful that she doesn't need anybody's assistance? Similarly, the media also remained silent. The opinion-makers never felt agitated against the abusive language used by Tikait. Probably, for them caste is dead and if they speak then they will have to accept that caste exists. On the contrary, the media tried to project that in punishing Tikait, Mayawati has misused the state machinery. Well, as we will see further in the chapter, the media is itself biased and has casteist overtones for Mayawati. Anyway, Mayawati has always been a victim of silence of the Indian women's movement and media. Whether she has achieved something in her life or she faced some upheaval in her life, both have been mute spectators. On the following lines, we will evaluate this silence of the Indian media and women's media. We will let the readers decide whether this silence emanates from caste prejudice or there is something else.

MAYAWATI'S ACHIEVEMENTS AND SILENCE OF INDIAN MEDIA AND WOMEN'S MOVEMENT

There is no doubt that Mayawati has emerged as a new Dalit icon of Dalit society in general and the Dalit movement in particular. A new epoch in the Dalit movement has begun because till now only Dalit males dominated the movement. There were a number of Dalit women icons such as Uda Devi Pasi, Jhalkari Bai Kori, Sukrao Bhangi, Ramabai Ambedkar, Shantabai Dani, etc., in the history of the Dalit movement. However, they were never visible in the movement and neither had they led any movement like Mayawati—who is the leader of the movement and also heads a government. This has given her visibility as well as space to prove her worth. It is on the basis of her struggle, sacrifice and substance that *Newsweek,* a US weekly magazine has declared BSP's President and UP's fourth time Chief Minister Mayawati one among the eight most powerful women in the world. Strangely enough, there was silence in the Indian media and women's movement on this account.

Barring the day when the news was published, the newspapers and news channels (Hindi, English or vernacular) failed to highlight her achievement by carrying the discussion forward. There were no newspaper articles or newsroom discussions by the so-called opinion makers. We all know that the media has been hostile to her personally and her government's programmes and policies since the day she has gained prominence in the politics. There are a number of incidents to prove the same. In the past, just when Mayawati had entered public life, the media twisted her argument related to Mahatma Gandhi. Similarly, the Hindi newspaper *Duinik Jugrun* tried to assassinate her character. And when party cadres led by Kanshi Ram *gheraoed* the said newspaper's Lucknow office, the newspaper tendered an apology and sit up was lifted. However, the press did not budge as again the same newspaper published derogatory news related to Mayawati. This time, its Noida (now Gautam Buddha Nagar, UP) edition published the news by her caste name, although the news by the specific Dalit caste name is prohibited under the Indian Press laws. Even in contemporary times, the media projects her negative image—a Mayawati, who believes in show and pomp, erects statues: statues of the social reformers of Bahujan Samaj. She makes parks and carves out new districts and changes names of universities and cities after the names of reformers belonging to Dalit and OBC communities. Mayawati recklessly transfers bureaucrats and ditches her political partners and so on so forth. The television has constructed her image of a politician who has unaccounted wealth in her name (The Taj corridor case is a case in point). Yet it is difficult to accept the silence of the Indian media on her phenomenal achievement. More so, when the foreign press has succeeded in recording the positive aspect of her personality.

It was not for the first time that the US media had highlighted Mayawati's personality in this positive manner. *The New York Times,* on 4 May 2003, had already emphasized her achievements by writing that, 'Mayawati is the Chief Minister of India's largest State, Uttar Pradesh .... It is home of 166 million people, which means that she governs more people than all but one woman in the world, Indonesia's President, Meghawati Sukamoputri'. Surprisingly, that time, the Indian media was even more silent. The silence of the Indian media on the positive achievement of Mayawati is really deplorable because the same media highlights Indian women who either win Miss World, Miss Universe, Miss Asia or even Miss India out of proportion. If a film actress sheds a few kilograms of weight or has an affair, gets engaged or gets married, it makes news. Lengthy articles are written about their lifestyle and even about their tastes of food, drinks, dress, hobbies, etc. The television channels will go for live telecast or have special bulletins on the subject.

In the same vein, the Indian media even carried a live telecast of protest against the implementation of the Mandal Commission's Report (Mandal I and II both) by so-called upper-caste girls, although these protests were submerged in the casteist overtones and symbols. The girls, who happened to be the so-called upper castes, were pretending to clean the roads with brooms and displaying placards that they would not get educated and employed husbands because of reservations. Latent meaning of this protest was that the jobs which were only reserved for the Dalits will be forced on them because of reservations. The weekly magazines have also blacked her out. Lift any special issue of an established weekly magazine (English or Hindi) on the completion of the decade or silver jubilee years in publication, you will find the names and big photographs of women with far fewer achievement than Mayawati. Their insignificant achievements are blown out of proportion, but you will not find a mention of Mayawati's achievement. Why this discrimination? No doubt Dalit leadership has termed Indian media 'Manuvadi'. Babasaheb Ambedkar had long ago commented on the prejudiced role played by the then Hindu Press in vehemently criticizing his leadership during the Indian freedom movement (Kadam 1993: 241) and head launched his own newspapers and magazines. In the late 1970s, Kanshi Ram declared the media as 'Manuwadi' for not carrying news items related to the achievements of Dalits and Dalit movements. That is why he also started his weekly newspapers in different languages of India.

We can understand the limitations of the Indian media because it is closely associated with the market. That does not mean that I am ruling out existing caste and gender biases in the Indian media. However, we have to understand and analyse the role played by the Indian women's movement to highlight and appreciate the achievements of Mayawati. Is it ready to own Mayawati and her achievements as a woman? Why is it silent? Can the general caste women now transcend class and caste in the name of sisterhood and celebrate the achievement of Mayawati as a woman or a Dalit woman? More so because, 'in the women's movement ... it was assumed that caste identities could be transcended by the larger identity of sisterhood among all women' (Rege 2006: 2). But I don't think that the women's movement in India will celebrate this. There are a number of reasons for the same. One has been rightly highlighted by the Dalit women's themselves. According to Rege (2006: 3), 'The writings and manifestoes of different Dalit women's groups underlined the fact that the unmarked feminism ... had, in fact been in the theory and praxis a kind of Brahmanical feminism'. Second, 'The common sense of the women's movement has often rendered Dalit women's narratives of struggle as not being feminist enough because of what is perceived as prioritization of community over women's own issues' (Rege 2006: 50–51). Last but

184 | Vivek Kumar

not least, the women's movement, though obliquely accepts direct relationship between caste and patriarchy, yet it is not prepared to launch any movement against discrimination based on caste. Why has the Indian women's movement failed to launch a movement against the caste system in Indian society?

CONCLUSIONS

To conclude, we can argue that the structural location of Dalits and their women in Indian society is unique. The exclusion and exploitation of Dalit women takes place because of their unique location in an hierarchical and caste-ridden society, which separates them from general caste women. However, what is commendable is that in spite of structural barriers, Mayawati—a Dalit woman—has emerged as an icon of the Dalit movement. But ironically, the Indian media, women's movement and the world society at large has failed to appreciate her achievement like any other daughter of the nation.

REFERENCES

Arun, Joe (2007). *Constructing Dalit Identity,* Rawat Publications, New Delhi.
Briggs, G. W. (1920). *The Chamars,* republished in 1990, by Low Price Publications, Delhi.
Ghurye, G. S. (1963). *The Scheduled Tribes,* Popular Prakashan, Bombay (Now Mumbai).
Gupta, Dipankar (1997). *Rivalry and Brotherhood: Politics in the Life of Farmers 'in Northern India,* Oxford University Press, New Delhi.
Jain, Ravindra K. (2003). 'Culture and Economy: Tamils on the Plantation Frontier in Malaysia Revisited, !998–1999' in Bhiku Paarekh (ed.) Culture and Economy in the Indian Diaspora, Routledge, New Delhi.
Kadam, K. N. (ed.), (1993). *Dr. B. R. Ambedkur the Emancipator of the Oppressed,* Popular Prakashan, Bombay.
Kumar, Vivek (2003). Uttar Pradesh: Politics of Change, *Economic & Political Weekly,* vol. XXXVIII, no. 37, 13–19 September, Mumbai.
———. (2005). Situating Dalits in Indian Sociology, *Sociological Bulletin,* Volume 54, Number 3, September–December 2005, New Delhi.
———. (2007a). Bahujan Samaj Party: Some Issues of Democracy and Governance, in Sudha Pai (ed.), *Political* Process *in Uttar Pradesh,* Pearson Longman, New Delhi.

————. (2007b). Governance and Development in the Era of Globalization: Understanding Exclusion and Assertion of Dalits in India, in Kameshwar Choudhary (ed.) *Globalization, Governance Reforms and Development in India,* SAGE Publications, New Delhi.

————. 2008. Mayawati: The Stateswoman, *Sahara Times,* August 16, Issue 273, p. 9, New Delhi.

Madanipour, A. (1998). 'Social Exclusion and Space' in A. Madanipour, G. Cars and J. Allens (eds.), *Social Exclusion in European Cities,* Jessica Kingsley, London.

Mayawati, Kumari (2006). *Mere Sangharshmai Jivan, Evam Bahujan Movement Ka Sugarmama—Part I* (Hindi), Bhaujan Samaj Party, New Delhi.

Murugkar, Lata (1991). *Dalit Panthers Movement in Maharushtra: A Sociological Appraisal,* Popular Prakashan Bombay.

Nadel, S. F. (1969). *The Theory of Social Structure,* Cohen and West, London.

Omvedt, Gail (1994). *Dalits and the Democratic Revolution: Dr. Ambedkar and the Dalit Movement in Colonial India,* SAGE Publications, New Delhi.

Oommen, T. K. (1990). *Protest and Change: Studies in Social Movements,* SAGE Publications, New Delhi.

Pinto, Sarah (2006). Division of Labour: Rethinking the 'Midwife' in Rural Uttar Pradesh, in Janet Chawla (ed.) *Birth and Birth Givers: The Power Behind the Shame,* Har-Anand Publications Pvt. Ltd, New Delhi.

Priyadarshini Vijayashree (2004). *Recasting the Devadasi: Patterns of Sacred Prostitution in Colonial South India,* Kanishka, New Delhi.

Ram, Nandu (2007). Caste System in South India: Genesis, Mechanism and Growth, RC-9 Dalits and Backward Classes, Indian Sociological Society, New Delhi.

Rege, Sharmila (2006). *Writing Caste/ Writing Gender: Narrating Dalit Women's Testimonies,* Zuban, New Delhi.

Rudloph, Lloyd and Susanne Rudolph (1987). *The Modernity of Tradition: Political Development in India,* Orient Longman, New Delhi.

Singh, Bhasha (2007). *Bhagwa Kaal Mein Jumo Sitam,* (Hindi), *Outlook Saptahik,* September 10, New Delhi.

Valmiki, Omprakash (2003). *Joothaa: A Dalit's Life* (Translated from Hindi by Arun Prabha Mukherjee), Samya, Calcutta.

Section V

Law and Violence

Sectional Introduction

Ghazala Jamil

The intricate relationship between law and social change lies at the heart of most aspects of struggle for gender equality. It can perhaps be said that for many decades the foremost aspect of the women's rights movement in India was to conceptualize law as a device to induce social change. It is interesting that after the colonial encounter with modern law as an oppressive force, the founders of the new republic, including women, put their faith entirely in the emancipatory potential of law. The exercise of drafting a postcolonial constitution was seen as a mode of delivering justice to the people of India (Baxi, 2000). Several decades following the promulgation of the Constitution of India, women's movement's engagement with law entailed evidencing a lag in social change and law—with prevailing gender attitudes in the society lagging behind 'more developed' laws. Later, women staked a claim to participate in law-making too.

But a feminist critique of law was to soon understand the limits of emancipation by law. Not only was the state lax in using law making and law enforcement to challenge patriarchal power and violence, but it was through law, aided by patriarchy, that state established its monopoly over exercise of violence (Uberoi, 1996). The monopoly worked through selective exercise of violence over groups of citizens to show them their place in the national narrative and landscape. It was often the bodies of women which were regulated and violated to raise this spectre of state power (Kannabiran & Menon, 2007).

The articles contained in this last section, chronologically and thematically bracket this entire volume. The debates on law, or violence and law, or even the violence of law are the most emblematic of the debates on gender in social change.

The first article in this section, 'Law and Women in India', was written by Durgabai Deshmukh, who was also a lawyer among other things. The article exemplifies the prevailing discourse about Indian women—she emphasized 'collaboration' over 'rivalry' and asserted that women's parity with men in India was not a result of any violence, rebellion or other aggressive revolutions, but as a 'respectful rebirth of the age-old culture, the ancient heritage of this land'. She highlighted that the Constitution of India accorded a status to women that was better than that of women in any other part of the world. The article is important because it reviews the status of social legislation at the outset of the constitution on 26 January 1950 and provides a summary of the legislation enacted during the first decade that followed. Also, importantly, Deshmukh asserts that beyond law-making, one of the key roles of the democratic state is to take steps to alter people's social consciousness. Without this, she argues, the project of social change would remain unsuccessful to the degree that regulation outweighs societal desire.

Between 1972, when Deshmukh's article was published, and 2007, when the second article in this section was published, numerous other articles were published in Social Change discussing legal issues related to specific gendered struggles that have been discussed in other sections and the volume introduction. The article 'Geographies of Indian Women: A Tale of Contesting Spaces' has been included in this section because it represents a fresh take in the pages of Social Change on endemic violence faced by women. The author, Nandini Rai, spatializes the exclusion of women within homes which are experienced as hostile spaces. The chapter uses the National Family Health Survey and National Crime Records Bureau data to elaborate on the manifestations of violence and its linkages with autonomy, including economic autonomy. Regional variation in incidents of familial violence is also evidenced, correlation with educational status and household decision-making is also established. One of the reasons this article is important is because the author's treatment of domestic violence problematizes the way the domestic-public binary is usually enacted in gender rights writing. The article is an example of how cultural critique of social institutions, such as family, by a senior generation of scholars is being built upon by a later generation of feminist researchers and scholars imaginatively.

In the next article 'A Gender Critique of AFSPA: Security for Whom?', Amit Ranjan deals with the incidents of rapes in areas where Armed Forces (Special Powers) Act, 1958 (AFSPA), is in force. He scrutinizes the text of the law for its points of failures. For example, despite the security clauses contained in AFSPA, the bulk of these crimes are committed with impunity by the armed forces personnel. The article makes its place in this volume because of the important questions it raises on the concept of 'security' and the selective public outrage, including from women's rights groups, on rape that seems contingent upon the identities of the victim and the perpetrator of the crime. Ranjan argues that this sexual violence has the tacit support of the dominant majority. He shows how the sexual violence perpetuates a cycle of violence because this illegitimate power by state actors gives the other parties a legitimate excuse to use counterforce. State violence obviously alienates civilians who are being targeted, and supporting state-centric security often puts the lives of non-dominant groups at risk in these areas. The article is important for its attention to the complicated civil-society interventions and problems of mounting a legal challenge against the cases of violence and the unjust law itself.

The last article in this section and volume is authored by Flavia Agnes. The article titled 'Has the Codified Hindu Law Changed Gender Relationships?' raises and attempts to answer the fundamental question pertaining to law as a driver of social change. Agnes revisits the debates that took place during the enactment of laws prohibiting child marriages and dowry and presents a comprehensive examination of these laws in action in the next six decades. Taking a position contrary to the usual assertions of revival of glorious traditions of gender parity, the article is important for its unqualified flagging of deep anti-women biases that have persisted in Indian society. The codification of Hindu laws is often posed as a revolutionary legalistic reform of the kind which has been resisted by the minorities. Agnes puts these positions to the test of law as a mode of social change and asks whether the said codification has been successful in bringing about a 'social transformation by posing a challenge to the brahminical patriarchy which was dominant at that point of time'. Going even further, Agnes shows that Hindu Code Bill is often misrepresented as a step towards Uniform Civil Code (UCC) while it actually gives statutory recognition to diverse Hindu customs practised across sects and regions.

The article is of importance because it frames this clearing of the popular misconception of the Hindu Code Bill even in the women's movement, in context of the debates around UCC and how it impacts women and society. Agnes presents a fine-grained story of the 'reforms' in which complicated semantics of resistance, opposition and continuity offset the claims of social change.

REFERENCES

Baxi, U. (2000). Postcolonial legality. In H. Schwarz, & S. Ray (Eds.), *A Companion to Postcolonial Studies* (pp. 540–559). Blackwell Publishing.

Kannabiran, K., & Menon, R. (2007). *From Mathura to Manorama: Resisting violence against women in India.* Women Unlimited.

Uberoi, P. (1996). *Social reform, sexuality, and the state.* SAGE Publications.

Chapter 14

Law and Women in India*

Durgabai Deshmukh

Oliver Wendell Holmes said, 'Legislation of today is to meet the social needs of yesterday.' Traditionally, law lags behind social system continually to a society which is constantly outgrowing so that the existing laws and the current needs of society may be called social legislation.

It is one of the primary functions of the modern state to take suitable and timely action to mould social consciousness of the people. If this is not done, to the extent legislation outruns social urge, it remains ineffective. All legislation, therefore, must be accompanied by the effort to bring about social preparedness by an intensive campaign of appeal to, and education of, the people with the purpose of breathing in them a faith in the ultimate utility of the particular legislative measures for promoting the common good and increasing the common welfare. It is only then that the law can give direction, form and continuity to social changes.

We had our Constitution written on 26 November 1949 that came into force in 1950. This declares India to be a sovereign democratic republic which rests on the four pillars of:

Justice (social, economic and political)
Liberty (of thought, expression, belief, etc.)
Equality (of status and opportunity), and
Fraternity (dignity of individual and unity of India).

---

* *Social Change* (March 1972), II, 7–22.

While ours is a sovereign democratic republic with plenary powers of legislation, it is nevertheless subject to the limits set by our Constitution to which all laws must conform. It declares certain inviolable principles which were given to be adhered to in making laws. It says that not all laws are in conformity with powers to pronounce on the validity of laws. All the constitutional validity of law is liable to be examined by it.

Part III confers certain fundamental rights on the citizens. Equality before the law and equal protection of law are guaranteed to all. Discrimination against any citizen on grounds of religion, race, caste, sex, place of birth, etc., is forbidden.

Part IV details the principles which should guide the state in promoting the welfare of the people. These principles are fundamental in the governance of the country. It is the duty of the state to apply these principles in making laws.

The state is required to secure all citizens'—men and women— equality, the right to adequate means of livelihood, equal pay for equal work, etc., right to work, to education and to public assistance in case of unemployment, old age, sickness or disablement, etc.

The Constitution itself provided for making special provisions for women and children. It has, likewise, indicated a priority for the interests of weaker section of the population. The problem of immoral traffic is a part of the problem of traffic in human beings. Beggary is a part of the children's problem.

Social laws would lack effectiveness unless they are backed by public opinion. Neither permissive laws like the Hindu Widow Remarriage Act nor the prohibitive laws like the Child Marriage Restraint Act have had much effect by themselves. This has to be brought out by a slow and gradual process of educating the public.

An attempt is made in this article to give a summary of the position of social legislation at the commencement of the Constitution, from 26 January 1950, and also to give a description of the legislation undertaken during the decade 1951–1961 and an assessment of the present position and prospects for the future.

Fundamental Rights in Chapter II proclaim the equality of all citizens before the law, more particularly equality of sexes. This is very significant in view of the subordinate position to which women were relegated under personal laws that were in force even after the Constitution came into virtue of Article 372. The rights and status of women had been left in a position of subordination. This constitutes a gross anachronism. Next, the Directive Principles impose an obligation on government to establish social justice.

POSITION OF WOMEN IN LAW

More than 2,000 years ago, the women of ancient Hindu community in India enjoyed a fair measure of equality with men in all spheres of human activity—spiritual and religious, teaching and learning, even war and statecraft.

The Rigveda, the Upanishads, Kautilya's *Arthashastra* and many other ancient writings which are available to us today will reveal this rather astounding truth to those who believe that the history of Indian women is one of ignorance, illiteracy and superstitions.

The Vedic tradition of equality of the two sexes continued in the Upanishadic age. The Upanishads expounded the idea of man and woman as the equal halves of a divine unity, each complement of and incomplete without the other. Learned women philosophers of the Upanishadic period like Brahmavadini, Gargi, etc., crossed swords in the conferences of rishis like Yagnavalkya convened at the court of Rajarishi Janaka of Videha. These are only a few illustrations of the truth that women were fully the equals of men.

The Buddhist age continued this Brahmanical tradition of the equality of sexes, and the Theri Nuns and Bhikshunis played an important part of the life of the entire community and did not impose any disability on women to acquire or propagate knowledge, aspire for spiritual eminence or serve in any field of public life.

Deterioration and decay, in this glorious equal status, set in during the past 1,500 years as a consequence of incessant invasions. Social institutions broke down and society suffered a cultural collapse resulting in women gradually losing their freedom and becoming dependent on men. Strict seclusion of women became the rule.

The decline of women's education and activities in public life, so common in Vedic India, of affairs had continued development of Indian society and stunting of women's personality.

The purdah system under which women lived in seclusion and isolated from men, the practice of Sati and the joint-family system under which women were excluded from succession to property were the root causes which gave the impression that Indian women are backward, suppressed and treated almost as chattels.

In the southern part of the sub-continent, which was free from continuous invasions, the position of women did not suggest such deterioration.

With the stabilization of social conditions by the 15th century, there was a revival of Hindu life and a consequent improvement in the status of women.

The advent of the British resulted in the introduction of an alien culture and new economic structure. The women of the middle classes began to adjust themselves to the new world and took to the new education. As far back as 1878, Indian girls studied in the universities and, a decade later, voyaged to far off countries to study medicine and law.

Provision for higher education for women was slow and halting for it was not favoured by the conservative British who were still imposing great many restrictions on women in their own country and had no intention of promoting such progressive measures in the colonies. In spite of every handicap, a new awakening crept into Indian womanhood due to the untiring efforts of social reformers and associations.

Eminent women like Mrs Margaret Cousins, Mrs Sarojini Naidu and many others by their work gave great impetus to this awakening. It was realized that the future of Indian women lay in the independence of the country. It was Mahatma Gandhi, the Father of the Nation, who brought a dynamic change among women, and it was at his bidding that they came out in large numbers to take part in the struggle for India's freedom. It was in the political awakening that we find the renaissance of Indian womanhood. In the 1936 elections, many women entered legislative assembles, municipalities and local boards. The women members of the Constituent Assembly made significant contributions to its deliberations.

The Constitution of the Sovereign Democratic Republic of India guarantees to everyone equality before the law and equal protection of the laws. All citizens are guaranteed equality of opportunity in matters of public appointments, etc. The Vedic ideal of perfect equality of man and woman is today guaranteed by the Constitution. The state can make special provisions for women and children (Article 15), and today, women in free India serve in every sphere of national activity. In conformity with their new status, women enjoy the franchise in equality with men. Universal adult franchise has been conferred by the Constitution, and in the general elections, women exercise their franchise in large numbers.

The next step consisted of reforming the personal laws by which the people are governed in the light of new developments. The laws of the majority community of the land (the Hindus) first received the attention of parliament as the first step in evoking ultimately a Uniform Civil Code for the entire Indian people. During 1955–1956, parliament passed statues reforming Hindu law relating to:

1. Marriage and divorce
2. Succession
3. Adoption
4. Minority and guardianship.

These changes were meant to confer equal status on women and also examine the position of non-Hindu women of the country in these respects.

The first Governor General of India, Warren Hasiting, had declared that as regards inheritance and marriage, caste and other religious usages and institutions, the laws of the Koran were to be administered for the Muslims and the laws of Shastras for the Hindus. Express recognition was given to this decree in the Act of Settlement of 1781. Attempts at modification at the instance of Macaulay were given up by the Second Law Commission which held that both Hindu and Muslim laws derived their authority from religion and that the British legislature was not entitled to make Hindu or Muslim laws.

Later, Queen Victoria laid down that in framing and administering the law, due regard should be paid to ancient rites, usages and customs of Hindus. Successive India Government Acts preserved these laws and Article 372 of the Constitution maintains this position.

Personal laws were supposed to be linked up with religion. The laws thus administered excluded women from all rights of inheritance.

DISABILITIES OF WOMEN IN LAW BEFORE 1955–1956

1. A woman came within the narrow limit of admitted heirs, she took only a limited interest in the divided property of a deceased;
2. Could not be a co-parcener;
3. She forfeited such right if she was unchaste;
4. Was not legally competent to adopt;
5. Her consent was not required to an adoption by her husband;
6. A widow could adopt only within the authority and direction given by her deceased husband;
7. The right of mother though recognized as guardian of her minor children could be defeated by any testamentary appointment made by her husband;
8. A mother could not give away validly her daughter in marriage;
9. She could not appoint a guardian by will;
10. A Hindu woman once married remained wedded to the husband in a tie not dissolved even by the death of her husband, a disability from which the husband was free even during the lifetime of the wife;
11. An illegitimate daughter had no claim against the putative father even to maintenance, whereas an illegitimate son among Sudras was admitted to a share in the putative father's property.

All these disabilities have been removed by four Acts passed in 1955–1956.

1. **Hindu Marriage Act 1955:** Came into force in May 1955.

    a. **Effects:** It codified the law relating to marriage among Hindus (which includes Buddhists, Sikhs and Jains).

    i. It makes monogamy the rule for men as well as for women.
    ii. Age of marriage fixed for women at 15 and for men at 18.
    iii. An idiot or lunatic cannot marry.
    iv. It provides for the registration of marriage.
    v. The grounds for annulment of marriage are very carefully defined. They could be available for either of them.

vi. The court may award costs and maintenance to either spouse against the other and make such other orders as may be deemed necessary for the maintenance and welfare of the children of the marriage.

2. **Hindu Succession Act 1956:** It repealed the Hindu Law to Property Act of 1937. The whole Law of Intestate Succession, which is wholly customary, is resolved into a well-defined set of rules. This Act purports to determine the heir on secular lists of consanguinity and affinity without any discrimination on the ground of sex. The limitations imposed by custom and tradition on the capacity of woman to hold, dispose and transmit have been done away with. It vests a Hindu woman with full ownership in all property, however acquired. The daughter, the widow and the mother now inherit property along with the son and take an equal share with him.

3. **Hindu Minority and Guardianship Act 1956:** Maintenance under the Act is defined to include food, clothing, residence, education, medical attendance and treatment.

   i. Maintenance

      (a) The wife is entitled to maintenance for life. She may live separately from her husband without forfeiting her right to maintenance on certain grounds.

      (b) Children, both legitimate and illegitimate, are entitled to be maintained by parents. This right is enforceable against those who inherit the estate of the deceased.

   ii. Adoption

      (a) Any male Hindu or female Hindu may adopt a son or a daughter.

4. **The Special Marriage Act 1955:** This succeeded an earlier Act of 1872 providing for a form of marriage for persons who do not profess the Christian, Jewish, Hindu religions. The Act of 1872 was amended in 1929 to permit intermarriage among Hindus, Buddhists, Jains and Sikhs. Succession to property is governed in the Indian Succession Act of 1925. The grounds on which either

party to the marriage may obtain judicial separation or dissolution of marriage are laid down in this Act and recourse to the Divorce Act in not necessary.

5. **Prostitution and Immoral Traffic Act 1958:** The policy of the Government of India in respect of prostitution provides for abolition as distinguished from regulation. As a signatory to the International Convention on the Suppression of Immoral Traffic in Women and Children at Geneva, 1921, the government had to undertake legislation to prevent immoral traffic. The Indian Penal Code (IPC) was accordingly amended in 1923 to make the procuring of a girl under 18 years of age for immoral purpose an offence.

Certain Police Acts and Municipal Acts prohibit soliciting in streets and public places and ban the working of brothels within certain defined limits. The Children's Acts enable the authorities to rescue minor girls who may be brought up for a life of prostitution. Certain provisions in laws as Prevention of Prostitution and Immoral Traffic Act have been in force in Bombay, Madras, U.P., Punjab, Bihar, Madhya Pradesh, etc. An All-India Act was felt necessary and such an Act was passed and enforced in 1958. However, it suffered from several drawbacks, because for this (a) the usual police machinery employed was wholly unsuitable and (b) proper benefits of rehabilitation were absent.

WOMEN AND EMPLOYMENT

Marriage

Indian society is still a heterogeneous complex consisting of communities belonging to different religious faiths governed by their respective personal laws. A vast majority of Indians are Hindu. According to Dharma Shastras, a Hindu marriage is a sacrament which creates a sacred and indissoluble tie. A wife does not cease to be a wife even if she is bartered away or deserted by the husband (Manu Smriti Chapter 9 Sloka 46).

Ancient Hindu law recognized eight forms of marriage, such as the Brahma, Daiva, Arya, Prajapatya, Asura, Gandharva, Rakshisa and the Paisacha. In the approved form of marriages, the essential ceremonies are:

1. The formal gift of the bride in front of the sacred fire, and
2. *Saptapadi*—the ceremony of seven steps taken together by the bride and the bridegroom by the recital of the prescribed vows of mutual fidelity.

The Shastras have laid many rules relating to the age of a girl, *varna* (caste), prohibited degree of relationship, etc.

Bigamy was permitted under certain restrictions. There does not appear to be any prohibition regarding the marriage of a widow. It could be safely inferred that in the ancient law of the Hindus, remarriage of a widow and the practice of divorce and remarriage were permitted but not considered to be desirable.

During the British rule, customs and usages of the Hindus had been given prominent recognition and were made the rule of decision in many cases, but certain reforms were effected in the Hindu law by legislative enactments.

1865. The Hindu Widows Remarriage Act was passed which validated the marriage for the dissolution of marriage on the conversion of one of the Hindu married couple to Christianity and the consequent refusal of the other to live with him or her.

1929. The Child Marriage Restraint Act of 1929 was passed to punish the persons concerned in the solemnization of the marriage of a child.

1946. Hindu Women's right to Separate Residence and Maintenance Act conferred on a Hindu woman the right to separate residence under certain conditions such as the husband suffering from loathsome disease, guilty of such cruelty as renders it unsafe, guilty of desertion, if he married another wife, if he keeps a concubine, etc.

POST-INDEPENDENCE REFORMS

The Hindu Marriage Act 1955: Introduced radical changes Hindus as defined under the Act constitute 80 per cent of marriage for all Hindus.

Monogamy is made the rule for man equally as in the case of woman.

For the dissolution of marriage petition for divorce may be presented either by the husband or wife on the ground that the other party (a) is living in adultery, (b) has ceased to be a Hindu by conversion, (c) has been of unsound mind for three years, etc. The wife can present a petition on two other grounds (a) the husband married again before the commencement of the Act or (b) the wife was alive who was married before the commencement.

The provisions of judicial separation as a matrimonial relief is another feature. The relief is equally available to both the spouses.

Another important feature is that difference in caste has become immaterial in regard to the validity of the marriage.

Special Marriage Act of 1954: This provides for a secular form of marriage. Two persons are entitled to marry irrespective of their religious affiliation and the dissolution of their marriage is governed by the provisions of the Act, and the succession to their property is governed by the Indian Succession Act.

MUSLIM WOMEN

The next important community is the Muslims. No progress worthy of mention has been made in giving better rights and status to Muslim women. There is reluctance on the part of government to do anything which may be even remotely considered as an interference with the religious rights of minorities. This, in the absence of a powerful movement of reform within the community itself, would lead to the continuation of the iniquitous and anomalous position of Muslim women. A Muslim man is entitled to have four wives at a time, but a Muslim woman is not entitled to have more than one husband at a time. He has unrestricted, unfettered and unilateral right to divorce at will. The dowry, sometimes, operates as a check against the exercise of divorce and secures proper treatment of the wife, as dowry is an essential part of Muslim marriage and the husband is bound to pay to the wife the agreed amount.

Shariat Act (Muslim Penal Law) Section 5—Dissolution of Muslim Marriage Act 1939, Sections 2 and 6, removed certain uncertainties regarding the grounds of dissolution which existed before, the grounds for a suit for divorce are clearly mentioned in that Act.

RIGHT OF SUCCESSION

The Hindu Succession Act of 1956—This came into force on 17 June 1956. The Act made radical changes in the Hindu law by conferring rights of succession to the daughter and mother simultaneously and equally with the son over both coparcenary property as well as separate property of the deceased.[1]

Section 19 abolished limited estate for women and granted full ownership in the inherited property with retrospective effect.

There was no uniform law applicable to all the Hindus with regard to succession to property, and diverse schools of law were in vogue. Spiritual and religious concepts overweighed considerations with men with regard to succession to property. Even when rights of heirship were conceded to them, there were ordinarily given a limited estate and not full rights of ownership.

The Hindu Succession Act, 1956, besides providing for a uniform set of rules for all Hindus, has introduced a revolutionary change in the law of intestate succession. The basis of heirship specified in the schedule to the Act is blood relationship. The son, daughter, widow and mother of a deceased male succeed together, each taking an equal share. In keeping with the general trend of equality of sexes, no discrimination is made in the matter of heirship on the ground of sex. The doctrine of limited estate, which denied absolute ownership to women inheriting under the prior law, has been swept away with retrospective effect. The son gets no inheritance. The daughter, who was given right of inheritance property with regard to the separate property of her deceased father only in default of a son, son's son, son's son's son or widow, and denied such right in the undivided interest of her father in the coparcenary property, today ranks equally with the son in regard to inheritance in either case. As in the case of a predeceased son in the case of a predeceased daughter, her children can represent her and take the share which she would have taken, had she been alive. These are considerable gains from the point of view of the daughter.

It ought to be mentioned here that in the case of coparcenary property, the law still recognizes the son's right by birth, and the equality conferred on the daughter is restricted to the father's interest in such property. 'Thus if a coparcenary consisted of a father and son and the father died, only half of the father's share in the coparcenary property, that is, one fourth of the total property'. The son will take three-fourths of the property, half in his own right and half of the other half as heir to his father.

The institution of joint-family property and the concept of coparcenary property still continue. But undoubtedly, the daughter today enjoys a much better position, whether the property be coparcenary or the separate property of the father.

Similarly, the mother's position in this respect has been improved, and she has been equated with the son, daughter and widow of the deceased. As a Class I heir, she has been preferred to the father who occupies a place only in Class II in the schedule to the Act.

The widow whose position was improved by an enactment of 1937, which made her an heir along with son with regard to the separate property of her husband, and conferred on her a limited estate in her husband's interest in the coparcenary property, now has an equal footing with the son and daughter.

Thus, the concept of equal status for the two sexes in the law of intestate succession as applied to the Hindu community is obvious. The female heirs take their share by inheritance with full ownership, and this has retrospective effect, that is, the estate of woman, inherited by her, prior to Act. A limited estate is now by operation of law enlarged into a full estate, provided the property was in her possession at the time of passing of the enactment.

Stridhana[2]: 'Nowhere were proprietary rights of women recognized so early as in India'.[3] But the concept of *stridhana* or the separate property of women, has become complicated and even bewildering, owing to the absence of the precise definition in ancient texts or an exhaustive enumeration of properties falling within its ford and owing to conflict between the various authorities. All that is material here is to observe that Hindu law had never subscribed to the view that women are not to be denied proprietary rights. However, only particular descriptions of property belonging to a woman constituted her *stridhana*.

Rules of succession to *stridhana* property, which were highly complicated, have been radically changed by the present Act.

Just as the daughter is given equal right to the father's property along with the son, so also the son, who was hitherto excluded by the daughter, is given equal rights of succession to the Act. 1956 has gone a considerable way in giving effect to the constitutional guarantee of equality of the sexes and realizing the Vedic ideal.

MUSLIM LAW

Rights of heirship of Muslim women in India are governed by Muslim law according to the Hanafi interpretation of the Koran as expounded in the leading text, the Sirajiyyah, in the case of Sunni Muslim. The Koran introduced reforms in the customary law of ancient Arabia, which excluded females and cognates from rights to heirship, by making (a) females and cognates competent to inherit, (b) the wife (or husband) an heir, though as a general rule females were given half of the share of a male.

Islamic law made no distinction between joint and separate property (as Hindu Law), or between movable and immovable property; nor did it confer a limited estate on females as the Hindu Law did; nor did it recognize any right by birth as in Hindu law, nor the principle of representation. Though it is beyond our scope to go into the details of the Islamic law of inheritance, it will suffice our purpose here to note that Muslim women have always had rights of inheritance and heirs in the second class.

The legislatures of the centre and states in free India have made no changes in the personal law of the Muslim community as pointed out earlier, though the constitution of Republic contemplates the coming into existence of a Uniform Civil Code for the entire citizens of this country—a great hope for which there seems to be no immediate prospect of realization, as the Indian legislatures appear to be reluctant to enter the field of the personal laws of religious minorities.

The Shariat Law, again based on the text of the Koran, proceeds on a footing of equality between relations and agnates are placed on a footing of equality.

Though a male heir takes twice as much as a female heir, it should be observed that this was a great reform introduced by the Koran on the pre-Islamic tribal law which denied any right to females.

CHRISTIAN, PARSI, JEWISH WOMEN

Women, other than those governed by the Hindu and Islamic laws, are brought under the Indian Succession Act.

Unlike the position in the personal laws of Hindus and Muslims, a woman's right to succeed on intestacy finds a satisfactory recognition under the Indian Succession Act. Those rules of intestacy are applicable to Europeans, Anglo-Indians, Jews, Armenians, Christians and to the succession of persons whose marriage had been solemnized under the Special Marriage Act and are based on the Statute of Distribution which governed the descent of personality in England prior to 1925.

Where the intestate has left a widow and also lineal descents, the widow is entitled to one-third of the property. The remaining two-thirds is divisible amongst children on the lineal descendants of the same degree equally. Thus, the distinction between the widow is entitled to half the property. These provisions are further subject to the rule in the case of Europeans, Anglo-Indians, Jews and Armenians, that where the net value of the property does not exceed ₹5,000 and where there are no lineal descendants, the widow is entitled to the whole property of the deceased.

ADOPTION AND INDIAN WOMEN

Hindu Law: Adoption in Hindu Law could be only of a son and not of a daughter. It was a 'process for obtaining the substitute of a son, and its purpose was spiritual'.

Women themselves were not allowed to adopt whether they were married or spinsters; and a woman could not be taken in adoption. This inability of the female to adopt or to be adopted is based on religious considerations varying in the different schools.

This disability has been done away with now by the Hindu Adoptions and Maintenance Act, 1956. That enactment has rendered the institution of adoption wholly secular and no longer religious and introduced radical changed in the law. The two changes of importance in our present context are the following.

1. Now, a woman has power to make an adoption—if she is a widow or spinster, or divorced, or if her husband has become an ascetic or apostate or has been declared to be of unsound mind by a competent court. This confers a new power on women.
2. Consent of the wife, of all wives if there be more than one, is necessary before a man, who has a living wife or wives and can make an adoption, unless the wife has become an ascetic or apostate or has been declared to be of unsound mind by a competent court.

Under the earlier law, no such consent was necessary, and a man could adopt even against the wishes of his wife. Today, the wife has almost a power of veto in the matter.

CONCLUSION

Thus, women in India occupy a position of equality with men, not as a result of any aggression, agitation or other violent movements, but as a peaceful revival of the age-old tradition, the glorious heritage of this land; and they worked with equal vigour and enthusiasm in every sphere of nation-building activity, not in any spirit of competition, but in a spirit of cooperation in keeping with ancient tradition. They occupy under the Constitution a position not inferior to that of women in any other part of the world.

Certain sections of the Constitution have been challenged on the ground of religion, caste and community.

Article 14 means that every law that the state passes shall operate equally upon all persons.

(1) Section 497 of IPC exempts a woman from being charged with the abetment of the offence of adultery—this is questioned as contrary to Article 14 of the Constitution. It was upheld in the High Court of Bombay by Justice Chagla saying that Article 15 (3) justifies the provision.

Article 15(1) If the legislature has discriminated only on the grounds of sex, race, caste, etc., and no other factor could possibly have been present, then the law would offend against Article 15(1). What led to the discrimination is not the fact that the woman had a sex different from that of man but that the woman is so situated that special legislation is required to protect her, so Section 497 does not intervene Article 15(1). The Constitution itself makes provision for special provision in the case of women and children by clause 3 of Article 15, which says,

'Nothing in the Article shall prevent the State from making any special provision for women.'

2. Providing maintenance to deserted women was questioned on the ground that it discriminates in favour of women and violates Article 15. Article 15(3) justifies it. It is said that a deserted husband should be awarded maintenance as in the case of a desertion by woman or wife.

3. Hindu Bigamous Marriage Act was questioned on the ground that all denominational legislation as applicable to particular communities' bases on religion is void. It was held by Bombay High Court that the words 'laws in force' in Article 13 did not take in personal laws which are continued in concurrent of a Uniform Civil Code for all citizens throughout the territory of India as an objective. There is nothing to prevent the state from making laws and applying them community wise and territory wise by virtue of 25 (1) to control religious practices. Article 25 (2) empowers the State to make a law for providing for social welfare and reform. The freedom to practise religion is not an absolute right but is subject to public order, morality and health.

4. The Communal (Government Order) of Madras was held to be ultra vires and void as based on community alone.

5. The refusal of admission of a girl student into a men's college under a scheme of better organization of both male and female education does not violate Article 15(1), the provision of separate women's colleges being permissible under 15(3). While the men students have no right of admission into a women's college, the right of women's admission into men's college is a matter of regulation by the authorities of the college.

NOTES

1. See Professor S. Venkatraman, The Hindu Succession Act 1956. Studies, 1956. S.C.J.P. 195–205.

   'Article 2, "Hindus" include Sikhs, Jains, Buddhists and all other religious with the exception of Christians, Muslims, Parsees and Jews, not spiritual or religious considerations.'

2. *Stridhana*—Personal property of women. Originally, their jewels and ornaments extended to other property, including that which was part of the husband's estate.

3. Sir Gooroodass Banerjee, The Hindu Law of Marriage and Stridhana, 4th edition, 1915. 337.

QUESTIONS FOR CONSIDERATION

1. How far have women availed themselves of the rights given to them in Parts III and IV?

2. To what extent have they exercised their rights when they are violated, or;

3. Has the legislation remained on the statute book, or has it been activity operating in practice/

4. Is education a determining factor?

5. Special Marriage Act and Indian Succession Act?
   Dr Sakuntala Myer's case.

6. Adult Franchise, etc. Would they be effective in the absence of education?

7. Does lack of education stand in the way?

Chapter 15

Geographies of Indian Women[*]
A Tale of Contesting Spaces

Nandini Rai

INTRODUCTION

The expansion of human capabilities is a necessary measure to translate economic growth into human progress. Human capability as defined by Sen is 'the ability of human beings to lead meaningful lives and also to enhance the substantive choice they have' (Sen, 1997: 1959). It means that if a violence-free environment makes a woman more efficient in delivering economic results, then it is indeed human progress. In the context of the developing world and especially India, various practices of atrocities against women, for example, rape, sexual harassment and wife beating are common across states. Male violence against women is considered in India as a common cultural practice and often described as a normal pattern of male behaviour.

Freedom from violence has remained a neglected issue in development studies, and it is necessary to have improved quality of life (Drkze and Khera, 2000; Mcllwaine, 1999). This may also be cited as the reason why developing countries like India, in spite of recognition regarding economic development, are still lagging behind in all-round human development. Thus, protection from violence may be thought of as one of the 'capabilities' that contribute to the quality of life (Sen, 1985). Scholars worldwide have recognized violence as a denial of basic human rights. And the fact that, in contemporary society,

[*] *Social Change* (September 2007), *37*(3), 78–91.

most of the physical violence is perpetrated against women further enhances the relevance of this issue.

The very extensive literature on gender and violence concludes that the pattern of violence is intrinsically associated with space and place (Evans and Herbert, 1989; Pain, 2000). Feminist geographers have explored and elaborated extensively their understanding on how place and space interact with the construction, practice and politics of gender. Women and men not only work and live in space, they also create social identities through space (Mackenzie, 1986). Such research exemplifies feminist geographers' concerns with how social identities, including gender, and the social production of space are mutually constituted in particular sites and places. It is reflected in my work on Delhi (Rai, 2006) that, in some neighbourhoods of Delhi, strong socio-spatial identities or sense of space among residents are implicated in the form of lower reporting of violence.

It is also true that under the framework of space situatedness of human relationships can be understood better, as the latter is an outcome of a continuous process of socio-spatial relation over the physical space.

Following the above propositions, the present chapter attempts to understand how place is central to the understanding of an event like violence at home. And similarly, the geographical place in understanding gender and also the extent to which geography matters to the study of gender and familial violence in India. Questions like the differences in places and its relation to violence—at local or regional scales, what sustains them and how they are changing will be addressed by analysing different data sets. This is relevant in the current context, as scholars have revealed the variations in gendered experience of violence across the globe. However, the central argument of the chapter is to explore the contested embodiments of spaces constructed in relationship to systems of gendered power relations. It can be elaborated by saying that gender practices of men and women are central to the ways in which spaces are constructed. The contestation is due to the dynamic practices which are constantly recreated and re-formed, as the spaces they construct are changed and transformed. Broadly, the chapter has tried to convey that gender on its own does not create inequality; the problem is power relations (Collins, 2002; Connell, 1995).

Along the lines of these themes, further arguments will be arranged by utilizing the information from the second and the third rounds of the National Family and Health Survey (NFHS) published in 1998–1999 and 2005–2006 respectively and the latest publication (2005) of the National Crime Records Bureau (NCRB). Indicators like violence by spouse and women participating in household decisions, that is, data on autonomy, have been used to elucidate the propositions related to the contesting nature of gender and violence in India. Here, the magnitude of autonomy exercised in different states of India has been used as an indicator for the present situation of power relations in the corresponding areas. The reason for choosing this as an indicator for power control is that autonomy determines the degree of access or control over materials within the family or in a society at large (Dixon-Mueller, 1978). Thus, before we proceed to a detailed discussion on the data, it will be appropriate to have a clear understanding of some of the principles on which the chapter is conceptualized.

GENDERED SPACES, VIOLENCE AND POWER RELATIONS

The trajectory of acknowledging gender as a developmental problem began to initiate its path towards the middle of the 20th century. Earlier, gender as an independent category was not recognized by academia and was merely treated as a biological difference between man and woman. Gender is constructed differently in different social locations because of its relational character, thus, acknowledging the role played by related social conditions. Social constructional changes have huge consequences for women depending on where they are situated, circumstances shaped by social structures of race, class and gender. It is accepted by scholars that women and men experience spaces and places differently and these differences shape the social constitution of gender as well as place. While discussing place, it is pertinent to mention the ways in which spatial division—that between public and private and between inside and outside—play such a central role in the social construction of gender divisions. The codification of place between private and public also drives its compartmentalization from the safety perspective. Until recently, private, which is exclusively to women—thus excluding her from public, has always been propagated as safe and violence-free.

But narratives from the daily lives of women in India reveal the fact that familial environment at home which is the only claimed place for women is not free of violence. Private places are the places around which women weave their identities, and that is also contested by exerting patriarchal control. It re-establishes the fact that places are made through power relations which construct the rules which define boundaries. The boundaries are both social and spatial—they define who belongs to a place and who may be excluded. Thus, spaces and places where we live are not fixed and they are not natural. The practice of exclusion and a separation between the 'domestic and public sphere' can be aptly understood within the framework of patriarchy.

Walby (1989) refers to the six structures of patriarchy, one of which is related to male violence. She opines that violence by men is not a random phenomenon but that it is connected with the social and structural elements of society. It is practised in a form of showing power of men over women. Spousal violence constitutes a set of various practices of potential power over women. This kind of violence is different, as it is not a result of a few deranged men but is a normal pattern of male behaviour. Overall, patriarchy has two forms, where one is based on the relative exclusion of women from social life and domination in the private sphere of home. However, one point that needs our attention is how male violence can be explained by the theory of patriarchy. One elaboration is that certain relations are gendered, and processes are more focused on the matrix of association between women and men than others. The fact is that gender is implicated in the fundamental constitution of life and it reflects on the daily practices in society.

CONCEPTUALIZING THE PROBLEM

Broadly, the central theme of the present essay is on gendered spaces and exploration of the contested embodiment of home space by Indian women. The chapter attempts to look at private spaces such as the home, as a site of exclusion and contestation. The home has traced the socially significant and contested place of women in India. Exclusion of Indian women from their own home by the practice of familial violence and suppression against them—where public is already claimed to be a restricted site for her—embodies the contested spaces of private and public. The construction of a hostile terrain inside the home and controlled spaces outside its boundary constructs a contestation of spaces.

Drawing on secondary data, I propose to discuss the contested location of Indian women within the framework of familial violence, primarily by analysing some facts from the latest publication of NFHS (2005–2006). The NFHS, since 1992–1993 has been conducting large-scale representative sample household data regarding emerging issues on family welfare. Issues like spouse violence and women's autonomy have also been addressed by the agency as a question of family welfare. The NCRB data regarding women-related offences will also be used to substantiate the arguments.

The main purpose behind this exercise is to explore how identity, meaning and power are constructed, bounded by, and contested through location.

SPACES OF THEIR OWN?

Social status of women is a by-product of the existing internal structure in the community. To take the obvious example, the sense of place for women is different from that for men. However, it can also be interpreted in other ways, as the sense of place for women is principally determined by cultural practices. And along such practices, spaces for women are also delineated in society. Social relations in different places are arranged along the internal structure of domination and subordination stretched out at every level from household to village. One of the earliest discussions of patriarchy reflects that the social map of patriarchy created uneven spaces. Spaces are constructed along certain activities and, thus, some places are called 'feminine' and others 'masculine'. Scholars have argued that possibilities for behaving in particular ways depend on the meaning given to femininity in particular discourses and those meaning are grounded in various socio-cultural spaces. And it has been found that present conditionalities of spouse violence in India can be studied under the framework of gender–space and power relations. The following paragraphs will throw some more light on this issue. The analysis is based on the various data sets mentioned earlier, brought out by the Government of India at regular intervals.

Table 15.1 *Cruelty by Husbands and Relatives against Women in India*

					Figures in %
S. No.	States	2005	S. No.	States	2005
1	Andhra Pradesh	12.5	10	Madhya Pradesh	7.0
2	Bihar	8.9	11	Maharashtra	9.3
3	Gujarat	7.6	12	Orissa	7.8
4	Haryana	4.8	13	Punjab	8.9
5	Himachal Pradesh	7.5	14	Rajasthan	9.5
6	Jammu and Kashmir	4.1	15	Tamil Nadu	13.7
7	Jharkhand	5.2	16	Uttar Pradesh	4.1
8	Karnataka	0.4	17	Uttarakhand	5.1
9	Kerala	0.1	18	West Bengal	3.2
	INDIA	5.2			

Source: NCRB, 2005.

It is reported by NCRB that there has been an overall increase in cases of cruelty to women by husbands and relatives (NCRB, 2005). However, the percentage share of the southern states is greater (Table 15.l), but northern states are also not faring any better.

Studies on violence have shown that aggression against women by their spouse is essentially an exercise of power difference (Deutsch, 2007). Various agencies have reported that aggression against women is spread across all kinds of spaces, that is, physical and personal. Table 15.1 shows that both northern and southern states of India have a dismal record of spouse violence. However, if we see the spread of violence over territorial spaces, western and central India do not perform as poorly as other parts.

The social arrangement of Indian society is such that in the southern states, women are positioned relatively better, while men seem to have obtained the locus of cultural value primarily in the northern region. Southern states also have a record of a better quality of life for women and, on various occasions, sense of personal spaces have been asserted by them by initiating activities like campaigns against drinking (anti-arrack movement in the early 1990s) and microfinance activities for less dependence on men. Thus, the process of 'reclaiming spaces' (Raju, 2007) has been initiated along the lines of creating awareness spaces by women in the southern states. Scholars are of the opinion that under such circumstances, women try to acknowledge abusive activities against them without hesitation and that may affect the magnitude of violence reported in the area. However, that does not mean that other areas reporting a lower number of cases have a lesser magnitude of violence. It can be mentioned, in passing, that the spatial approach in studying gender issues has been criticized, that, contemporaneity of gendered spaces could be understood better by seeing it more as a social process of symbolic encoding and not by geography imposed by patriarchy. But it is also true that however conventional the approach of patriarchy is, it provides a better explanation for spousal violence in India.

At the outset, the current report by NFHS (2005–2006) displays exclusionary practices against women across the states. Though it is acknowledged by the author that it entails a limitation of a relatively small, sample-based survey, but since the issues are of serious concern to women, the data can be used to throw some light on their situation. The picture emerging from the analysis is that there has been a significant rise in the number of cases reported (Table 15.2). The dividing line between north and south India, that is, Rajasthan, Madhya Pradesh, Bihar and West Bengal have reported a steep rise in the number of cases of spousal violence. While in the 21st century, India is aspiring to achieve gender equity in all sectors, women's spaces have been contested.

While discussing representation of spaces, Lefebvre (1991) talks about lived spaces which are appropriated and altered by society. Women in India have hardly been able to appropriate and alter the spaces in order to claim their rights. The process has been slow due to the higher proportion of illiterate women in Indian society. The lower the literacy, the higher will be the exclusionary attempts (Merry, 2003). Both the second and third rounds of the NFHS surveys depict that illiterate women experience more incidences of violence at the hands of their spouses (Table 15.3). It is also true that as they progress educationally, the number of such incidences reduce.

Table 15.2 *Spousal Violence in Major States of India*

S. No.	States	NFHS 2[a]	Figures in % NFHS 3[b]
1	Bihar	24.9	59.0
2	Rajasthan	9.8	46.3
3	Madhya Pradesh	19.7	45.8
4	Uttar Pradesh	20.8	42.4
5	Tamil Nadu	36.0	41.9
6	West Bengal	15.7	40.3
7	Orissa	22.9	38.5
8	Jharkhand	–	37.0
9	Andhra Pradesh	21.2	35.2
10	Maharashtra	16.7	30.7

Source: NFHS.
Note: [a]1998–1999, 2nd round; [b]2005–2006, 3rd round.

Table 15.3 *Women's Educational Status and Spouse Violence in India*

S. No.	Educational Background	NFHS 2	Figures in % NFHS 3
1	Illiterate	23.6	42.0
2	Less than middle	16.7	33.1
3	Middle complete	12.1	28.2
4	High school complete and above	5.9	17.6

Source: NFHS.

At the state level also, the level of literacy and frequency of violence has a strong relationship. It is reflected in Table 15.4 that illiteracy leads to exclusionary practices. Women who are illiterate are more vulnerable to violence at the hands of family members. The beta value from the linear regression model value suggests that a rise in the illiterate population may cause increased disharmony in spousal relationships.

Table 15.4 *Relationship between the Level of Education and Spousal Violence*

Variables	Illiteracy	Less than Middle	Middle Complete	High School Complete
Spousal violence	0.97[a]	0.95[a]	0.96[a]	0.87[a]

Source: NFHS, 2005–2006.
Note: [a]Significant at 0.01

Recent investigations by scholars have revealed that power and control of the wife are the central issues in the incidence of marital violence. Abusive husbands have a more stereotypical attitude to sex roles and also try to control women's space. The issue of controlling women's spaces can be understood with the concept of 'autonomy'. Although the concept of autonomy is about her strength in the family, it is also true that despite the active role that women have played in challenging oppressive structures, it is they who are first marginalized in the social sphere. Present study has concluded that increased female autonomy is correlated to an improved quality of living. The information pertaining to autonomy has been drawn from the recent publication of NFHS–3, where questions related to normal household decision-making have been asked of female respondents. Various dimensions of autonomy have been covered and issues pertaining to who takes the decision on how to spend money, decisions about healthcare, household purchases, visiting relatives, etc. were elaborately covered. It is interesting to observe that in the Indian context, merely taking decisions on the above aspects cannot be declared as empowerment. Though it is just a tip of the iceberg, it does reflect some existing reality. However, various studies have tried to relate the dimensions of autonomy with marital violence. The authors have also tried to investigate this factor with the threat of violence by their husbands (Byrne, 1992). Most of the studies have tried to situate the contest between women 'who are seen to be the repository of tradition, and their inviolability has been a powerful tool as a cultural defence against modernization' (Verma, 1995). Nonetheless, the control over a woman's body as the symbolic space has often involved oppression.

NFHS–3 shows that places of regions that have offered higher responsible roles to women have recorded better familial conditions. Areas with a higher degree of autonomy for women show fewer chances of spousal violence.

Table 15.5 shows that areas possessing traditional patriarchal values have offered minimal amount of autonomy to their women inhabitants. Here, the most common belief shared in order to control women's sexuality is of confining them within the home and placing them in predominantly subordinate and familial positions as daughters and sisters.

Table 15.5 *Women Facing Spousal Violence and Participating in Household Decisions in the Major States in India*

			Figures in %
S. No.	States	Spousal Violence	Autonomy
1	Bihar	59.0	46.7
2	Rajasthan	46.3	46.3
3	Madhya Pradesh	45.8	47.4
4	Uttar Pradesh	42.4	51.3
5	Tamil Nadu	41.9	69.2
6	West Bengal	40.3	40.2
7	Orissa	38.5	55.3
8	Jharkhand	37.0	59.0
9	Andhra Pradesh	35.2	55.7
10	Maharashtra	30.7	63.8
11	Chhattisgarh	30.0	52.1
12	Uttarakhand	27.9	48.2
13	Gujarat	27.6	56.7
14	Haryana	27.3	56.3
15	Punjab	25.4	52.3
16	Karnataka	20.0	47.9
17	Kerala	16.4	62.5
18	Delhi	16.3	69.5
India		37.2	52.5

Source: NFHS, 2005–2006.

A graphical presentation of autonomy scale and practice of spousal violence in India shows that areas with a low concentration of violence have a better record of women's autonomy (Figure 15.1). Autonomy as a determinant to threat at home is similar in the context of both rural and urban areas (Figures 15.2 and 15.3).

Places of women are contested in discourses of resistance. Mapping patriarchy highlights their social construction and their potential for multiple interpretations. The construction of 'sexual space' paralleled

Figure 15.1 Women's Autonomy (Urban)   Women Facing Spouse Violence (Urban)

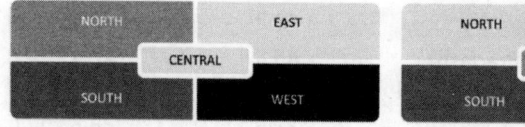

Figure 15.2 Women's Autonomy   Women Facing Spouse Violence

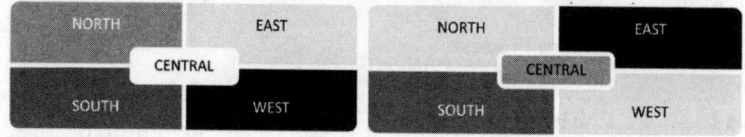

Figure 15.3 Women's Autonomy (Rural)   Women Facing Spouse Violence (Rural)

Source: NFHS, 2005–2006.

	Highest	North, consist of states like Delhi, Haryana. Himachal Pradesh, Jammu and Kashmir, Punjab and Rajasthan
	Higher	
	Medium	South: Andhra Pradesh, Karnataka, Kerala, Tamil Nadu. Central: Madhya Pradesh, Uttar Pradesh
	Lower	East: Bihar, Orissa, and West Bengal
	Lowest	West: Goa, Gujarat and Maharashtra

the construction of space to be colonized and also in terms of 'sexual control'. In the urban Indian context, more urbanized states such as Maharashtra, Tamil Nadu and Kerala have reported higher autonomy for women. Here, the contestation is present in the sense that spaces of women are resisted by higher spousal violence in spite of the fact that they enjoy greater freedom of expression (especially in Tamil Nadu). If we take a cursory look at this aspect, we find that the empowerment is working in the form of better reporting of such cases. Another reason that may be sited is that these states are experiencing 'role reversals', where women are taking over (Deutsch, 2007). Such interactions may redefine gendered spaces in India. On a similar path, rural areas in Bihar and Rajasthan have the worst record of women's autonomy and threat to violence is higher. It has been generally evidenced in rural areas and it is also found in research that abusive husbands hold more traditional sex-role stereotypes than others, and this creates a greater likelihood of violence. Women face more alienation from the people and from the possibilities of unmediated social interaction and thus increased control by men over the production and use of space. Here, women are placed within the domestic sphere where they are associated with reproduction, cleaning, cooking and sexual and ego-servicing, which are not regarded as 'economic' and therefore are unpaid. Mental work performed by men is romanticized as superior to such work and this leads to exploitation within the private sphere.

CONCLUSION

The situation of familial violence in India clearly demonstrates that gender disparity prevails in its spatial structure. The situation calls for an urgent stand as spaces that are traditionally identified as feminine, exhibit a greater amount of vulnerability. Women are marginalized in public spaces as it is claimed to be non-feminine, but spaces other than this also seem to be contested. To a great extent, and in innumerable ways, women in our society are made vulnerable, economically and socially, by gendered cultural practices across the nation. In some parts (the patriarchal heartlands of the north), women have often internalized their oppression so well that they hardly view it as an oppression of their rights. It is evidenced in the chapter that northern Indian states registered a phenomenal rise in incidences of spousal violence, refuting the claims of empowerment and revealing their disadvantageous situation. Gender embeddedness seems so pervasive that even those women who are in places of higher learning have not been able to escape these constraints. However, information related to education and the magnitude of gendered violence by NFHS exhibits an encouraging picture. Women with higher literacy face less oppressiveness, even though the overall framework of patriarchy seems to dominate the region. Hence, it appears that women in India retain their primary identity as producers, and their capacities and activities in privatized spaces of the household are contested.

REFERENCES

Andersen, M. L. August 2005. 'Thinking About Women: A Quarter Century's View', *Gender and Society*. 19 (4): 437–455.

Bhat, R. L. and Namita Sharma. 2006. 'Missing Girls: Evidence from Some North Indian States', *Indian Journal of Gender Studies*. 13 (3): 351–374.

Bipul Malakar Roy and Tapa Roy. 2005. 'Reproducing Human Capital', *Social Sector Development in India*. pp. 145–162. New Delhi: Deep and Deep Publications.

Blunt, A. 2006. 'Home, Community and Nationality: Anglo-Indian Women in India', in Raju, S., M. Satish Kumar and Stuart Corbridge (2006) *Colonial and Post-Colonial Geographies of India*, pp. 49–69. New Delhi: SAGE Publications.

Byrne, Christina, A. and Ileana Arina. 1992. Autonomy as a Predictor of Marital Violence, http://www.eric.ed.gov, 20 July 2007.

Collins, P. H. 2002. Symposium of West and Fenstermaker's 'Doing Difference.' In S. Fenstermaker and C. West (eds.), *Doing Gender, Doing Difference: Inequality, Power and Institutional Change*. New York: Routledge.

Connell, R. W. 1995. *Masculinities*. Berkeley: University of California Press.

Deutsch, F. M., February 2007. 'Undoing Gender', *Gender and Society*. 21(1): 106–127.

Dixon-Mueller, Ruth. 1978. *Rural Women at Work: Strategies for Development in South Asia*. Published for Resources for the Future. Baltimore: Johns Hopkins Press.

Drtze. J. and Khera. R. 2000. 'Crime. Gender. and Society in India: Insights from Homicide Data.' *Population and Development Review* 26 (2). 335–352.

Dutta, A. 2005. 'MacDonaldisation of Gender in Urban India: A Tentative Exploration', *Gender, Technology and Development*, 9 (1): 125–135.

Dyson, Tim and Mick Moore. 1983a. 'On Kinship Structure, Female Autonomy and Demographic Behaviour in India.' *Population and Development Review.* 9: 35–60.

Estrada, William. D. 1999. 'Los Angeles' Old Plaza and Olvera Street: Imagined and Contested Space', *Western Folklore.* 58 (Winter): 107–129.

Evans. D. J. and Herbert. D. T. (eds.) 1989. *The Geography @Crime.* pp. 1–15. London: Routledge Publications.

International IDEA (2002) The Challenge of Women's Political Participation in Guatemala. http://www.idea.int/ 30 July.

Jayawardena, K. and Malathi de Alwis. 1996. *Embodied Violence: Communalising Women's Sexuality in South Asia,* pp. ix to xxiv. New Delhi: Kali for Women.

Lefebvre. H. 1991. *The Production of Space.* Oxford: Blackwell Publications.

Longhurst, R. 2002. 'Geography and Gender: A 'Critical' Time? *Progress in Human Geography,* 26 (4): 544–552.

Massey, Doreen. 1994. *Space, Place and Gender,* Minneapolis: University of Minnesota Press.

McDowell, L. 1999. 'Gender, Identity and Place: Understanding Feminist Geographies', United Kingdom: Polity Press.

Mcllwaine, Cathy. 1999. 'Geography and Development: Violence and Crime as Development Issues', *Progress in Human Geography.* 23 (3): 453–463.

Michell, D. March 1995. 'The End of Public Space? People's Park, Definitions of Public and Democracy', *Annals of the Association of American Geographers,* SS (1): 108–133.

Mukherjee, C., Preet Rustagi and N. Krishnaji. October 27, 2001. 'Crime Against Women in India: Analysis of Official Statistics,' *Economic and Political Weekly,* 4070–4080.

National Crime Records Bureau. 2005. 'Crime Against Women', *Crime in India,* New Delhi: Ministry of Home Affairs, Government of India.

National Family and Health Survey. 2005–2006. http://www.nfhsindia.org/factsheet.html

Nussbaum, M. C. 1995. 'Human Capabilities, Female Human Beings' in Martha, Nussbaum and Jonathan Glover *Women, Culture and Development: A Study of Human Capabilities,* pp. 61–104, Oxford: Clarendon Press.

Nussbaum, M. C. 1995. 'Human Capabilities, Female Human Beings', in *Women, Culture and Development: A Study of Human Capabilities,* pp. 61–104 in Nussbaum, M. C. and Jonathan Glover (eds.). Oxford: Clarendon Press.

Pain, R. 2000. 'Place, Social Relations and the Fear of Crime: A Review'. *Progress in Human Geography.* 24 (2): 365–381.

Rai, N. 2006. 'Social Space and Crime in Delhi', unpublished thesis submitted to Jawaharlal Nehru University.

Raju, S. 2006. 'From Global to Local: Gendered Discourses, Skills and Embedded Urban Labour Market in India', in Raju, S., M., Satish Kumar and Stuart Corbridge (2006), *Colonial and Post-Colonial Geographies of India,* pp. 99–119. New Delhi: SAGE Publications.

Raju, S. 2007. 'Reclaiming Places and Spaces: The Making of Gendered Geography of India'. Paper presented at the national seminar on *Gender and Space: Discourses on Women in India*. New Delhi: India International Centre.

Ray, Sawmya. 2006. Legal Construction of Domestic Violence, *Sociological Bulletin*, 55 (3): 427–448.

Safilos-Rothschild, Constantina. 1980. 'A Class and Sex Stratification: Theoretical Model and its Relevance for Fertility Trends in the Developing World', pp. 189–202 in C. Holn and R. Machensen (eds.) *Determinants of Fertility Trends: Theories Re-Examined*. Ordina Edition: Liege.

Sally, Engle Merry. 2003. 'Constructing a Global Law-Violence against Women and the Human Rights System', http://www.journals.uchicago.eduJ/u,l y 30, 2007.

Schmelzkopf, Karen. July 1995. 'Urban Community Gardens as Contested Space', *Geographical Review*, 85 (3): 364–381.

Scmidt, Elizabeth. December 1990. 'Negotiated Spaces and Contested Terrain: Men, Women, and Law in Colonial Zimbabwe, 1890–1939', *Journal of Southern African Studies*, 16 (4): 622–648.

Sen, A. 1997. 'Editorial: Human Capital and Human Capability', *World Development*, 25 (12): 1959–1961.

Sen, A. 1985. *Commodifies and Capabilities*. North Holland: Amsterdam.

Townsend, Janet. G. March 1991. 'Towards a Regional Geography of Gender', *The Geographic Journal*, 157 (1): 25–35.

Verma, R. R. 1995. 'Femininity, Equality, and Personhood', *Women, Culture and Development: A Study of Human Capabilities*, pp. 433–443 in Nussbaum, M. C. and Jonathan Glover (eds.). Oxford: Clarendon Press.

Walby, S. May 1989. 'Theorising Patriarchy', *Sociology*, 23(2): 215–234.

West, C. and Don H. Zimmerman. June 1987. 'Doing Gender', *Gender and Society*. 1 (2): 125–151.

Chapter 16

A Gender Critique of AFSPA*
Security for Whom?

Amit Ranjan

INTRODUCTION

On the night of 16 December 2012, a young paramedical student was raped and murdered by five men and a youngster in New Delhi, India. Though this was not the only rape and murder that took place that year, it shook the conscience of the nation, leading to strong countrywide protests over the issue of exacerbating crimes against women in India. What compelled/impelled a large number of people—who usually remain silent or apathetic—to join in the protests in Nirbhaya's[1] case was the space and the time of the incident: the rape and murder was committed on the roads of south Delhi, the centre of India's socio-economic and political power. It also took place at a time when the government of the day was under pressure because various allegations of corruption had been surfacing against its ministers. The rape provided an opportunity for people to vent their anger against a recalcitrant political establishment. Reacting to the situation, the government set up a commission, under former Chief Justice of India J. S. Verma, to look into the issue of growing sexual violence against women and come out with some recommendations on how to control this menace. As a result, debates over a comprehensive definition of rape entered the public domain. In some public debates, and in the Justice Verma Commission report, the issue of rapes in areas which came under the

* *Social Change* (December 2015), *45*(3), 440–457.

Armed Forces (Special Powers) Act (AFSPA) too figured. In those debates, demand for revoking such draconian Act was made by a few participants.

In the middle of the ongoing public debate on rape, suddenly another headline flashed on the news channel: two Indian Army soldiers had been killed and mutilated at the India–Pakistan border in Jammu and Kashmir (J&K). One had even been decapitated. This incident put an end to all media debates on sexual violence and laws and moved to what steps India must take to give befitting reply to its 'enemy'? Political spin doctors exploited this incident to enhance the feeling of nationalism, thus isolating the voices strenuously demanding laws to protect women from the region under the AFSPA. About the beheading, television journalist Barkha Dutt, in 'Confession of a War Reporter', first published in *Himal South Asian* (2001), wrote that such mutilations are not an aberration but a practice commonly carried out by soldiers from both countries.[2] This barbaric act is undertaken to display each country's 'valour' over the other. This news not only stemmed the agitation on the Nirbhaya incident but, more significantly, it even stopped future discussions on rapes in regions under AFSPA. For people from the 'mainland',[3] rapes in those areas are a part of 'collateral damage' to secure the territorial integrity and sovereignty of the country.

In this article, an attempt has been made to address the following questions. What is security? Why do rapes take place in areas under AFSPA? Why do people, including many women groups, remain silent or give their tacit consent to such rapes? Apart from the introduction and conclusion, this article is divided into three main sections.

The first section discusses the conceptual and theoretical aspects of security and how and why AFSPA is actually a paradoxical instrument of security. The second is divided into two sub-sections in which rapes carried out by security forces in the Kashmir Valley and the North-East have been discussed. In the third section, reasons for the silence over rapes in areas under the AFSPA are discussed. In this article, the term armed forces is used for both the army and paramilitary personnel. The word North-East is used for the general area and does not imply a particular state or states, as the study is about rapes in the region and not in any individual state, where AFSPA is in operation. Appendices have been used to furnish provisions of important reports discussed in this article.

SECURITY AND AFSPA: THE PARADOX

The word security is derived from the Latin word *securitas*, which, in its primary classical use, means the condition of individuals of a particularly inner sort. It denotes composure, tranquillity of spirit, freedom from care—the condition that Cicero called the 'object of supreme desire' or 'the absence of anxiety upon which the happy life depends' (Rothschild, 2007). The new idea of security as principally a collective good, to be ensured by military or diplomatic means—the idea that came into European prominence in the period of the revolutionary and Napoleonic wars—is strikingly different. In its new content, individuals and the state are being been seen as similes for one another (Rothschild, 2007). After the emergence of a new understanding of state-centric security, the individual(s) have become subservient to the state, which is an abstractly imagined entity. A shift from state-centric security policy was made in 1991, after the disintegration of the Soviet Union. A bewildering array of issues, including demographics, resource scarcity and global warming, were now seen as having security implications (Bajpai & Pant, 2012: 2). As a result of the broadening of concept, security is now being defined as the absence of insecurity and threats, that is, freedom from both 'fear' (of physical, sexual or psychological abuse, violence, persecution or death) and 'want' (of gainful employment, food and health). It therefore deals with the capacity to identify threats, to avoid them when possible and to mitigate their effects when they do occur (Tadjbakhsh & Chenoy, 2009: 39). But despite making the definition more inclusive, the state remains the main actor in any form of security architecture.

Paradoxically, in all its variants, the nation state, which is responsible for providing security to its citizens, is a repository of violent means and has the legitimate authority to use them, and it has used them even against its own citizens. The state is a human community that (successfully) claims the monopoly of the legitimate use of physical force within a given territory (Gerth & Mills, 1991: 78). Anthony Giddens (1985: 20) defines the state as a political organization whose rule is territorially ordered and which is able to mobilize the means of violence to sustain that rule. To legitimize the use of violence, the state constructs threats and defines security in terms of insecurity. The given threats do not just exist out there but have to be created (Dibyesh, 2012).

In the modern world, most of nation states have created situations and constructed threats to use violence against their ethnic, sectarian religious minorities. In Chile, during Auguste Pinochet regime (December 1974–March 1990); in China, during the Cultural Revolution (1966–1976); in Bosnia (April 1992–December 1995); in Pakistan (in 1971 and also presently, in the name of fighting against terrorism); and the latest, in Syria, since 2013, the state has not shied away from using lethal weapons to kill its own citizens. Most of the large-scale violence confronting the world after 1989 is intra-state as opposed to inter-state, and for a significant portion of the world's population, the state is the main source of insecurity (Bajpai & Pant, 2012: 2).

THE IMPLEMENTATION OF AFSPA IN KASHMIR AND THE NORTH-EAST

The Indian state is not different from other countries. It has used violent means in many parts of the country but the North-East[4] and J&K[5] are different. Here, special powers have been given to the armed forces under the AFSPA, which came into force in 1958. It was first applied to the north-eastern states of Assam and Manipur and was amended in 1972 to extend to Tripura, Meghalaya, Arunachal Pradesh, Mizoram and Nagaland (Singh, 2007: 310–311). In 1991, the Kashmir Valley was put under this Act, to fight against the rise of militancy which erupted in 1989, followed by Jammu in 2001.

Tracing its history, AFSPA is based on a colonial law—(The) Armed Forces (Special Powers) Ordinance, 1942. Soon after independence, this law was implemented to fight Naga insurgency. What really transpired Pandit Jawharlal Nehru to support such Act is not very clear.[6] In many of his letters to the Governor of Assam, Sayid Fazal Ali, Chief Minister of Assam, Bishnu Ram Medhi and the Army Chief show that Nehru was not in favour of a military solution to the problem.

In his letter to B. R. Medhi, dated 13 May 1956, Nehru wrote:

There can be no doubt that an armed revolt has to be met by force and suppressed. There are no two opinions about that and we shall set about it as efficiently and effectively as possible. But our whole past and present outlook is based on force by itself being no remedy. We have repeated this in regard to the greater problems of the world. Much more, we must remember this when dealing with our own countrymen who have to be won over and not merely suppressed. (Nehru, 2004: 171–174)

In another letter to B. R. Medhi, dated 27 August 1956, Nehru wrote:

I still adhere to my opinion that large armed forces should not be maintained in the Naga Hills. Of course an adequate number have to be sent there or kept there, but a situation like this is not met by numbers but by techniques. I do not think those different techniques have been employed satisfactorily yet. I hope in future we shall do it. (Nehru, 2005: 172–173)

Nehru was fully cognizant of the fact that laws included in AFSPA had an 'invasive' potential and would impact human rights, yet in parliamentary debates, he upheld the security and unity of the country as paramount (Dam, 2013: 80–81).

Introducing the Bill, the then Home Minister, Govind Ballabh Pant, said:

Certain misguided sections of the Nagas were involved in arson, murder, loot, dacoity (robbery) etc...so it has become necessary to adopt effective measures for the protection of the people in those areas...in order to enable the armed forces to handle the situation effectively when such problem arises hereafter, it has been considered necessary to introduce this bill. (Chasie & Hazarika, 2009: 6)

At that time, some Members of Parliament (MPs) from Manipur and other places opposed the Bill. L. Achaw Singh, an MP from Manipur, said it was 'an unnecessary anti-democratic measure...a lawless law' (Chasie & Hazarika, 2009). The most vocal opponent of the Bill in Parliament was Surendra Mahonty from the political party Gantantra Parishad. Opposing it, he said:

If anybody analyses this bill, one will find that it seeks to indemnify any person for any act done for quelling disturbance in an area declared so by either the Governor of Assam or the Chief Commissioner of Manipur within their jurisdiction...[W]e want a free India. But we do not want a free India with barbed wires and concentration camps, where *havaldars* (sergeants) can shoot any man. If that is the concept of free India, I think I may as well be a traitor. (Subramanian, 2011)

Since then, AFSPA has been debated and interpreted in different ways. It is justified by the Government of India on the grounds that the region is an integral part of India, which many groups in the North-East do not recognize, so it cannot be permitted to secede (Menon & Nigam, 2004: 141). Technically, AFSPA is implemented after an area is declared disturbed under the Disturbed Areas Act, which facilitates the summoning of armed forces to the aid of civil authorities when they are unable to control armed insurrection. The call can be made by the state government or the centre (Hazarika, 2013). This law consists of six sections (see Appendix), of which the most damning are to be found in the fourth and sixth sections. The former enables security forces to 'fire upon or otherwise use force even to causing of death'. The latter says no criminal prosecution will lie against any person who has taken action against any person under this Act Hazarika, 2013. Due to the immunity given to the personnels acting under this law, in the 54 years of its operation, not a single army, or paramilitary officer or soldier has been prosecuted for murder, rape or destruction of property Hazarika, 2013. In his representation to the Justice Reddy Committee, a (retired) major general stated that of the 55,000 cases registered against the armed forces, there have been only three convictions (S. Chakravarti, 2012: 262). In 1997, in the Naga People's Movement for Human Rights *vs* Union of India, the only case where the constitutional validity of the AFSPA was challenged, the Supreme Court of India granted its legitimacy.

RAPES IN AREAS UNDER AFSPA

Rape, as a practice in war zones, is embedded in the patriarchal construction of a woman's body as a symbol of the territory or 'property' of the enemy which has to be violated (Chenoy, 2002: 28). This phenomenon's timeless ubiquity can be traced back to early accounts in the Torah, in Homer, in the Anglo-Saxon chronicles and in mythological events like the rape of the Sabine women. The most well-documented historical wars include examples of mass rape. Rape is well documented in the war between Jews and their enemies described in the Bible, in Anglo-Saxon and Chinese chronicles, in medieval European warfare during Crusades, in Alexander's conquest of Prussia, in Viking marauding, in the conquest of Rome by Alaric in pithy wars of ancient Greeks and so on (Gottschall, 2004: 129–136). Rape is also a form of power used by a community or a group over the other by carrying out violent acts on the others' women, who are supposed to be protected by their menfolks; raping them means that their men are not of valour. There is also a concept of 'colonizing'[7] an area through rape or the impregnation of women. To get rid of it, many post-war societies carry out mass abortion programme, which is just another form of violence but for a different cause. For centuries, the international community has overlooked this issue, until in 1998, the International Crime Tribunal set up by the United Nations (UN) for genocides in Rwanda made a landmark decision by defining rape as a crime of genocide under international law.[8]

To be fair, not all rapists want to commit this act; some are forced into it by their superiors. Some captive rapists who have been interviewed have substantiated this: Borislaw Herek, from Sarajevo, who admitted to raping and shooting three unarmed women, said that if he did not do it, his superiors would have sent him 'to the worst frontline' or to jail and that they would have taken away the Muslim's house that had been given to him (Card, 1996). Also during the Bangladesh war of liberation, in 1971, many soldiers from west Pakistan saved the lives of women from east Pakistan (Mookherjee, 2006).

Rape during any form of group violence has deep roots in India. In modern times, during Partition-related violence in 1947, which started as an ethnic cleansing (Ahmed, 2011: 4–6), 75,000 women were thought to have been abducted and raped by men whose religions were different from their own; and indeed, sometimes by men of their own religion too (Butalia, 1998: 5). Butchery was carried out against women by their family members to secure individual or community's 'honour'. Women who were raped were either killed by their rapists or by their family members or they committed suicide. In Thoha Khalsa, in Rawalpindi district, 90 Sikh women and children committed suicide Butalia, 1998. The inhumanity did not stop even after people settled down in their respective areas. Since 1947, during all communal riots, rapes have been carried out against women from the 'other' community. Shockingly, the state or the community has never filed complaints against the perpetrators of rape because by doing so, the individual or group would be labelled 'weak' as compared to the rival group. Besides this, there have been incidents when security forces carried out rape to establish the power of the Indian state over the aggrieved group. In March 1979, the tribal women from Santhal Pargana were raped by the personnel of the Central Reserve Police Force (CRPF) to emasculate an ongoing agitation which sought to reclaim tribal land under the leadership of the Jharkhand Mukti Morcha—then a minor political party (Kumar, 1993: 142).

In areas where AFSPA is enforced, rape, security and patriarchy are intertwined. The Indian state defines rape to secure its patriarchal interests[9]; therefore, perpetrators in uniform do not get convicted and punished for their crimes. Like other parts of India, in regions under AFSPA, the onus to prove that rape has been committed lies with the victim and not on the accused; but unlike other parts, in areas under AFSPA, the accuser or victim can be alleged to be a foreign agent, a militant or a supporter of a terrorist group. And for that reason, she can be killed, as happened in Thangjam Manorama's rape case. False evidence, like a grenade and other items, were produced by the Assam Rifles to prove that she was a part of a militant group. Reason for a murder after rape is often cited as a move to erase the evidence, but it is more than that: the murder of women after rape symbolizes cultural violence in the society (Galtung, 1990: 291–305).

RAPES IN THE KASHMIR VALLEY

After AFSPA was clamped down in 1991 in the Kashmir Valley, the molestation of women during army crackdowns were seen as 'normal' acts. While the army did not expect them to leave their houses during crackdowns, Kashmiri women, fearing harassment, preferred to do so as they do not want to be alone inside when security forces raided their homes. During search operations, security personnel have been known to leer, extort, initiate unsolicited physical contact, psychologically torture and sexually assault girls/minors and women (Chakravarti, 2002). In 1997, in Wavoosa, seven women were reportedly raped during a 'routine cordon and search operation'. In 1991, between 23 and 100 women, including minors and elderly, those pregnant and those with disabilities, were allegedly raped by the 4th Rajputana Rifles unit in Kunan Poshpora (Chatterji, 2012). Apart from these two cases, there are many other infamous rape cases perpetrated by security forces in the Kashmir Valley, including Chhanpora and Pazipora (1990); Chak Saidpora (1992); Haran (1992); Theno Budapathary Kangan (1994); Bihota (2001); Handwara (2004); and Kazi (2009). One of the latest cases was in May 2009 when two residents of Shopian, Asiya Jan and Nilofar Jan, were raped, reportedly by more than one person, and murdered. They were 17 years and 22 years of age, respectively (Chatterji, 2012). After the incident, the police did not file even a first information report. Instead of speaking out against this flagrant violation of human rights, particularly the rights of women to live safely and with dignity, and instead of taking speedy and firm steps to bring the perpetrators to book, the state and the new administration, first, denied the rape of the women and then, attempted to justify it by saying that the women went there on their own and their murder was an accident or a suicide (South Asian Citizens Web, 2009).

Indeed, in all rape cases, the state's machinery has sided with the perpetrators and not with the victim. One of the early examples of this was the Press Council of India's *Crises and Credibility* report on Kashmir, set up under B. G. Verghese, after the Kunan Poshpora rape incident in 1991. The report's findings echoed the arguments made by security forces; the committee concluded that the rape incident was concocted and 'women tutored and coerced into making state-ments derogatory to their own honour and dignity' (Manchanda, 1991). In his book *Curfewed Night*, Basharat Peer has mentioned about the rape of Mubeena Ghani, who was raped by a group of soldiers from the Indian paramilitary force, a few hours after her marriage in May 1990. The incident reminded him Sadat Manto's classic *Khol Do*.[10]

The security issue in Kashmir highlights the irony and enduring contradiction in the state's attempt to secure Kashmir, which becomes synonymous with bodily insecurity for Kashmiri women—a contradiction that undermines democracy, institutional integrity and state legitimacy each day, every year (Kazi, 2009). In his testimony presented at the 52nd UN Commission on Human Rights, Professor William Baker said: 'Rape in Kashmir is not the result of a few undisciplined soldiers but rather an active strategy of Indian forces to humiliate, intimidate and demoralise the Kashmiri people' (Parvez, 2014). In 2013, the then Chief Minister of J&K, Omar Abdullah, responding to a question raised in the Legislative Assembly, gave a statement that more than 5,000 cases of rape have been registered since 1989. In 2013 alone, 70 cases of sexual violence were registered against the security forces Parvez, 2014.

As a result of the prevailing situation in the Valley, women face many sorts of restrictions on their attire or movements and they are being denied many of their natural and civil–political rights. The age of marriage has dropped down to 14–15 years, which, before 1991, was 21–22 years. Once a girl has been raped, it becomes impossible for her to marry, so parents are eager to marry off their daughters at a younger age (U. Chakravarti, 2002: 113–148).

RAPES IN THE NORTH-EAST

The other region with same experience under the AFSPA is the North-East. The Kashmir Valley has an advantage that it is a disputed territory between India and Pakistan over which wars have been fought and therefore, it gets regular media coverage, unlike the ongoing conflicts in Manipur or Nagaland, which are shrouded in mystery (Kak, 2011). The term North-East was formalized by the British colonial administration as a frontier region. It was subsequently endorsed and retained by the Indian state under the 'native' vocabulary as Purvanchal. Today, the North-East is a unique (more aptly a strange) ghettoized entity (Bhagat, 2009).

Unlike the Kashmir Valley, most of the rape cases in this region are unknown to the outside world. The only case which has attracted the attention of civil society was that of Thangjam Manorama. She was taken from her residence in the early hours of 10 July 2004 by three Assam Rifles personnel. A few hours later as daylight began, her body, bearing signs of torture and rape, as well as bullet wounds, was recovered 4 km from her house (Vajpeyi, 2009). This incident gained publicity because, reacting to this rape and murder, about 30-odd middle-aged to elderly women came out and stood naked in front of the headquarters of the Assam Rifles in Kangla, Manipur, on 15 July 2004. They carried banners that read 'Indian Army Rape Us', 'Indian Army Take Our Flesh', etc. Vajpeyi, 2009. As the protests became more vocal, the Justice Upendra Commission was set up by the Manipur government to inquire into her death. Even the Government of India, after a barrage of protests from human rights groups, set up the Justice Jeevan Reddy Committee which was mandated to look into the utility of the AFSPA. It recommended repealing of the Act. However, the AFSPA has remained intact and in operation Vajpeyi, 2009. Recently, in April 2015, an allegation was made that soldiers had raped a 13-year-old girl and molested her mother and grandmother, who tried to rescue the teenager (Bagchi, 2015). This incident took place in the Karbi Anglong district of Assam.

A report on incidents that have occurred during 2004–2008 was compiled by a group of serving and retired judges associated with the district courts in Manipur. One particular incident that was submitted by the Manipur government to the Supreme Court triggered fresh demands from human right activists for a probe by a special investigation team into the nearly 1,700 extra-judicial killings that have occurred in the past 35 years (Nair, 2014). The report says:

Crimes against women, more particularly relating to sexual harassment committed by armed forces, are now increasing in some states like ours. They (armed forces) think themselves placed at the elevated status of impunity by the legislation and think wrongly they are given licence to do whatever they like. (Nair, 2014)

After a probe, Manoj Kumar Singh, District Judge of Imphal East, confirmed the rape of a 15-year-old schoolgirl by two army personnel on 4 October 2004. She committed suicide the same day. Upendra Singh, a retired district judge, reported the death of Amina, a young mother who was shot by CRPF personnel while putting her baby to sleep at home Nair, 2014.

Besides rapes and molestations by soldiers, women in these areas also face the ire of various groups fighting the army and villagers. Such groups force their rules over individuals, especially women, restricting their movements and rights. In the Kashmir Valley, militant groups from time to time issue fatwas dictating dos and don'ts for girls. The Dukhtaran-e-Millat (Daughters of the Nation), under the leadership of Asiya Andrabi, acts as an instrument of social control over women's activities in the Valley. In these areas, relationships develop between soldiers and local women. Such a situation does not get accepted by the locals.[11] These women are looked at suspiciously by other villagers. To fulfil their dream, in some cases, these women have to leave the village to marry their soldier husbands (Sundar, 2014: 37).

AFSPA, due to its provisions, has attracted the ire not only of members of the civil society and/or human rights bodies but also by the Indian judiciary and various commissions set up to look into it or deal with its cases. In April 2013, while looking into a case where two Border Security Force, a paramilitary organization, personnel were engaged in the killing of a Kashmiri teenager in 2010, the Supreme Court held that the provisions of AFSPA could not summarily replace general laws and that all such cases need not be tried in defence services court. It asserted that AFSPA's protection was limited to acts conducted in the line of duty. Rape and murder were 'normal crimes' that should be prosecuted in criminal courts (Sen, 2013). The Justice Verma Committee, in its 2013 report, also cited the Supreme Court's observation that security forces should not be given protection under AFSPA, especially in cases of rape and sexual assault. It said, 'systematic or isolated sexual violence, in the process of internal security duties, is being legitimized by AFSPA which is in force in large parts of our country' (Ramachandran, 2013; also, see Appendix).

FRACTURED IDENTITY AND GROUP-BASED DISCRIMINATIONS

As rapes occur frequently in areas under AFSPA and culprits are never found guilty, the question arises: Why there are no mass protests against such incidents in the North-East or the Kashmir Valley? One possible reason is a fractured, multi-ethnic society in India and 'imaginations'. Though all communities are part of the country, not all are considered to be equal members. Some groups are considered to be pillars of the nation, while others become a part simply because of territorial reasons. The former dominate, sketch out and narrate (Said, 1993) the idea of India, which is then imposed and followed by the others. Putting it more clearly, Paul Brass observes that the Indian state is pluralist only in relation to cultural groups which remain within the broadly defined Hindu fold, but discriminates against non-Hindu minorities and groups such as some tribals whose Hindu identity is marginal. Certain groups are considered to be 'enemies' of the nation; and security is needed against them. This links security closely with identity politics. How we define ourselves depends on how we represent others. The other gets reduced to being a danger, and hence an object that is fit for surveillance, control, policing and possibly extermination (Dibyesh, 2012).

It is well known that many people from the so-called 'mainland' of India carry biased perceptions about people from Kashmir and the North-East. Kashmiri Muslims are seen as unpatriotic and as owing allegiance to an entity other than India. 'They are considered as "intimate and viral other"', who can never be fully trusted and must be assimilated into the norm to become obedient national subjects' (Chatterji, 2012).

About the people from the North-East, the derogatory term *chinki* is used. This popular assertion of difference is translated into being 'dangerous', invoking the label 'disturbed' for the region where control through extraordinary measures becomes imperative. The people of the region are seen as defiant tribes who have to be assimilated and Indianized. Thus, movements for self-determination, sovereignty and autonomy in various parts of the region are addressed by the state, with its coercive might, by using counter-insurgency measures backed by laws like AFSPA (Singh, 2007: 310–311). The democracy for which India prides itself comes alive in the North-East only during elections. The young tribal boy or girl grows up with the Indian soldier as the living symbol of a country; they begin to hate from the day their village is first raided (Bhaumik, 1998).

In the Kashmir Valley, the security forces find that Muslims here form the majority, making this area demographically different from any other part of India. In the North-East, people are ethnically different from the 'mainland'. These differences allow the security forces to freely unleash violence against them. The discrimination in terms of imposition of this sort of laws was seen when the army declined to carry out such a large-scale operation against the Maoists in central India—an area considered to be the heartland of the country. Another tangible example of discrimination against people from the North-East is the way the state is treating Irom Sharmila, who has been on a hunger strike for the last 13 years against the killing of 10 civilians by paramilitary forces near Imphal, the capital of Manipur. Her only and constant demand has been the repeal of AFSPA. Instead of engaging with her in a democratic way, she has been ignored by the state and various cases have been imposed against her.

IDENTITY AND THE GENDER ISSUE

In such background, these perceptions and identity play a significant role on what is considered to be a gender issue. Though gender itself is an identity, in India, it is subservient to religion, caste and ethnicity. This has led to the participation of women in identity-based riots and to remain silent or even support the rapes of women from the 'others' group. The gradual communalization of women made them actively participate in the Ram Janambhoomi–Babri Masjid movement. During the post-Godhra riots in Gujarat, prominent women leaders in the Bharatiya Janata Party remained indifferent to the rape and humiliation of Muslim women, and refused to take a gender-sensitive stand on the state government's brutal attitude and the calculated inaction of the police forces (Dutta, 2003). This trend repeated itself in 2014 during the Muzaffarnagar riots where a few Muslim women were raped by Hindu men. There is an increase in number of women directly participating in communal programmes. In 2008, during tensions over the Amaranth shrine's land transfer issue, Dogra Hindu women participated in large numbers. They shouted abusive anti-Kashmiri and anti-Muslim slogans. They were seen beating their chests, displaying swords and *trishuls* (tridents) and taking pledges that they would keep going till the land was restored back to the Amaranth Shrine Board (Bhatia, 2009).

Against such a background, it is difficult to garner solidarity over the issue of rapes in India. A few left-wing groups, women organization and some individuals have been vociferous in their protests, but their voices against rape in the impacted areas almost get drowned out. They are not powerful enough to challenge the security discourse set up by the majority. The feeling of otherness is strong in Indian society, which is socially, culturally and religiously based on the practice of discrimination against the outsider, though this keeps on changing according to the wishes of the dominant group. Ethnic groups in the North-East and Muslims, especially from Kashmir, in the popular imagination, are seen as the 'other', so if anything untoward happens in these areas, it does not disturb the popular definition of 'security'.

CONCLUSION

In this article, the question that has been raised is: whether AFSPA provides security to individuals or to the state? Answers may differ but, largely, the response would be in the negative. The force used by the state gives a justified reason to the other groups to use counter-force. As civilians face the brunt of AFSPA in form of rapes, physical violence and so on, they get alienated and start supporting or sympathizing with forces challenging the presence of any symbol of the state. This has been happening in the Kashmir Valley and in the North-East. Many youths from Kashmir studying in various parts of the country are happy when India loses a cricket match. This symbolic opposition is because they have witnessed the brute face of the Indian state and have developed a hatred towards anything related to Indian nationalism.

In this article, it has been argued that supporting state-centric security often jeopardizes the lives of non-dominant groups. The treatment of people from Kashmir and the North-East, both regions under AFSPA, is an anti-thesis to any theory of security. Even Chanakya, who is praised by the proponents of Indian nationalism and a state-centric security establishment, gives importance to the citizens of a country, even when they are in a mood to rebel. He writes:

When the local persons are abetting (with foreigners) the means to be employed to suppress them are conciliation (*sama*) and gifts (*dana*). The act of pleasing a man with a high rank and honour is conciliation;

favour and remission of taxes or employment to conduct state works is what is termed as gift. (Kautilya, 1956: 384)

There are institutions which have stakes in the continuation of AFSPA. They relate every debate on the AFSPA with 'national security', where no lapses and compromises can be made. Civil society has almost accepted this thinking. As a result, rapes or murders in areas under AFSPA are rarely questioned. Pressure to revoke this Act has never been put by people on their democratically elected leaders. This is the position not only in the 'mainland' but in the areas under AFSPA too: A few co-opted individuals and stakeholders are present who are using this law for their personal benefit. This class does not worry about atrocities carried out against marginal communities.

APPENDIX

THE ARMED FORCES (SPECIAL POWERS) ACT, 1958

(Act 28 of 1959)

An Act to enable certain special powers to be conferred upon members of the armed forces in disturbed areas in the States of Assam, Manipur, Meghalaya, Nagaland and Tripura and the Union Territories of Arunachal Pradesh and Mizoram.

BE it enacted by Parliament in the Ninth Year of the Republic of India as follows.

1. Short title and extent—

    (1) This Act may be called the Armed Forces (Special Powers) Act, 1958.
    (2) It extends to the whole of the State of Assam, Manipur, Meghalaya, Nagaland and Tripura and the Union Territories of Arunachal Pradesh and Mizoram.

2. Definitions—In this Act, unless the context otherwise requires,

    (a) 'armed forces' means the military forces and the air forces operating as land forces, and includes any other armed forces of the Union so operating;

(b) 'disturbed area' means an area which is for the time being declared by notification under s.3 to be a disturbed area;

(c) All other words and expressions used herein, but not defined and defined in the Air Force Act, 1950 or the Army Act 1950, shall have the meanings respectively attached to them in those Acts.

3. Power to declare areas to be disturbed areas—If, in relation to any State or Union Territory to which this Act extends, the governor of that State or the administrator of that Union Territory of the central government in either case, is of the opinion that the whole or any part of such State or Union Territory, as the case may be, is in such a disturbed or dangerous condition that the use of armed forces in aid of the civil power is necessary, the governor of that State or the administrator of that Union Territory or the central government, as the case may be, may, by notification in the official gazette, declare the whole or such part of such State or Union Territory to be a disturbed area.

4. Special powers of the armed forces—Any commissioned officer, warrant officer, non-commissioned officer or any other person of equivalent rank in the armed forces may, in a disturbed area:

(a) if he is of opinion that it is necessary so to do for the maintenance of public order, after giving such due warning as he may consider necessary, fire upon or otherwise use force; even to the causing of death, against any person who is acting in contravention of any law or order for the time being in force in the disturbed area prohibiting the assembly of five or more persons or the carrying of weapons or of things capable of being used as weapons or of fire-arms, ammunition or explosive substances;

(b) if he is of opinion that it is necessary so to do, destroy any arms dump, prepared or fortified position or shelter from which armed attacks are made or are likely to be made or are attempted to be made or any structure used as a training camp for armed volunteers or utilized as a hideout by armed gangs or absconders wanted for any offence;

(c) arrest without warrant, any person who has committed a cognizable offence or against whom a reasonable suspicion exists that he has committed or is about to commit a cognizable offence and may use such force as may be necessary to effect the arrest;

(d) enter and search without warrant any premises to make any such arrest as aforesaid or to recover any person believed to be wrongfully restrained and confined or any property reasonably suspected to be stolen property or any arms, ammunition or explosive substances believed to be unlawfully kept in such premises, and may for that purpose use such force as may be necessary.

5. Arrested persons to be made over to the police—Any person arrested and taken into custody under this Act shall be made over to the officer in charge of the nearest police station with the least possible delay, together with a report of the circumstances occasioning the arrest.

6. Protection to person acting under Act—No prosecution, suit or other legal proceeding shall be instituted, except with the previous sanction of the central government, against any person in respect of anything done or purported to be done in exercise of the powers conferred by this Act.

7. Repeal and saving

(1) The Armed Forces (Assam and Manipur) Special Powers Ordinance, 1958, is here by repealed

(2) Notwithstanding such repeal anything done or any action taken under the said ordinance shall be deemed to have been or taken under this Act, as if this had commenced on the 22nd day of May, 1958.

Source: http://indianarmy.nic.in/Site/RTI/rti/MML/MML_VOLUME_3/CHAPTER__03/457.htm

JUSTICE (RETD) J. S. VERMA COMMITTEE ON RAPES IN AREAS UNDER AFSPA OFFENCES AGAINST WOMEN IN BORDER AREAS/ CONFLICT ZONES

1. We now address a very important, yet often neglected, area concerning sexual violence against women—that of legal protections

for women in conflict areas. Our views on this subject are informed by the plight of a large number of women from areas in Kashmir, the Northeast, Chhattisgarh, Odisha and Andhra Pradesh who were heard at length in the course of preparing our report. We are indeed deeply concerned at the growing distrust of the State and its efforts to designate these regions as 'areas of conflict' even when civil society is available to engage and inform the lot of the poor. We are convinced that such an attitude on the part of the State only encourages the alienation of our fellow citizens.

2. At the outset, we notice that impunity for systematic or isolated sexual violence in the process of internal security duties is being legitimized by the AFSPA, which is in force in large parts of our country. It must be recognized that women in conflict areas are entitled to all the security and dignity that is afforded to citizens in any other part of our country. India has signed the International Convention for the Protection of All Persons from Enforced Disappearance, which has to be honoured. We therefore believe that strong measures to ensure such security and dignity will go a long way not only to provide women in conflict areas their rightful entitlements, but also to restore confidence in the administration in such areas leading to mainstreaming.

3. To this end, we make the following recommendations for immediate implementation:

    (a) Sexual violence against women by members of the armed forces or uniformed personnel must be brought under the purview of ordinary criminal law;

    (b) Special care must also be taken to ensure the safety of women who are complainants and witnesses in cases of sexual assault by armed personnel;

    (c) There should be special commissioners—who are either judicially or legislatively appointed—for women's safety and security in all areas of conflict in the country. These commissioners must be chosen from those who have experience with women's issues, preferably in conflict areas. In addition, such commissioners must be vested with adequate powers to monitor and initiate action for redress and criminal prosecution in all cases of sexual violence against women by armed personnel;

(d) Care must be taken to ensure the safety and security of women detainees in police stations, and women at army or paramilitary checkpoints, and this should be a subject under the regular monitoring of the special commissioners mentioned earlier;

(e) The general law relating to detention of women during specified hours of the day must be strictly followed;

(f) Training and monitoring of armed personell must be reoriented to include and emphasize strict observance by the armed personell of all orders issued in this behalf;

(g) There is an imminent need to review the continuance of AFSPA and AFSPA-like legal protocols in internal conflict areas as soon as possible. This is necessary for determining the propriety of resorting to this legislation in the area(s) concerned; and

(h) Jurisdictional issues must be resolved immediately and simple procedural protocols put in place to avoid situations where police refuse or refrain from registering cases against paramilitary personell.

Source: http://www.thehindu.com/multimedia/archive/ 01340/ Justice_Verma_Comm_1340438a.pdf

NOTES

1. The real name of the girl who was raped and murdered by six people on 19 December 2012 in New Delhi was Jyoti Pandey. She is called Nirbhaya because, according to Indian law, a rape victim's real name cannot be disclosed by the authorities or the media.

2. In her article, Dutt talks about beheaded bodies during the Kargil conflict between India and Pakistan in 1999.

3. This term is used by scholars from peripheral regions for people living in north and central India (see Baruah, 2005).

4. Though the term indicates homogeneity, the reality is different. The area is heterogeneous with many differences amongst the ethnic groups. The northeast comprises eight states: Assam, Sikkim, Manipur, Meghalaya, Mizoram, Arunachal Pradesh, Tripura and Nagaland. AFSPA is enforced in parts of Assam, Manipur and Nagaland.

5. J&K is under the AFSPA, but it is the Kashmir Valley where militancy is present. The tortures and rapes mainly take place in the Valley and not in

Jammu. The Kashmir Valley is inhabited by Muslims, while the majority in Jammu are Hindus.

6. The 1950s saw a growing number of Chinese incursions in the north-east border. There were also reports of Pakistani engagements in the region. Simultaneously, there was a rise in the number of separatist groups. All these factors might have contributed and influenced Nehru to promulgate AFSPA.

7. One of the reasons to rape women from 'other' group is to impregnate her. As the child she gives birth to contain sperms of male from 'other' group, the linkage between two remains intact for the future. This is one of the reasons why mass abortion programme was launched in some post-mass raped societies.

8. Available at http://www.unictr.org/Portals/0/English%5CAnnualReports% 5Ca-54315.pdf

9. In India rape has been redefined many times. This has become possible because of feminist groups, which from time to time have challenged the then existing partial definition of rape. See Baxi (2014); also, see Agnes (2002).

10. During Partition-related madness, a father finds his daughter in a hospital ward a few days after she has gone missing. The doctor in the ward asks her father to open a window, *khol do*, for his daughter. When she hears the doctor's phrase, the daughter drops down her pants. Having being repeatedly raped, she associates the phrase *khol do* (open up) with the rapist's command to undress.

11. Such cases have occurred in many war zones. See Mookherjee (2011). In this chapter, she has also disclosed that a few Bengali women were saved by Balochi soldiers posted in east Pakistan because of the relationship they developed. Also, some Bengali women went to Pakistan and married the soldiers they loved.

ACKNOWLEDGEMENT

The author is thankful to Dr Jinee Lokaneeta, Associate Professor at Drew University, for going through the first draft and valuable suggestions.

REFERENCES

Agnes, F. (2002). Law, ideology and female sexuality: Gender neutrality in rape laws. *Economic & Political Weekly*, 37(4): 844–47.

Agnihotri, I., & Mazumdar, V. (1995). Changing terms of political discourse: Women's movement in India, 1970s–1990s. *Economic & Political Weekly*, 1869–78.

Ahmed, I. (2011). *Punjab bloodied, partitioned and cleansed: Unravelling the 1947 tragedy through British reports and first person accounts*. New Delhi: Rupa Publications.

Anderson, P. (2013). *The Indian ideology*. New Delhi: Three Essays Collective.

Bagchi, S. (2015, April 13). Protests in Guwahati against army after 'rape' of minor. *The Hindu*. Retrieved from http://www.thehindu.com/news/national/other-states/protests-in-guwahati-against-army-after-rape-of-minor/article7096056.ece

Bajpai, K., & Pant, H. V. (Eds.). (2012). *India's national security: A reader*. New Delhi: Oxford University Press.

Baruah, S. (2005). *Durable disorder: Understanding the politics of Northeast India*. New Delhi: Oxford University Press.

Baxi, P. (2014). *Public secrets of law: Rape trials in India*. New Delhi: Oxford University Press.

Bhagat, O. (2009). Preparing for a cohesive Northeast: Problems of discourse. In S. Baruah (Ed.), *Beyond counter-insurgency* (pp. 25–48). New Delhi: Oxford University Press.

Bhatia, M. (2009). Women's mobilisation in the Jammu agitation: Religion, caste and gender identity. *Economic & Political Weekly*, 44(26–27): 447–453.

Bhaumik, S. (1998). North East India: The evolution of a post colonial region. In Partha Chatterjee (Ed.), *Wages of the freedom: Fifty years of the nation-state* (pp. 310–27). Delhi: Oxford University Press.

Butalia, U. (1998). *Other side of silence: Voices from the partition of India*. New Delhi: Penguin.

Card, C. (1996). Rape as a weapon of war: Women and violence. *Hypatia*, 11(4): 5–18.

Chakravarti, S. (2012). *Highway 39: Journey through a fractured land*. New Delhi: Harper Collins Publications, Fourth Estate.

Chakravarti, U. (2002). Kashmir diary: Seven days in armed paradise. In U. Butalia (Ed.), *Speaking peace* (pp. 113–48). New Delhi: Kali for Women.

Chasie, C., & Hazarika, S. (2009). *The state strikes back: India and Naga insurgency*. East-West Centre. Retrieved 2 February 2015, from http://www.eastwestcenter.org/fileadmin/stored/pdfs/ps052.pdf

Chatterji, A. (2012). Witnessing as feminist intervention in India-administered Kashmir. In Ania Loomba & Ritty Lukose (Eds.). *Feminisms in South Asia: Contemporary interventions* (pp.181–203). New Delhi: Zubaan.

Chenoy, A.M. (2002). *Militarism & women in South Asia*. New Delhi: Kali for Women.

Dam, S. (2013). *Presidential legislation in India*. Cambridge: Cambridge University Press.

Dibyesh, A. (2012). The violence of security: Hindutva's lethal imaginaries. In Rowena Robinson (Ed.), *Minority studies in India* (pp. 287–304). New Delhi: Oxford University Press.

Dutt, B. (2001, June). Confession of a war reporter. *Himal South Asian*. Retrieved 4 January 2013, from http://old.himalmag.com/component/content/article/5140-confessions-of-a-war-reporter.html

Dutta, N. (2003). Gujarat and majority women. In Krishna Chaitanya (Ed.), *Fascism in India: Faces, fangs and facts* (pp. 355–358). New Delhi: Manak Publications.

Galtung, J. (1990). Cultural violence. *Journal of Peace Research*, 27(3): 291–305.

Gerth, H. H. & Mill, C. W. (1991). *From Max Weber: Essays in sociology*. London: Routledge.

Giddens, A. (1985). *The nation state and violence: Volume two of a contemporary critique of historical materialism*. Cambridge: Polity Press.

Guha, R. (2007). *India after Gandhi: The history of the world's largest democracy*. London: Macmillan.

Gottschall, J. (2004). Explaining wartime rape. *The Journal of Sex Research*, 41(2): 129–36.

Hazarika, S. (2013, February 12). An abomination called AFSPA. *The Hindu*.

Kak, S. (2011). What are Kashmir's stone pelters saying to us? *Economic & Political Weekly*, 45(37): 12–16.

Kautilya. (1956). *Arthashatra* (5th Ed.). Trans. R. Shamasastry. Mysore: Mysore Printing and Publishing House.

Kazi, S. (2009). Shopian: War, gender and democracy in Kashmir. *Economic & Political Weekly*, 44(49): 13–15.

Kumar, R. (1993). *The history of doing: An illustrated account of movements for women's rights and feminism in India 1800–1990*. New Delhi: Kali for Women.

Manchanda, R. (1991). Press Council report on the army in Kashmir. *Economic & Political Weekly*, XXVI(3): 1899–900.

Menon, N., & Nigam, A. (2004). *Power and contestation: India since 1989*. Hyderabad: Orient Longman.

Mookherjee, N. (2006). Remembering to forget: Public secrecy and memory of sexual violence in the Bangladesh war of 1971. *The Journal of the Royal Anthropological Institute*, 12(2): 433–450.

———. (2011). Love in the time of 1971: The furore over Meherjaan. *Economic & Political* Weekly, 46(12): 25–27.

Nair, H. V. (2014, October 4). There is no respect for human life: Armed forces 'raped or killed' nearly 2,000 Manipur civilians in 35 years, say judges. *Daily Mail Online*.

Nehru, Jawaharlal (2004). *Selected Works of Nehru Vol. 33*, ed. by H.Y. Sharada Prasad, A.K. Damodaran and Mushirul Hasan. New Delhi: Jawaharlal Nehru Memorial Foundation.

———. (2005). *Selected Works of Nehru Vol. 34*, ed. by H.Y. Sharada Prasad, A.K. Damodaran and Mushirul Hasan. New Delhi: Jawaharlal Nehru Memorial Foundation.

Parvez, A. (2014, October 15). On the fringes of India's political and moral consciousness. Retrieved 28 January 2015, from http://www.warscapes.com/opinion/fringes-india-s-political-and-moral-consciousness

Peer, B. (2008). *Curfewed nights*. New Delhi: Random House.

Ramachandran, S. K. (2013, January 24). Don't allow army men to take cover under AFSPA, says Verma. *The Hindu*. Retrieved from www.thehindu.com/multimedia/archival/01340/justice_verma_comm_130438a.pdf

Rothschild, E. (2007). What is security? In Barry Buzan & Lene Hansen (Eds), *International Security, Vol. III* (pp. 1–34). New Delhi: SAGE Publications.

Said, E. (1993). *Culture and imperialism.* New York: Vintage.

Sen, M. (2013, June 19). Right to rape. *The Telegraph.*

Sharada Prasad, H. Y., Damodaran, A. K., & Hasan, M. (Eds.). (2004). *Selected works of Jawaharlal Nehru, Vol. 33.* New Delhi: Jawaharlal Nehru Memorial Foundation.

———. (2005). *Selected works of Jawaharlal Nehru, Vol. 34.* New Delhi: Jawaharlal Nehru Memorial Foundation.

Singh, Ujjwal Kumar. (2007). *The state, democracy and anti-terror laws in India.* New Delhi: SAGE Publications.

South Asian Citizens Web. (2009, June 21). Women's groups condemn state cover-up in Shopian case (in Kashmir). Accessed on 2 April 2014, from sacw. net/article 976.html

Subramanian, S. (2011, November 21). The long view: AFSPA's bitter roots. NYtimes.com. Retrieved 24 January 2015, from http://india.blogs.nytimes. com/2011/11/21/the-long-view-afspas-bitter-roots/?_r=0

Sundar, N. (2014). *Buried history of Indian democracy.* New Delhi: Critical Quest.

Tadjbakhsh, S., & Chenoy, A. M. (2009). *Human security: Concepts and implications.* London and New York: Routledge and Taylor and Francis.

United Nations International Crime Tribunal on Rwanda. Retrieved 21 January 2015, from http://www.unictr.org/Portals/0/English%5CAnnualReports% 5Ca-54-315.pdf

Vajpeyi, A. (2009). Presenting the Indian state: For a new political practice in the North East. In S. Baruah (Ed.), *Beyond counter-insurgency* (pp. 170–187). New Delhi: Oxford University Press.

Varshney, A. (2003). Ethnic conflict and civil society: India and beyond. In Carolyn M. Elliot (Ed.), *Civil society and democracy: A reader* (pp. 424–456). New Delhi: Oxford University Press.

Chapter 17

Has the Codified Hindu Law Changed Gender Relationships?*

Flavia Agnes

INTRODUCTION

In order to explore whether the enactment of the Hindu Code Bill has changed gender relationships, we need to first revisit the debates which were centre stage at the time of enacting these laws and the compromises that were made; then examine how these enactments played out on the ground during the last six decades, and finally list out the anti-women biases which still prevail today as part of the Hindu cultural ethos which adversely impact women's rights. The question this essay has attempted to address is whether the codified Hindu laws were instrumental in bringing about a social transformation by posing a challenge to the Brahminical patriarchy which was dominant at that point of time.

THE HISTORICAL CONTEXT

In 1950, we gave ourselves a Constitution that mandated equality and nondiscrimination as non-negotiable fundamental rights and protected the human rights of every citizen, irrespective of sex, caste and religion. Within five years, we violated that mandate which prohibited discrimination on the basis of religion by enacting a code

* *Social Change* (2016), *46*(4), 611–623.

only for Hindus. What was the political expediency driving the agenda of Hindu law reform at that time? Volumes have been written on this; however, this article addresses only a few and limited concerns.

As Hindu women lagged far behind, their counterparts from other religions who already had two important rights—the right of divorce and the right to inherit property—reforms for Hindus could not wait till a consensus was reached for enacting a Uniform Civil Code (UCC) across all religious denominations as mandated by Article 44 of the Constitution.

Given the urgency, it would be logical to assume that the process of enacting a gender-just code for the majority community would have been smooth and expeditious and the nationalist leadership (predominantly Hindu) would be united in this mission. But alas, it was not so. It turned out to be a long-drawn and extremely contentious process spanning over 15 years. The reforms met with severe opposition from conservative nationalistic leaders who opposed introducing the concept of divorce within the Hindu law, based on the premise of a sacramental marriage, and awarding equal property rights to daughters as it violated the Hindu ethos of treating daughters as *paraya dhan*. There was an apprehension that if Hindu women were granted the right of divorce and property inheritance, strict sexual control over them would loosen, and women would go 'astray' and the Hindu social fibre would disintegrate.

The reforms were opposed, among others, by the then President and Constitutional head Dr Rajendra Prasad and senior Congress leaders like Pattabhi Sitaramayya, Sardar Patel and P. D. Tandon (Lateef, 1994). Dr Rajendra Prasad declared that he would not sign on the dotted line if the concept of Hindu Undivided Family (HUF) property was abolished as it would fragment rural agricultural landholdings. As Prime Minster Jawaharlal Nehru kept vacillating in the face of stiff opposition within the ruling Congress, even after India's first general elections gave an overwhelming majority to the Congress party, Dr B. R. Ambedkar, who had been spearheading the campaign, resigned as the law minister in utter frustration. This mounted pressure to finally enact a set of piecemeal statutes rather than a composite Hindu Code which would govern family relationships as was initially envisaged.[2]

Though the liberation of women was the stated agenda, there was also a hidden political agenda. There was an urgent need to bring a culturally diverse and pluralistic society, divided along caste, sects and regional lines under one law and wrest the power to legislate in family matters away from the religious leadership (Parashar, 1992). So the statutes created a legal fiction and defined Buddhists, Jains, Sikhs, Brahmo, Arya and Prarthana Samajis (all of whom had broken away from the Hindu fold through various social reform movements at different historical points during pre-colonial and colonial period) as 'Hindu'. Resultantly, the net of legal Hinduism was cast very wide, and no one could escape, not even an atheist.[3]

Even if two Hindus married under the secular statute—the Special Marriage Act, they would still be governed by the Hindu Succession Act so that the Hindu male was not ousted from the privileged position of belonging to the HUF property and the resulting tax benefits could be preserved even when married under a secular statute.[4] But if he married a person from the Muslim, Christian, Parsi or Jewish community, he could be denied his rights to the ancestral property.

Archana Parashar has argued that while enacting a code for Hindus, the attempt was not to abandon ancient scriptural law or established community customs but to assimilate them within a Code along with the principles of English law and, while doing so, establish the law-making authority of the newly independent nation, which was, until then, vested with the heads of various religious sects (Parashar, 1992). The only people who were left out from the application of these statutes were the people of the Book—Muslims, Christians, Parsis and Jews, who were governed by their own respective personal laws.[5] The reforms privileged modernization, codification and unification as key elements of progress and development. Hence, several pro-women customary practices were discarded for the sake of uniformity (Derrett, 1999, p. 107).

Since the political impediment to reforming the Hindu law was grave, several balancing acts had to be performed. Crucial provisions empowering women had to be constantly diluted to reach the level of minimum consensus. While projecting the reforms as pro-women, male privileges had to be protected. While introducing modernity, archaic Brahminical rituals had to be retained. While claiming uniformity, diverse customary practices had to be validated. Only by adopting such manoeuvring tactics could the state reach its goal of Hindu law reform.

UNFOLDING OF THE STATUTES

The codified laws continued to reflect the patriarchal ideology and validated Brahminical rituals. Despite their claims, they did not bring in uniformity or gender equality as they provided a statutory recognition for the diverse customs and usages followed by various sects, communities and regions.

Under Section 5 of the Hindu Marriage Act, which stipulated conditions for contracting a Hindu marriage, and under Section 7, which prescribed the ceremonies for performing a valid Hindu marriage, customs and usages were awarded due recognition, Brahminical rituals, such as *vivaha homa* (the sacrificial fire), *saptapadi* (seven steps round the fire) and *kanyadaan* (offering the bride to the groom)[6] as essential ceremonies were prescribed. While Section 13 of the Act provides for a judicial divorce, Section 29 (2) validates customary divorces. The provision for registering the marriage under Section 8 is optional. Hence, despite the law being codified, a Hindu need not approach any state authority, either for solemnizing the marriage or for dissolving it, a position not very different from that prevailing under the uncodified Muslim law. Only through retaining the fluidity of customs of the pluralistic Hindu society, could the reforms be pushed through.

Yet, despite the lacunae, the reforms were projected as modern, secular, gender-just and uniform. It is interesting to see how these statues unfolded on the ground in subsequent years.

CONTRADICTIONS AND THE LACUNAE

The Hindu Marriage Act brought in monogamy, prevented child marriage by stipulating a minimum age of marriage and brought in the concept of contract by introducing an element of consent, even though the sacramental aspect of Hindu marriage was retained. Premised on the concept of gender equality, it awarded rights of divorce and other matrimonial remedies on the same and similar grounds of cruelty, desertion, bigamy and so on and also ancillary reliefs such as maintenance and child custody for both men and women, though the socially sanctioned gender roles and responsibilities within marriage were vastly different for men and women.

Since the concept of division of matrimonial property upon divorce was not introduced, women's economic rights after divorce were confined to a meagre maintenance, and even this provision carried a rider of sexual purity. If the husband's allegations of adultery or promiscuity were accepted by the court, the woman could be deprived of her right even to that small maintenance amount. So for women, in most cases, opting for divorce meant opting for destitution.

Under the Hindu Succession Act, the property inherited by widows became their absolute property and could not be taken away upon remarriage. The daughters were given a limited right of inheritance in a self-earned parental property. The concept of testamentary succession was introduced and the property could be willed away depriving legal heirs which often meant depriving daughters of their share in the self-earned property of the parent. As women were excluded from the Hindu coparcenary, the notion of equal inheritance rights was illusory. After a sustained struggle, in 2005, through an amendment to the Hindu Succession Act, this gross injustice to women was rectified and they were granted an equal right in ancestral property. While this was an important development, in reality, it is cosmetic as property continues to be consolidated in the hands of male relatives.

Due to the retention of the HUF property, Hindus alone were awarded the privilege of special tax benefits, an evident discrimination against all other religious minorities. (However, this issue is seldom discussed during public discourse as a 'Hindu' privilege.)

Despite the compromises and loopholes, the misconception that Hindus have forsaken their personal laws and have embraced a secular, egalitarian and gender-just code, which must now be extended to minority communities to liberate 'their' women, persists. Adverse comments in some Supreme Court rulings have added fuel to this tension. For instance, in the Sarla Mudgal judgement,[7] while examining the issue of polygamy by Hindu men by converting to Islam, the Supreme Court endorsed this view and commented, totally out of context, that oneness of the nation, as well as loyalty to it, would be at stake if different minority groups followed different family laws.

THE REMEDY OF RESTITUTION OF CONJUGAL RIGHTS

Restitution of Conjugal Rights (RCR), a remedy in English law, which has its base in the medieval church of Europe, viewed marriage as a permanent and indissoluble sacrament. If a wife left the board of her husband, she could be brought back and restored to his custody by church authorities, a position akin to slavery. This was based on the premise that the wife is the property of the husband. But by 19th century, when civil law was introduced, the position changed, and since women were awarded the right of legal separation and divorce, RCR could not be used to restore a wife back to her husband.

However, during the colonial rule, this principle was applied to Hindu and Muslim marriages. The most famous case here is that of Rukhmabai in 1882–1885.[8] Married as an adolescent upon attaining maturity, she refused to join her husband. In a case filed by her husband for restitution of conjugal rights, the trial court refused to grant him the remedy on the grounds that ancient Hindu law did not recognize this reinstatement. But in an appeal, and under pressure from some Hindu revivalists, a division bench of the Bombay High Court ordered the wife to join her husband and fulfil her conjugal obligations. Rukhmabai defied the order of the colonial court and was ready to face imprisonment, thus creating a furore even in faraway England as it tarnished the image of the colonial rulers as 'saviours' of women. Finally, the matter was settled after Rukhmabai agreed to pay her husband compensation (Chandra, 1998; Agnes, 1999).

Through Section 9 of the Hindu Marriage Act, this remedy was included in the codified Hindu law[9] but was made applicable to both parties. In the following two decades after the enactment, using this remedy, several husbands approached the courts to prevent their wives from taking up gainful employment in a place of their choice, despite the fact that they were the main bread winners of their families. While upholding the husband's unconditional right, under a codified Hindu law, the courts made the following comments: 'A wife's first duty to her husband is to submit herself obediently to his authority and to remain under his roof and protection.'[10] 'The Hindu law imposes on the wife the duty of attendance, obedience, and veneration to the husband,

and to live with him wherever he chooses to reside.'[11] 'According to Hindu law, marriage is a holy union for the performance of marital duties with her husband where he may choose to reside and to fulfill her duties in her husband's home.'[12]

Finally, in 1978, a full bench ruling of the Delhi High Court[13] departed from the position advocated by the earlier judgements and granted women the right to reside separately from their husbands if they were gainfully employed. However, the notion that the husband is 'lord' and 'master' and his wife should be subservient to him (the *pati parameshwar* concept) still dominates divorce proceedings.

In 1983, in *T. Sareetha* v. *T. Venkata Subbiah*,[14] the Andhra Pradesh High Court struck down this offensive section and declared it unconstitutional. While the wordings of this section do not discriminate against women, examining the social context in which it operates, Justice P. A. Choudary, in a pro-women ruling, held that the provision violates the right to privacy and human dignity guaranteed under Article 21 of the Constitution and causes the grossest form of violation of an individual's right to privacy. It has the impact of denying a woman her free choice whether, when and how her body is to become the vehicle for the procreation of another human being.

However, in 1984, the Delhi High Court, in *Harvinder Kaur* v. *Harminder Singh*,[15] upheld this provision, invoking the legal dictum that personal laws are immune to the test of Part III of the Constitution and ruled:

> Introduction of Constitutional law in the home is most inappropriate, it is like pushing a bull into a china shop. It will prove to be a ruthless destroyer of the marriage institution and all that it stands for. In the privacy of the home and married life, neither Article 21 nor Article 14 has any place.

Later in the same year, the Supreme Court, in *Saroj Rani* v. *Sudarshan Kumar Chadha*,[16] affirmed the ruling of the Delhi High Court and overruled the more-progressive, Andhra Pradesh ruling which had invoked the principles of human rights. So, the provision remains and can be conveniently invoked to defeat the wife's claim to maintenance during court proceedings.

THE WORKING OF HINDU MONOGAMY

While examining developments in Hindu law, Professor Werner Menski, an expert in this area, commented that Hindu law has always been a people's law. Hence, something as complex as Hindu personal law could not be reformed and abolished by a statute, nor could its influence as a legal normative order, that permeates the entire Indian socio-legal field, be legislated into oblivion. Though the law was codified, in reality, all that happened was that while official Indian law changed more and more, Hindu law went underground, populating unofficial law. The conceptual framework and ideologies underpinning multiple ways of life and hence the entire customary social edifice of Hindu culture remained largely immune to the powerful wonder drug of legal modernization (Mensky, 2003, pp. 24–25).

Within a pluralistic society, the Hindu Marriage Act validated diverse customary practices. However, the notion of a valid custom remained that of ancient and time immemorial, as stipulated under the English law. This mingling of Brahminical rituals and customary practices with English legal principles resulted in absurd rulings regarding the validity of Hindu marriages, and women have been the worst sufferers.

In the process of urbanization, most customary forms have been modified and urban communities living in close proximity have adopted a synthesis of marriage rituals. The forms range from exchanging garlands, applying *sindoor* on the bride's forehead to declaring themselves married by signing a stamped paper, or by taking an oath before a deity in a temple. Television serials and Hindi films have added to the confusion by projecting these as valid rituals.

Such ambiguity provides a Hindu male ample scope to contract bigamous marriages. As the law recognizes only monogamous marriages, the women in polygamous relationships are denied their rights. In the absence of any clear proof, the man has the choice of validating either his first or the subsequent relationship as a valid marriage to escape from any financial liability towards the other woman. A Hindu husband can routinely deny the marriage or plead that the woman is not his wife and hence deny her claim to maintenance, as there is no official record of any of these rituals. It is left to the lawyer to formulate an adequate strategy that can turn fiction into fact and fact into fiction.

When a man refuses to validate the marriage, the woman loses not only her right to maintenance but also her status as a 'wife' and faces humiliation and social stigma as a 'mistress'. An examination of law journals reveals how widely prevalent this ploy, of refusing to validate the marriage in maintenance proceedings, is.

So, the progressive sounding provision of monogamy not only turned out to be a mockery but in fact even more detrimental to women than the uncodified Hindu law which had recognized rights of wives in polygamous marriages. For instance, in a case for maintenance where the husband pleaded that as the woman was his second wife, he is not obligated to pay her maintenance, the court took recourse to the uncodified Hindu law and held that as the couple is governed by the ancient Hindu law which permits bigamy and under which the second wife is entitled to maintenance[17] and not by the reformed code. This judgement speaks volumes for a law that was ushered in with much fanfare as an instrument of social change and women's empowerment.

The flip side of this predicament in maintenance proceedings is the dilemma faced by women in criminal proceedings in cases of bigamy. Here, years of litigation have failed to end in conviction for the errant male due to the courts adopting a rigid view that the Brahminical rituals, *vivaha homa, saptapadi* and *kanyadaan,* were essential ceremonies for solemnizing a Hindu marriage. The husband could wriggle out of conviction, despite proof of cohabitation, the birth of a child or the community accepting the couple as husband and wife, if these ceremonies could not be proved by the first wife in respect of her husband's second marriage (Agnes, 1995). This was absurd as Hinduism, as explained earlier, was defined in the widest terms including castes, sects and religions that did not follow Brahminical rituals. Furthermore, among many communities, the ceremonies prescribed for a second marriage differed vastly from those prescribed for the first marriage of a virgin bride. But the law did not have the scope to take these minute intricacies into consideration.

An official report brought out in 1974 (Government of India Publication, 1974), almost 20 years after the enactment of the Hindu Marriage Act, Towards Equality highlighted the disturbing fact that polygamy among Hindus, Buddhists and Jains (communities governed by the codified Hindu law) was higher than among Muslims.[18] The statistics revealed the huge number of Hindu wives who were trapped in legally invalid marriages were denied their basic rights of maintenance and sustenance as their husbands were able to plead that the woman was his mistress.

DILUTION OF MONOGAMY

Contrary to the feeling of perceived disentitlement (as compared to Muslims), it is the Hindu husband who enjoys a privileged position of denying maintenance to a woman with whom he has not only cohabited but also produced children, merely by pleading, during court proceedings, that he has violated the mandate of monogamy without any criminal consequences visiting him. In comparison, the Muslim woman in a bigamous marriage fares better than her Hindu counterpart, as she is entitled to rights of maintenance, shelter, dignity and equal status. She cannot be discarded as a used doormat. The reported cases in law journals bear testimony to the frequency with which Hindu men adopt this tactic while sympathetic and sensitive judges constantly try to find ways by which to secure rights for women trapped in such marriages and provide them dignity. The following judgement is an example.

In 2005, in *Rameshchandra Daga* v. *Rameshwari Daga*,[19] the Supreme Court, while trying to grapple with this problem and while awarding maintenance to a woman whose husband had challenged the validity of their marriage on the grounds of a previous marriage, conceded that despite codification and introduction of monogamy, the ground reality had not changed and that many Hindu marriages, like Muslim marriages, continued to be bigamous. Furthermore, the Court commented that though such marriages were illegal, as per the provisions of the codified Hindu law, they were not 'immoral', and hence, a financially dependent woman could not be denied maintenance on this ground (Agnes, 2011).

In the same year, in order to redress the injustice caused to Hindu women in legally invalid marriages and to bring them within the fold of legality, the Protection of Women from Domestic Violence

Act, 2005 (PWDVA) introduced the concept of a 'marriage-like relationship', popularly referred to as a 'live-in relationship'. However, a Supreme Court ruling by Justice Markandey Katju, *D. Velusamy* v. *D.Patchaiammal*[20] proved to be a dampener. The court was dealing with an appeal by a Hindu man whose wife had been awarded maintenance under Section 125 of the Criminal Procedure Code (Cr.PC) by two lower courts. While setting aside these orders and denying the woman her right to maintenance, the judge also narrowed the scope of the term 'marriage-like relationship' under PWDVA and held:

> If a man has a 'keep' whom he maintains financially and uses mainly for sexual purpose and/or as a servant, it would not, in our opinion, be a relationship in the nature of marriage... No doubt the view we are taking would exclude many women who have had a live-in relationship from the benefit of the 2005 Act, but then it is not for this Court to legislate or amend the law.

By a stroke of his pen, the judge undid several earlier rulings that had attempted to find a way of securing some relief to women who were ensnared in such relationships. However, dissenting from Justice Katju's judgement, in 2014, in *Badshah* v. *Urmila Badshah Godse*,[21] Justices Ranjana Desai and A. K. Sikhri upheld the right of a Hindu woman who had been duped into a bigamous marriage and thwarted the attempt of her husband to subsequently deny her maintenance. The judgement emphasized that while dealing with the application of a destitute wife under this provision, the court is dealing with the marginalized sections of society. The purpose is to achieve 'social justice, the constitutional vision enshrined in the Preamble of the Constitution of India. The Preamble clearly signals that we have chosen the democratic path to secure for all its citizens justice, liberty, equality and fraternity. It specifically highlights achieving social justice. Therefore, it becomes the bounden duty of the courts to advance the cause of social justice. There is a non-rebuttable presumption that the legislature, while making a provision like Section 125 of the Cr.PC to fulfil its constitutional duty in good faith, had always intended to give relief to the woman becoming 'wife' under such circumstances.

As an example, the judgement cited the journey from Shah Bano[22] to Shabana Bano,[23] which granted maintenance rights to divorced Muslim women. The judge was referring to the developments within Muslim law in recent times, which have secured the post-divorce economic rights of Muslim women through important rulings such as Daniel Latifi[24] and Shabana Bano[25] and also Shamim Ara,[26] which invalidated triple *talaq* by stipulating strict Quranic conditions for pronouncing *talaq* under Islamic law.

In yet another ruling of 2015, a bench of Justices Vikramajit Sen and A. M. Sapre dismissed a petition by a man who claimed that since he was already married before entering into the live-in relationship, his partner could not claim the status of a wife and was not entitled to maintenance (Choudhary, 2015). The man, who works in Bollywood, had challenged an order of the Bombay High Court, which had held that his live-in partner of nine years and the child were entitled to maintenance. He argued that as he was legally married to another woman for the last 49 years, his live-in partner was not entitled to maintenance as she was well aware of his marital status. He pleaded further that his live-in partner was a 'call girl' and that she had decided to live with him out of her own wish since 1986 and a child was born to them in 1988. The judges slammed the man for referring to his former partner as a 'call girl'.

These recent judgements indicate a change of judicial attitude towards women who used to be humiliated and stigmatized during court proceedings, while rewarding the errant husbands by absolving them of their obligation to maintain their former partners. Despite this reality, the popular trend (within media and progressive groups) is in the reverse direction, with a demand to abolish Muslim polygamy and bring Muslim women on par with Hindu women, while turning a blind eye to these legal developments.

CONTEMPORARY CONCERNS

This brings me to the concluding point of my essay. As we enter the debate on the enactment of a UCC there is a view that the codified Hindu law will form its base. There is also a parallel view that the best elements from all personal laws must be incorporated into this ideal code. Tested against this formulation, how will Hindu law, which is applicable to the mainstream majority, fare? Apart from the elaborate discussion above on unfolding of the Hindu law within our courts, there is also the need to bring into context certain other vital indicators of gender justice.

According to recently released census data, India has 12 million married children under the age of 10. According to a news report and to place it in context, this number is equivalent to the population of Jammu and Kashmir. The most disturbing part of the report is that 84 per cent of this number were Hindus, while 11 per cent were Muslims (Saha, 2016). What do these figures indicate in the context of the current debate on UCC which is focused primarily on reforming the oppressive Muslim law?

As per the Child Marriage Prohibition Act, 2006, as well as the Hindu Marriage Act, the minimum age of marriage for a Hindu girl is 18 years, while the principle applicable under Muslim law is 'age of reason' which is deemed to be achieved a little after puberty. Yet the figures for child marriage do not reflect a social transformation taking place due to the codification of Hindu law.

Though child marriage is prohibited, it is not void. Some groups have been campaigning for a total ban on child marriage and for declaring all child marriages void. But from the context of social justice, what will be the impact on young Hindu girls who are married upon reaching puberty and are deserted even before they become majors? When a destitute girl, with a baby in her arms, approaches our courts, would it be in the interest of justice to declare, as the marriage is void, that she is not entitled to the basic and fundamental right of maintenance?

While this is a legal concern, there is also a social aspect to it. The belief that a girl should be married before reaching puberty is still dominant among various rural Hindu communities. The concept of a virgin bride prevails and the fear of any sexual assault which will taint the girl and render her impure and unfit for marriage still persists; parents are afraid to take the risk of keeping an unmarried girl at home. The fear of the girl eloping with a boy of her choice and bringing dishonour to the family also haunts parents due to which they prefer to marry off their daughters at a young age. This often exposes young, vulnerable girls to sexual and domestic abuse in her marital home. It also results in an early pregnancy, one of the main causes of maternal mortality in our country. Yet the fear of sexual purity and sexual defilement overrides concerns for the girl's health and security while marrying off an underage daughter.

The reformed Hindu law has not been able to bring a change within this deeply engrained notion. It is not a question of criminalizing child marriage and declaring it void but of providing adequate facilities for education, both formal and informal, skill training and a secure environment for a young girl to grow up in until she reaches the age of 18 years, along with a change in the parental mindset, regarding the notion of virgin bride are measures which are needed.

A Hindu father still believes that marrying his daughter is a pious obligation which he must perform to attain salvation. Apart from encouraging child marriage, this concept also gives a boost to the dowry system, despite our laws criminalizing dowry and dowry-related violence. The pressure to marry off their daughters at any cost drives parents to meet the demands for dowry made by the groom's family, rather than bear the stigma of having an unmarried daughter. Despite the legislative reforms to curb dowry deaths and suicides, the figures are constantly rising. In an informal study of dowry deaths which reached the Supreme Court and the Bombay High Court, conducted by Majlis, Mumbai, over 95 per cent cases of dowry death were among Hindus.

While the system of dowry has spread to lower castes and minority communities, its roots in Hindu cultural tradition cannot be overlooked. Ironically, Muslim law started with the notion of *mehr,* a financial amount which must be stipulated in the marriage contract as a future security to the bride. Unfortunately, while the community has accepted the anti-women Hindu custom of dowry, *mehr* amounts have been reduced to mere tokens rather than anything more viable to secure the future needs of the bride.

The age-old dictum still prevails that a girl who enters a bridal home in a wedding procession must leave the home only in a funeral procession. So, despite acute domestic violence, girls are sent back to their homes even at the risk of them being killed or driven to suicide. Despite amendments to the Hindu law, which rendered the Hindu marriage contractual, the sacramental aspect still dominates the social

psyche and parents prefer to send the daughter back to her matrimonial home rather than risk having a divorcee on their hands.

In contrast, a Muslim marriage is always regarded as a civil contract. While the Christian marriage started on the premise of a permanent and dissoluble sacrament, gradually due to education and exposure, the perception about sacramental marriage has changed. While among the urban, middle- and upper-class Hindus, divorce is gradually gaining acceptance, there is greater likelihood of women opting for divorce when faced with domestic violence. In rural areas, however, where conservative views of sacramental marriage still dominate, women are less likely to opt for divorce even when faced with cruelty, desertion or their husband's adultery as marriage is deemed to offer protection to women.

The concept of permanency of marriage and husband as the 'lord' and 'master' still dominates not only in our public life, but also in litigation in family courts where women are constantly advised to return home to save their marriage even at great risk to themselves: at times, the judges themselves endorse this view. Women too believe that even if their husbands are abusive, violent or alcoholic they prefer to remain married, as the symbols of marriage worn by them, such as the *mangalsutra* (black-beaded necklace) and *sindhoor,* are perceived as marks of respect, status and protection against advances from other men.

Despite the enactment of PWDVA, the only advice given to most women in counselling sessions, conducted by the police or social workers located in police stations, is to opt for reconciliation and return to her matrimonial home. This appears to be the most viable solution as the state has not attempted to evolve alternate support structures to help women to make the transition from a housewife to an independent and self-supporting person (Agnes & D'Mello, 2015). When there is a resumption of violence, the women are in a state of acute depression. A recent international study which covered 187 nations revealed another disturbing fact that suicide among married women is the leading cause of death among married women aged between 15 and 49 years in India, replacing death due to maternal disorders (Liat, 2016). And a majority of these cases are likely to be urban Hindu housewives.

While all religions are patriarchal and believe in maintaining a strict control over a woman's sexuality, the hold of Brahminical patriarchy

262 | Flavia Agnes

reaches a high pitch when we examine the phenomenon referred to as honour killings. In this, a girl is brutally killed by her own parents or at their stance, for transgressing the caste boundaries and marrying a man/boy from a lower caste—a reality captured in a recent popular Marathi movie *Sairat*. Earlier, this phenomenon was believed to be prevalent only in north India but now several southern states have also started regularly reporting such occurrences. The young couple often is also killed for contracting *sagotra* and *sapinda* marriages within certain north Indian communities.

Against this overarching evidence of anti-women social practices, can we assume that the codified Hindu law has been instrumental in bringing social transformation and changed gender relationships and provided the necessary foundation upon which a strong edifice of a uniform and gender-just family code for India can be built? This is the challenging question that confronts us today.

NOTES

1. This is the text of the 2016 Durgabai Deshmukh lecture delivered on 15 July 2016 and organized annually by the Council for Social Development, New Delhi.
2. The four enactments which constitute the reformed family laws for Hindus are: The Hindu Marriage Act, 1955, The Hindu Succession Act, 1956, The Hindu Minority and Guardianship Act, 1956 and the Hindu Adoption and Maintenance Act, 1956.
3. See the definition of who the Act applies to in Section 2 of the Hindu Marriage Act where the net is cast wide which I refer to as 'legal Hinduism'. A similar definition is found in all four statutes enacted at that time.
4. This was introduced through an amendment to the Special Marriage Act in 1976.
5. Tribal communities in various states are also excluded from the application of these statutes and are permitted to govern themselves through their own internal mechanisms.
6. A ritual which reinforces the notion that women are property to be handed over from fathers to husbands.
7. *Sarla Mudgal* v. *Union of India* (1995) 3 SCC 635.
8. *Dadaji Bhikaji* v. *Rukhmabai* (1885) ILR 9 Bom 520.
9. This because the matrimonial remedies of the codified Hindu law were borrowed from the then prevailing English family law. Though a few years later, this remedy was abolished under the English law but was retained under

the Hindu law. This remedy is frequently used by husbands to defeat the claim of maintenance of their deserted wives.

10. *Gaya Prasad* v. *Bhagwat Prasad*, AIR 1966 MP 212.
11. *Surinder Kaur* v. *Gurdeep Singh*, AIR 1973 P&H 134.
12. *Kailash Wati* v. *Ayodhia Parkash*, ILR (1977) 1 P&H 642 FB.
13. *Swaraj Garg* v. *K.M. Garg*, AIR 1978 Del 296.
14. AIR 1983 AP 356.
15. AIR 1984 Del 66.
16. AIR 1984 SC 1562.
17. *Anupama Pradhan* v. *Sultan Pradhan*, 1991 Cri.L J 3216 Ori.
18. Muslims 5.6 per cent, Hindus 5.8 per cent, Jains 6.7 per cent, Buddhists 7.9 per cent.
19. I (2005) DMC 1 SC.
20. *D. Velusamy* v. *D. Patchaiammal* 2010 (10) SCC 469.
21. 2014 (1) SCC 188.
22. *Mohd. Ahmed Khan* v. *Shah Bano Begum*, AIR 1985, SC 945.
23. *Shabana Bano* v. *Imran Khan*, AIR 2010, SC 305.
24. *Daniel Latifi* v. *Union of India* (2001), 7 SCC, 740 FB.
25. Cited above.
26. *Shamim Ara* v. *State of UP*, 2002 (7), SCC 518.

REFERENCES

Agnes, F. (1995). Hindu men, monogamy and the Uniform Civil Code. *Economic & Political Weekly, XXX*(50), 3238.
———. (1999). *Law and gender inequailty.* New Delhi: Oxford University Press.
———. (2011). The concubine and notions of constitutional justice. *Economic & Political Weekly, XLVI*(24), 31.
Agnes, F., & D'Mello, Audrey. (2015). Protection of women from domestic violence. *Economic & Political Weekly, L*(44). Review of Women's Studies, 31 October 2015. Retrieved from http://www.epw.in/review-womens-studies/protection-women-domestic-violence. html
Chandra, S. (1998). *Enslaved daughters.* New Delhi: Oxford University Press.
Choudhary, Amit Anand. (2015, May 6). Supreme Court upholds maintenance for live-in partners. New Delhi. *The Times of India.* Retrieved from http://timesofindia.indiatimes. com/india/Supreme-Court-upholds-maintenance-for-live-in-partners/articleshow/ 47169351.cms
Derrett, D. J. M. (1999). *Religion, law and the state in India.* New Delhi: Oxford University Press.
Government of India. (1974). *Towards equality—the report of the status of women committee.* New Delhi: Government of India.
Lateef, S. (1994). Defining women through legislation. In Z. Hasan (Ed.), *Forging identities: Gender, communities and the state.* New Delhi: Kali for Women.

264 | Flavia Agnes

Liat, Clark (2016, March 27). Suicide is number one cause of death among young women in India. *WIRED*. Retrieved form http://www.wired.co.uk/news/archive/2013-03/27/suicidewomen-india

Mensky, W. (2003). *Hindu law beyond tradition and modernity*. New Delhi: Oxford University Press.

Parashar, A. (1992). *Women and family law reform in India*. New Delhi: SAGE Publications.

Saha, D. (2016, June 1). India has 12 million married children under age ten. *The Wire*. Retrieved from http://thewire.in/2016/06/01/of-12-million-married-children-under-age-ten-84-are-hindus-39885/

About the Editors and Contributors

SERIES EDITOR

Manoranjan Mohanty retired as Director, Developing Countries Research Centre and Professor of Political Science, University of Delhi, in 2004. A political scientist, China scholar and a peace and human rights activist with special interest in China, India and global transformation, he is editor of *Social Change* and distinguished professor, Council for Social Development, New Delhi. He is chairperson, Development Research Institute, Bhubaneswar and honorary fellow and former chairperson of the Institute of Chinese Studies, Delhi. He has taught or researched in many universities including California, Oxford, Copenhagen, Moscow, Lagos and Beijing. He is the author of many publications including *China's Transformation: The Success Story and the Success Trap, Ideology Matters: China from Mao Zedong to Xi Jinping* and edited or co-edited many publications, including *People's Rights, Class, Caste, Gender, India-Social Development Report, 2010, Exploring Emergent Global Thresholds* and *China at a Turning Point*.

VOLUME EDITOR

Ghazala Jamil is Assistant Professor at the Centre for the Study of Law and Governance, Jawaharlal Nehru University. Prior to this, she was Associate Fellow at the Council for Social Development (2014–2015) and has served as book reviews editor of *Social Change* (2014–2019). She has earlier taught at the Department of Social Work, University of Delhi, and School of Planning and Architecture, New Delhi. She is the author of *Accumulation by Segregation* (OUP, 2017), *Muslim Women Speak* (SAGE Yoda Press, 2018), and co-translator of Intizar Hussain's *Dilli Tha Jiska Naam* from Urdu to English titled, *Once There Was a City Named Dilli* (Yoda Press, 2017).

CONTRIBUTORS

Sanghmitra Acharya is a Professor at the Centre for Community Health and Social Medicine at JNU. She has also served as director, Indian Institute of Dalit Studies, New Delhi. Her research includes health and discrimination; vulnerability among youth; gender in urban spaces and caste–gender intersectionality.

Flavia Agnes is a women's rights lawyer. She is a co-founder of MAJLIS, a legal and cultural resource centre providing quality legal services to women and children. She has worked and written extensively on gender and law providing incisive analysis of many social trends and legal reforms including domestic violence, minority law reforms, secularism and human rights.

Uma Chakravarti is a feminist historian. She writes on Buddhism, early Indian history, the 19th century and on contemporary issues. She is closely involved with the women's movement as well as the movement for democratic rights in India and has been part of many fact-finding teams to investigate human rights violations, communal violence and state repression.

Durgabai Deshmukh (1909–1981) was a social worker and a lawyer. She was also a freedom fighter who managed to obtain a law degree while participating actively in the freedom struggle. She established Andhra Mahila Sabha in 1937, which is still working towards welfare and education in South India. She was a Padma Vibhushan awardee.

Anita Dighe has researched and written extensively on India's experiences with literacy and adult education. Her current interests include the use of information and communication technologies in adult learning. She also served as joint director of the Council for Social Development and as director of Extension Education at the Indira Gandhi National Open University in New Delhi.

Devaki Jain is a development economist, activist and a writer. She taught economics at the University of Delhi and, later, became the director of Institute of Social Studies which played an important role in the women's studies movement.

Maniben Kara (1905–1979) was a trade unionist, social worker and freedom fighter. She was the founder and president of Hind Mazdoor Sabha and also established Seva Mandir. Kara was also a member of the CSWI. She was honoured with the Padma Shri in 1970.

Maithreyi Krishnaraj is an expert in economics, sociology and education, and regarded a pioneer in developing women's studies. She was formerly the director of Research Centre for Women's Studies, SNDT Women's University, Mumbai.

Sanjay Kumar is Professor at the Centre for the Study of Developing Societies, Delhi. His core area of research expertise is electoral politics and voting behaviour. His wider research interest extends to issues related to Indian youth, women in politics and democratic politics.

Vivek Kumar is a Professor of Sociology and Chairperson of Centre for the Study of Social Systems at JNU, New Delhi. He received Tree-Sararu award and, also, is a consultant at Harvard.

Vina Mazumdar (1927–2013) was the Member Secretary of the Committee on the Status of Women in India, and the founding Director of the Centre for Women's Development Studies (CWDS). Her disciplinary training was in political science.

Usha Mehta (1920–2000) was a Gandhian activist and scholar. She was a freedom fighter and ran underground radio. She started her law studies but dropped it midway to participate in the Quit India Movement. She later went on to earn doctorate degree from Bombay University, where she also taught political science.

Sujata Mukherjee* is a UGC Senior Research Fellow, Department of Journalism and Mass Communication, University of Calcutta, Kolkata.

---

* Affiliation at the time this contribution was published in *Social Change*.

Farah Naqvi is a feminist, author and activist. She has worked for over 30 years on gender rights, caste and minority issues, towards justice, equality, democratic rights and freedom from violence. She was a member of the Post-Sachar Evaluation Committee (Kundu Committee).

Nandini Rai* is an Associate Fellow, Council for Social Development, New Delhi.

Praveen Rai is a Political Analyst and expert in election studies and survey research. His key areas of interest include politics, electoral competitions and opinion polling in India. He is currently working at the Centre for the Study of Developing Societies, Delhi.

Amit Ranjan is Research Fellow at Institute of South Asian Studies, National University of Singapore. He has a doctoral degree in South Asian Studies from School of International Studies, Jawaharlal Nehru University, New Delhi.

Kumkum Roy is Professor of ancient Indian history at Centre for Historical Studies, JNU. Her other area of interest is the gender studies. She has been the sectional president, Ancient History, Indian History Congress, 2009.

Mina Swaminathan is an expert on early childhood care and education. She was the chairperson of the Central Advisory Board of Education Committee (1972) which led to the Integrated Child Development Services (ICDS).

---

* Affiliation at the time this contribution was published in *Social Change*.

Index